Her royal-blue-robed arm rose from her lap. The precise tip of her napkin swept the corners of her mouth; within the linen, her fingers never moved. I don't think there were even any crumbs to brush off. I couldn't see any, and I was watching. Closely.

Sister Antonia Marie must have been of noble descent. She moved regally, never in a hurry. Her black eyes, deep as a mystic's in trance, told me every thing and absolutely nothing. I was supposed to divine what they meant. My whole soul was listening to who she might be, for clues as to why God had made such a face and what He wanted me to know about it.

The day she moved her napkin was December eighth, the feast of the Immaculate Conception. It was the major holy day of our order. That was why the postulants were eating dinner with the novices in the refectory; that's how I got to read Antonia's eyes all evening.

A LESBIAN NUN STORY

KICKING THE HABIT

AN AUTOBIOGRAPHICAL NOVEL BY
Jeanne Córdova

MULTIPLE
DIMENSIONS
Hollywood, California

Kicking the Habit: A Lesbian Nun Story
by Jeanne Córdova

Published by
Multiple Dimensions
1604 Vista Del Mar
Los Angeles, CA 90028
U.S.A.
(213) 469-4454

Cover design by Cher Martin
Typesetting by Plain Rap

Printed in the United States of America, First Edition

ISBN 0-9625080-0-4 Paperback

This book is

dedicated to my

Higher Presence

and yours.

Acknowledgments

As we were editing this book shortly after midnight, a week before *Kicking the Habit* went off to publishers heaven, my friend and writing group cohort, *Nancy Tyler Glenn,* turned to me bleary-eyed and said, "Bet ya didn't know how many people it takes to write a book!"

"No, I didn't," said I, the first-novelist. "And no one told me I'd have to rewrite it four times either."

I am now very sure writing a book takes 10% talent, and 90% hard work. And equally sure that *Kicking the Habit's* sisterhood of particular friends was the invaluable support team that kept me glued to the computer screen for a year and a half.

I wish to say a heartfelt thank you to that sisterhood:

My Thursday Night Writers Group II, notably *Barbara Chesser, Nancy Tyler Glenn,* and *Sharon (Shair) Cho,* for making me re-write this book four times. Thursday night has been the centerpiece of my life for a year. No budding novelist ever had as much fun, friendship and ego-deflating hard work as I did being a part of this true collective-of-words.

Secondly, I wish to thank *Patricia Kelly*, budding editor and dear friend, who pretended my first draft made sense—just barely enough sense—to convince me to rewrite, rewrite, rewrite. I thank her for adopting and nurturing the *Habit* through its adolescence.

Writers Group I: *Karen Wolman* and *Nancy Robinson* for their invaluable critique, "great book here . . . even if your wild tangents don't relate to the main story-line."

Caryn Goldberg, Managing Editor of the Community Yellow Pages, for going to work so I could stay home and write. And for reading this manuscript so many times that she became convinced that she wrote it.

Michelle Callahan and *Del Martinez* for their roles as living characters in my habit.

Terry Wolverton, Katherine Forrest, and *Eloise Healy* for their early critical, yet well-tempered, support.

Karen Kircher, Robin Tyler, and *Ariana Manov* for their promotional and editorial "important friendly advice."

Dina Bachelor for her spiritual assistance in helping me pry open my past and this story, and for believing in me as a writer.

Aleida Rodriguez, my editor, for unscrambling my atrocities of metaphor and syntax, and for her tenacious attention to rectifying my complete ignorance of punctuation.

Cher Martin, graphic artist, for conceiving and birthing Sister Mary Marti on the cover.

Sally Stewart for her love and her presence. In front of every woman who creates something special is another woman who clears the brush, and stokes the homefires that warm the pages of *Kicking the Habit.*

My Spirit Guides, *Tomasino,* for her literary advice, and *Angus* for his "medicine" . . . and to their *Higher Presence* and mine, for blessing *Kicking the Habit,* and the rest of my dreams.

Thank you, my friends.

Foreword

by

Rosemary Curb, Coeditor, *Lesbian Nuns: Breaking Silence*

Jeanne Córdova's autobiography, *Kicking the Habit*, dramatizes her search for self in a world which overvalues conformity. As a tenaciously naive baby butch, Jeanne may be able to catch softballs that fly her way, but she misses the subtler meanings of words, looks, and touches that older nuns, and her peers in the convent, toss her way.

With an irrepressible sense of humor, Córdova family pride, and the protection of her own bravado, Jeanne immediately dives deep into the medieval dogmas and rules still prevalent in mid-twentieth century American convents. Much too quickly, from her point of view, she is missioned back out into the secular world she thought she had left for good. There she must suddenly confront the hungers and violence of an inner city ghetto without the protection of convent walls or religious habit. Through all of this, Jeanne discovers a sexual and spiritual identity far different from what she thought she was seeking.

When she finally recognizes her lesbian self as an intrinsic part of her personality, Jeanne rejoices. Suddenly she sees all of the players on the ballfield of her heart, to paraphrase Meg Christian's "Ode to a Gym Teacher," in their respective positions. Jeanne understands that her commitment to social change, her passion for the life of spirit, and her relentless intellectual curosity weave together in her lesbian self.

What Jeanne Córdova has created in *Kicking the Habit*, many of us who contributed to *Lesbian Nuns: Breaking Silence* (1985), would like to do for ourselves and the world we move through. In the earlier anthology, we had space for only a sliver of the fifty lives which narrate the often painful process of lesbian self-discovery in a Church which tells us we do not exist, or, if we do, we must be evil or loathsome. Those of us who felt called to a religious life, and who later discovered ourselves lesbian, found that the weights which kept us down were heavy in many ways. Women from various races, classes, and backgrounds of all sorts are daily struggling to rise from a sea of socially constructed gynephobia to gasp the fresh air of self-esteem.

The international lesbian community can boast many women with Jeanne Córdova's curiosity and courage. Jeanne, however, has the wit and wisdom to show us the progress of her life in full color. Telling our stories flies in the face of patriarchal assumptions about women's roles and limitations. Jeanne's life, and her clever telling of it, proves that any woman can define her own identity, resisting both compulsory heterosexuality, as well as the passivity expected of nuns.

Kicking the Habit causes the rawest nerve of patriarchy to shudder because it shows a woman taking power independently and resisting male control. The lesbian sisterhood takes from within the self and the circle of selves.

Winter Park, Florida
November 1989

iv

Foreword

Nancy Manahan, Coeditor, *Lesbian Nuns: Breaking Silence*

Lesbian Nuns: Breaking Silence (1985) offered glimpses of fifty lesbians' experiences in the convent. *Kicking the Habit: A Lesbian Nun Story* takes one of those snapshots and develops it into a full-length story—funny, perceptive, and, at times, lyrical. I've always liked Jeanne Córdova's writing. I devoured nearly every issue of her monthly magazine, *The Lesbian Tide*. Rosemary Curb, my coeditor, and I chose Jeanne's story to begin *Lesbian Nuns: Breaking Silence* because it was one of the best pieces we received.

Even so, after five years of editing and promoting *Lesbian Nuns*, I thought I had read and said everything I'd ever want to on the subject. So I was not eager to read this book.

But I found myself absorbed by *Kicking the Habit*. I was

reminded of my own convent experiences, chuckling with appreciation at Jeanne's fine eye for detail. I identified with her shocked disillusionment that nuns could break any vow as long as they were discreet.

Anne Wilson Schaef, Ph.D., and Father Matthew Fox have written recently about the Church as an addictive organization replete with the characteristics of an active addict. *Kicking the Habit* is a powerful description of three of those most prominent traits: denial, dishonesty, and image management. Jeanne's dawning recognition of how her religious community fostered these traits is at the heart of her book. So is her tribute to those women—in and out of her community—who have dared to live their lives honestly.

In the end, I was moved by the integrity of Jeanne's story. It is an important step in breaking the silence about the lives of women, of lesbians, of nuns, and of ex-nuns. This book tells the truth!

Napa, California
November 1989

Author's Prologue

Genesis says God created man in his own image. Karl Marx, who, of course, is on the Catholic Index of forbidden authors, said creation combusted quite the other way around: Man created his own opiate. I figure if one really believes in either God or 'man,' it's possible both world views are correct. Perhaps in our universal collective unconscious there is no duality. God and humankind are of the same stuff, a chicken-and-egg cosmic synthesis. Or, as the heresy painted on the wall of Sister Corita's convent studio said that winter of 1967:

"You are god,
and you are not,
it's good not to get the two confused.
It is one."

Paradoxes like this have haunted my life since it began. My mother was perfect, yet there was always something missing. The Church offered immortality, yet I could not survive in it. My generation went to war and marched for peace. My very own patron saint, Jeanne d'Arc, was both a general and a witch.

Once I believed things only had one name. The Holy Roman Apostolic and Catholic Church for instance, had its parameters cemented in two thousand years of infallibility. This was the rock upon which I based my life.

CHAPTER 1

Montecito: A Place Apart

All of my life I had been waiting for September 6, 1966. My limbo was now over. Our gold Cadillac convertible swept beneath the convent portal. "Welcome to the Novitiate of the Immaculate Heart of Mary," the sign read. Immersed in my eighteen-year-old passion, I jumped up off the back seat and screamed, "I'm home!"

Neither my parents nor my twelve siblings paid any attention to me or the sign. They continued to scream and yell as though we were bound for the circus.

Swerving sharply, perhaps in an unconscious attempt to unload half his offspring, Dad took a curve in the novitiate's seemingly interminable winding drive, almost careening the Cadillac into a serene grotto of Jesus and His Sacred Heart.

"Joan, I told you we shouldn't have brought them all. Please check and see if the Cordovan made that turn onto San Ysidro Lane with us," he said.

The Cordovan was a late-model, bright red-and-white striped Chevrolet van Dad had customized as the family vacation vehicle. Even with the top down, and Mom almost literally stuffing us into the Cadillac like turkey dressing, there wasn't nearly enough room for all of their twelve children in one car.

"Yes, it's back there, Fred. It's easy to spot through the trees," Mom answered. She leaned over Zoe and Vincent to gently pat her exasperated husband's shoulder. "I know this is a lot of trouble, Fred, but it's the most important day of Jeanne's life. We all need to be here."

Since grade school, I'd marked each calendar I'd owned with the day I was to enter the convent. In a couple of hours, after the picnic and formal orientation, I was to meet my future sisters. The portal sign had read, "Welcome." Did that really include me? The branches of the ancient oaks surrounding the novitiate's gardens whipped the sides of the car, impatiently urging me onward. Except for summer camp, I'd never really been away from home. It's peculiar how the obvious never shows up until the last moment. I was always sure about wanting to join the convent but hadn't reckoned that meant leaving my family.

The Cadillac finally emerged from a mysterious orchard of barren fruit trees and screeched to a stop in a crowded circular parking lot. Other families were already picnicking on a grassy knoll nearby.

"We're here! Open the damn door and get out the food. I'm starving." Bill leaned across me and flipped the door handle.

"William, don't swear," Mom admonished. Mom never swore until we moved from Europe to "the land of barbarians" twelve years ago. Californians ran around barefooted and wore "indecent" swimsuits. Since living among the Philistines, she too had culturally degenerated, adopting "damn brats" as her collective noun for us during times of high stress. But not in a convent.

"Darnation!" I screamed, as Bill's scramble flung me into the cactus patch immediately beneath the open door. But I hardly felt the needles in my rear end—I couldn't take my eyes off the edifice of Montecito.

There have always been inner sanctums in all great religions—secluded estates of the divine, convents and monasteries, where men and women come to marry God. The tradition of solitude breeds mysticism. Ancient man had rites of seclusion. The Spirit Guardians of North American Indian legend protected warriors in their wilderness of isolation. Even my favorite mystic, Thomas Merton, patron saint of the godless twentieth century, cherished the lifestyle, "which empties the heart of all earthly attachments so it can be free, be silent, hear God, and pray always." Seeing Montecito now for the first time in my life, my heart emptied and refilled with awe.

The castle rose before me. The stately entrance and sprawling main house crowned the vast fifty-acre estate given to the Immaculate Heart Order by the Dupont family. The main house appeared to have several wings linked by inner courtyards evoking another epoch's romance. The stone-block walls met terra-cotta roof tiles, which were topped by steeples that rose in prayer toward the heavens. Slim green vines laced the castle from ground to steeple tops. The serene magnificence of the building was fortified by a dramatic six-foot-wide oak-and-iron door. This antique could have been hauled to this spot at the behest of Father Junipero Serra in the late eighteenth century by the Chumash Indians. The entrance was at the end of a shrouded tiled passageway as holy as Moses' path up Sinai. The sanctified grounds, which I could barely glimpse peeking out from behind the main house, were replete with gently rolling rock gardens and alcoves.

This was my Paradise *Found*. Montecito appeared to be the very promise of Merton: a place "in which to dare to penetrate my own silence, and . . . advance without fear into the solitude of my own heart." It was, every sacred stone and beveled stained-glass window, exactly what Sister Veronica Mary, my high school mentor, had led me to dream about in her poem:

3

Montecito

A Place Apart . . .
Where I fear not to be myself,
Away from the money lenders and conscience tabbers
Away from the pharisees and sadnesses of my life.

A Place Apart . . .
Where the saint may forgive
And the sinner may praise
Where nature in her multicolored sunsets
Spreads out an ocean of brilliant silvers,
Interrupted only by the white shear
Of an orchard path winding its way
To a solitude and silence I learned to hold for true.

A place where I was first introduced to humility
And her odd ways of behaving
Where Love blossomed into meaningful depth
And friendship ideas searched for greater meaning.

I was alone, not lonely.
I was myself, not conscious of paltry pettiness,
I was God's and this began
To be my only boast,
And I guess shall always be.

In a few short moments Serra's wrought-iron-and-oak entrance
would miraculously open, beckoning me, a bride of Christ. Already
I could feel Montecito, Merton's "intimate union." Would I refill my
soul here with the wine of mystics? My rapture went unnoticed as I
stood there speechless. Family and crowds swirled around me; they
dwelled on the earthly plane.

The Immaculate Heart of Mary community was founded in
1848 by Father Puig in Spain. The sisterhood crossed the Atlantic
and came to rest in San Francisco in the 1920s.

The microphone sputtered to life and a tall, robed figure
mounted the dais in front of the gathering. "Good afternoon, dear
families," said the shrill voice. "My name is Mother Mary Caritas."

4

Plastic picnic forks stopped in mid-air. There were no rules of etiquette for how to listen to your child being received into religious life, but my parents stood up.

"On behalf of the sisterhood of the Immaculate Heart of Mary, I would like to welcome the fifteen members of our postulant class of 1966."

I tried to ferret out of the crowd my fourteen other mates—their faces must be as tense as my own. My only other real clue was that they'd likely be my own age, since most candidates entered the convent directly after high school. Catholic mythology held that if you let young girls escape as far as college, Sodom and Gomorrah would corrupt their souls and render them irrevocably unfit.

I felt someone staring and half-turned to my left. The short, frail girl appeared as innocent as I. Even from a distance she looked like an aspiring postulant. Except that her attention was focused on me rather than Mother Mary Caritas. I smoothed my windblown hair into place and checked my collar. I was dressed more neatly than usual, so why was she staring? The girl put her hand over her eyebrows, as if to shade them from the sun, but it was cloudy. She flicked one finger back and forth over her eyes like a windshield wiper. Was it a signal to me? Perhaps she found my James Dean wrap-around sunglasses amusing. Mom told me not to wear them, "out of place," she'd commented. But I always wore my sunglasses, rain or shine, when I was nervous. I nodded to the bemused stranger deliberately and arrogantly, *Yes, and I'm going to keep them on, thank you!* The girl tilted her head coquettishly and smiled.

"I know you've all been looking forward to this day," the bony Mother Superior's voice abruptly commanded my attention, "but perhaps you parents are even more anxious than your children. I want to assure you they are safe here in God's hands."

I already had my doubts about being safe in Mother Caritas' hands. It was terror at first sight when I'd met her three months before at my acceptance interview in Los Angeles. An elongated being with a pinched, red-and-white blotched complexion, Mother

5

Caritas' bony fingers sliced the air in slow motion when she spoke. Her facial skin was stretched back severely as though she'd made a ponytail of the excess flesh at the nape of her neck. Her hair was coifed and veiled, of course, so my speculation was not verifiable. Mother Caritas spoke in a high-pitched whine that sounded like the last molecules of oxygen were escaping from her collapsed lungs. Her voice was unearthly; it had a supernatural echo, a tortured Anne Bancroft anguishing through a Cecil B. De Mille kind of epic.

"My title, Mistress of Postulants," she continued, "may sound odd. It's an old Latin translation that simply means I will be your daughters' direct Mother Superior during their first year. 'Postulant' comes from the Latin verb *postulare,* meaning one who proposes, one who is an apprentice, a candidate. Today, your postulant daughters begin a two-year novitiate to become fully professed nuns. They will spend those years here in Montecito . . . in an extensive on-the-job-training program."

I laughed out loud at the juxtaposition of Latin and President Johnson's war-on-poverty jargon. The frail stranger who didn't like my sunglasses was smirking to herself also. I wanted to wait until she looked at me again, to exchange smirks. Mom stared at me briefly. I guess it wasn't a joke.

"For the first year," the Mistress continued, "they will wear a modified habit, the postulant's habit—a navy blue skirt and blazer, and a plain white cotton blouse. Two sets of this uniform will be issued to each of them tomorrow."

Dad nodded his somber approval. As a West Point graduate, he had often said the world would be eternally simplified, more morally upright, not to mention more cost-efficient, if everyone wore a uniform from birth to the grave. He thought the convent—in addition to being a holy calling—was a "well-disciplined outfit." In the-gospel-according-to-Dad, discipline, not cleanliness, sat at the right hand of God. Discipline ensured character as well as salvation. Drilling in his point, he used to play reveille through the house intercom to wake us up every morning. He'd followed his prerecorded West Point morning hymn with tender admonishments such as, "Sunrise in the swamps, boys!" and "Up and at 'em, another day, another dollar!" There would be no bugles in the convent, I was sure.

"Upon completing their postulancy next July, your daughters will make a private retreat in preparation for their First Vows—the vows of poverty, chastity, and obedience. We'll be sending them home to you for a week of self-evaluation before making this major decision. Those who return to Montecito will become novices. They will don the habit you see me wearing, except that they will wear a white veil rather than the black of the fully professed." Employing her first visual aid, Mother Caritas used a bony finger to point to her own black headdress.

I was not pleased with this news about the postponed habit. The silly postulant uniform didn't sound much different from our girls' uniforms at Bishop Amat, my high school. I'd have to wait almost a year before I *looked* like a nun! Somehow it felt easier to be holy underneath a real habit.

Still, wearing any kind of uniform was probably a good idea—for me. Dressing had always been problematic. I hoped the socks would be starched, since I'd never liked folding them down around my ankles and they'd never stayed up around my calves if they weren't starched. To Mom's chagrin, I always returned home from school with my shirt untucked and hanging out around my hips, the sleeves rolled up so they wouldn't bother me playing softball. I combed my abundant and wild black wavy hair once a day as prescribed, but it never seemed to do much good. My shoes were always badly scuffed. I ran into things, and my jacket was more often on the ground than on my back. Luckily, I'd inherited a nice dose of my parents' good looks, Irish features in a light Spanish complexion, so I got away with being called "messy" rather than "ugly." But the convent would probably not tolerate messy.

"The novices are at prayer now," Mother Caritas continued. "Although they do share a few classes together, we maintain a separation of novices and postulants because they are at different stages in their spiritual development."

7

Not good. I shook my head in disappointment. Earlier I'd seen two white-veiled figures emerge from a side door in the main house. My attention was drawn to the one with a guitar slung over her shoulder. Short, with a stately carriage to her shoulders, she had jet black hair that poked out from around the white-starched coif that framed her face, forehead to chin. As they stood laughing and pointing toward the crowd, I could see the deep set of dimples cut into the guitarist's cheeks. Her smile was enchanting. I had been looking forward to meeting her at dinner, if not sooner. I'd always wanted to learn to play the guitar. But, according to Mother Caritas, there would be no early introduction . . . perhaps we'd have a class together.

Mother Caritas continued highlighting my future. "Next fall, as novices, their training and spiritual studies will deepen as they prepare to become fully professed nuns. During their novice year they will also begin their certifications as teachers or nurses. The Immaculate Hearts are a secular, rather than a cloistered order, which means we go out into the world to perform our missionary service."

I had some doubts about my abilities as a nurse or teacher. I had no bedside manner. I agreed with Mom's perspective on injury and health: if it's not bleeding, you're fine. I enjoyed most of my teachers at Bishop Amat, especially the Immaculate Hearts who were always the most witty, bright, and otherwise perfect academics. But I never felt a vocation to teach. In my family, teaching mostly boiled down to crowd control. Left to baby sit when Mom and Dad had Church work, I'd stalk the bedroom corridors imitating my father, the would-be general, "No TV until I see finished pages!" "A night with no homework is a good night for a book."

The Blessed Virgin save my future students! I had decided to join the IHM order because they had missionary houses in the ghettos. I wanted to become a postulant, make my First Vows, become a novice, and then after a year take on the black veil of the fully professed, and leave Montecito with some assignment serving the disenfranchised. I felt my specific vocation was to be a crusader for the poor like Francis of Assisi or St. Damien, who labored among the lepers. I wanted to right some of the world's wrongs, not spend my life lecturing the suburban middle class on the ABC's of Christian affluence.

Even after profession in two years, I knew I'd have to wait another five years before taking Final Vows. Good God in heaven! It would be seven years in all before my postulant class made that final lifetime commitment. Seven years to decide something I'd already committed to ten years ago. Still, this had been part of the Holy Rule for centuries. I shifted my weight against the picnic table and wondered if there was some rule about not sitting down while Mother Superior talked.

"Lastly, a word about our Holy Rule," Mother Caritas persisted. I craned my neck to pay closer attention. I'd heard about the Holy Rule but no one had spoken to me about it in detail. "During the novitiate, your daughter's daily routine will be regulated by a schedule of prayer, work, study, and silence. The daily routine of a nun is critical to her spiritual development. The Holy Rule sets the tone and pace for close communion with God and self.

In the Middle Ages nuns were given such penance as self-flagellation, but whips were out in the twentieth century. Perhaps Mother Caritas would make us keep Grand Silence for the rest of our lives or crawl around the rock gardens on our hands and knees.

"Sisters arise at 5:00 AM to meet in Chapel for Matins, which are morning prayers, and Mass. Breakfast follows, then classes and chores. At noon we come together again for Lauds, during which we sing the praises of the Lord for each day. Sacramentology, theology, or secular classes are held in the afternoons." Mother Caritas looked directly at me as she arranged my life.

"Yes, we do educate them," she said. "We are primarily concerned with their metaphysical development, but Immaculate Hearts do not neglect the mind. All of our sisters attain at least a Bachelor of Arts degree from our college in Los Angeles, many of us have gone on to achieve our master's and doctorates."

Dad reached around Mom and gave me a congratulatory slap on the shoulder. He had approved of my choosing the IHM's because they were emphatic about higher education. Dad's version of higher education was "as far as your mind can take you." Woe be unto the Córdova who thought required education ended with high school. It would be simpler to drop out of the family than to drop out of college. I knew he wanted me, like my older sister France, who had just completed her freshman year at Stanford, to at least obtain a master's degree. This sat well with me. I loved school. Graduating with honors and as vice-president of Amat's California Scholarship Federation, I was looking forward to college with a passion.

"In the evenings before dinner," Mother Mary Caritas continued, wrapping up the Holy Rule, "we chant Vespers together. We occasionally have special lectures in the evenings from visiting priests, or we share communal recreation—singing or reading. Compline, our closing prayers of the day, gives the sisterhood an opportunity to say goodnight to the Lord and to one another. Postulants then retire to their cells."

Traipsing between chapel and classes singing, especially in Gregorian chant, and studying all day sounded like my kind of life. It would just be a continuation of everything I'd been practicing for years. It was exactly what I'd been led to believe about religious life. How delightful!

Except for the 5:00 AM part. That would be a cross. I was positive God had invented the dawn as shock therapy, a prelude to purgatory. I hated mornings. I couldn't see, I couldn't think, and God help the fool who tried to get me to talk before breakfast. "Jeanne is an unadulterated crab in the morning!" Mom diagnosed when I was in the fourth grade and had failed to outgrow what she called my "birth defect." My sister France had assured me that many college classes didn't begin until 10 AM. Apparently I had picked the wrong college. Ah well, God would have to provide.

"Before I bid you good evening, please know that our sisterhood is indeed grateful for the dowry you have given us on

10

behalf of your daughters." Mother Superior brought up the topic Mom hadn't wanted to mention. One never discussed money publicly. It was, Mom said, uncouth. "This donation will help us care for your child and spread God's Word through our teaching."

"Joan," Dad said, prodding Mom's shoulder, as I twisted my neck again, this time trying to overhear them. "Do you think we gave enough? Jeanne didn't get straight A's in conduct you know." Dad was a problem at times. And I thought Mom exaggerated my personality disorders.

"One day, when Jeanne was five," she would explain to friends. "I overheard her sitting there talking to herself on the back porch. She was debating going barefoot. She said, 'The Devil tells me to take off my shoes. Mommy says to keep them on. But it's hot, so I'll take them off anyway.'"

Today Mom was less anecdotal. "Yes, Fred, I added a little more than the five hundred dollars they requested."

The Mistress of Postulants declared, stepping away from the podium, "Thank you all for coming. Postulants, you will have one hour now to say goodbye to your family and to your previous life."

On this ominous note, no one clapped.

CHAPTER 2

The Tower of Babble

I never really wanted to leave Mom. While Dad was most often in Europe or preoccupied at the office, Mom was as present, as long-suffering, as all-purposely Mom as Holy Mother the Church herself. We thought she was infallible. All the neighbors said the woman with twelve kids was Supermom. Leaving her, I naturally sought perfection again in my next love object. The Blessed Virgin Mary appeared to be my best alternative.

Alone on the picnic blanket, I sat cross-legged on the grass and propped my elbows on my knees. Mom was demurely picking her way through my siblings, chiding and attempting to keep our corner of the convent grass in some holy order.

Perhaps it was the nuns at her convent school who taught Mom that duty was a deeper love than words. We were always well-fed, well-dressed, well-cared-for in body and mind, but she was rarely emotionally intimate. "I love you," and its awkward corollaries, came infrequently. By the age of one or two each of us was supplanted by the most recent arrival. Weaning was abrupt.

My mother seldom referred to her own childhood. That was "too personal and impractical" since she "wasn't a child anymore." I suppose having twelve children, a demanding husband, and a prayer book full of Church and social obligations meant self-analysis wasn't a top priority. After all, we had to have clean socks every day, twenty-four little clean socks to be exact. Twenty-six if you count Dad's. My mother rarely got personal with me either, except at major growth points in my life. Then she simply uttered the impersonal, "No, you can't . . . go barefooted, play Little League baseball, grow up and drive in the Indianapolis 500, watch TV on a school night, have a slumber party, have a boyfriend until high school, stay up until midnight, stay out overnight, go on vacation with a friend's family, or learn to drive a car."

I didn't need to know her autobiography to see why my father had married her twenty years ago. She was as white as he was brown, as rich as he was poor, as "arrived" in her birthright as he was yet to establish his own. In a word, he married "up." This was just the beginning of why, we all agreed, Mom was the best thing that ever happened to Dad. Dad agreed. At thirty-nine she was still stunningly beautiful. The neighbors concurred, "You'd never believe she's the mother of twelve!" Petite and ever-poised, a small smattering of gray strands had just begun to accent her jet-black Irish locks. They fell down her back in gentle undulations. Even though she rarely combed her hair—too much combing might amount to the sin of vanity—her mane was lustrous. Creamy-white skin created the backdrop for her self-possessed blue eyes, giving her a delicate look. But it was Mom's strong mind that dominated her personality, offering a counterpoint to any who would think Dad had married her simply for her looks. Our sibling argument over whether Dad was smarter than Mom, or vice-versa, was a source of continuous debate.

I don't know how it came to pass that my mother knew the biography of every saint ever martyred by a Roman gladiator, or the historical and theological etiology of every nook and cranny of Catholic doctrine. Her mother, Frances McGuinness, was a bona fide Irish Catholic—she worshipped nuns. Perhaps the seeds of Mom's encyclopedic knowledge came from the nuns at her school in Queens, New York. Despite all of us, come evening she always had her head in a book and boasted a Catholic library that was eventually donated to the local bishop. Had there been a Catholic Smithsonian, Mom, her books, and her saintly pet projects—such as a larger-than-life mural of the Last Supper on the kitchen wall—would have qualified for inclusion. There was no Catholic Smithsonian, so the twelve apostles remained on the wall and joined us for hard-boiled eggs each morning.

Brushing the flies off someone's leftover sandwich, I thought about the three-hour drive from West Covina this afternoon. It had offered an extensive, if chaotic, period of contemplation. Growing up, I'd learned to think and pray without missing a synapse—under conditions rivaling a world war. Still, the journey hadn't lasted long enough. I had a lot of good-byes to whisper there in the back seat, staring at Dad's head.

Last night our fourteen bodies had adorned the huge dinner table like rosary beads. Until today the dinner table was the center-piece of my life. Dad sat at the head of the table with Mom on his right. It had always been so. Breaking form with the Last Supper, we twelve were arranged in chronological order; the six youngest were propped next to Mom and Dad so they'd learn that being one of a dozen doesn't mean you can eat spaghetti with your knife. "The Middle Kingdom," the girls—Marianne, Leslie, and Louise, served as a buffer zone between the babies and "the Big Three," the eldest triumvirate to which France, Bill, and I belonged. Mom arranged us into reference groups like "the Middle Kingdom" in hopes of persuading the neighbors that her procreation held some order, if no sanity. But there was no sanity at our family dinner table, only verbal cannibalism.

14

"Mom, what's the doctrine of predestination?" France asked, leaning forward with full attention on Mom while thrusting a handful of peas to Louise, who dutifully stuffed them on the ledge underneath the table.

"Jeanne, I mean Marianne, I mean Frances Córdova, who told you that word? That's heresy!" My father exclaimed, glaring at France. He could never remember our names when he got emotional. Heresy was always emotional.

"She probably read about it in some book Larry, her *boyfriend,* gave her!" Bill chimed in on cue. A nasty fifteen, Bill fought the family's matriarchal dominance by picking on all of his sisters—except me. Bill and I were partners in hooliganism.

"I told you to stop seeing that atheist!" Dad continued. "Joan, do something about your daughter."

"Predestination is a heresy that eclipses free will." Mom did something about our education. "It comes out of seventeenth century Calvinism, which . . ."

". . .was popularized by John Calvin," Dad interrupted, "who was a German heretic and a forerunner of Karl Marx!" (Karl was Head Heretic.) "It's fundamentally atheistic because it says there is no such thing as free will, all things are pre-determined."

"Then it's similar to the Church's Doctrine of Infallibility, which says the Pope is always right," I interjected, grabbing my opening in the debate.

"No, Jeanne, it's not similar!" Mom eyed me suspiciously, trying to figure out if I was mocking or serious. "Papal infallibility is the Divine Word of Christ: 'Thou art Peter, and upon this rock I will build my Church.'"

Mom paused to replace a fork right-side-up in Zoe's little fist. "Predestination," she continued, "says there is no such thing as free will, that secular evolution predetermines man's behavior and thought. It also negates the concept of Original Sin, Adam's fall from Grace, and it denies man's moral reclamation of heaven through faith."

15

"But," I retorted, holding my ground, "Socrates says there is no such thing as morality in the abstract. So how can the Pope dictate morality for all the peoples of the world, through all times and cultures? Socrates says . . ."

"Oh, Jeanne, even Plato says there are definitely absolutes in the universe," France countered. France and I definitely had little in common except our mutual enjoyment of the *Index*, the Catholic list of forbidden authors. "Darwin also suggests . . . " France continued.

"Joan, where are these kids getting these books?" Dad shouted, motioning to Mom to fix him a highball. Despite his Mexican heritage, or Spanish, as he preferred to call it, Dad was some kind of non-Catholic before he met Mom. We'd heard rumors that Grandpa Córdova believed in reincarnation. But when we tried to explore Dad's own mysterious religious past, he'd regale us with funny stories about his being a Holy Roller, barreling up and down the aisles of a mythical canvas church in south Texas. The rigidification of his intestines, ileitis, at the end of his college years at West Point, put an end to his fundamentalism, his military career, and, very nearly, his life.

Mom said she'd have married him even if he hadn't become a Catholic. "I was in love," she'd simply state. Short, dark, and handsome my father's grace on the dance floor and his sword-and-saber Anthony Quinn dash literally swept her off her feet. Twenty years later, all twelve of us would sit in rapture as Dad still waltzed Mom around the kitchen. Mom also told us that she figured Dad for a "man of substance" because he must have had brains to get into West Point. In those prenuptial years, Mom said Dad was vivacious and aggressive and, unlike her first boyfriend, who wouldn't take her to a Donald Duck movie, my father was thoughtful. In the friendship that preceded their courtship, Dad even arranged blind dates for Mom. Very thoughtful, I thought.

Hospitalized the day after graduation, Dad was given an honorable military boot. Hearing he was going to die, he became a deathbed convert to the faith of his betrothed. It was not a spurious

16

decision. Since he couldn't become a general, he arose from his deathbed hell bent on becoming a saint. The collective consensus of his children was that Mom stood a better chance of canonization.

"What exactly is faith, Mom?" I continued relentlessly. "Socrates maintains that the Greek belief system was no more than a cultural phenomenon, begotten to help his people interpret their world. He says faith is a rationalization for life."

"Faith," Mom said, in summation, "is the eternal and internal, most private and most sublime Inner Knowledge of God in His Wisdom. And faith . . ."

" . . . is akin to free will," Dad finished. Their one-mindedness was sometimes frightening. Luckily, their osmosis did not extend to child raising. Depression-born, Dad would have had us walk to school in snowshoes if there had been any snow in Southern California. He took the Catholic interpretation of Original Sin seriously and treated us like his twelve personal bad seeds. Mom, on the other hand, insisted baptism had redeemed her children.

"Free will is what separates men from animals," Dad continued, delineating the only difference he recognized between us and Pipeline, the family dog. "Free will is our soul's . . . "

"Where is the soul in our psyches?" I asked, taking off on a new jag. Mom rose to clear the table and motioned us to follow suit. I wanted to talk all night; I always did. My family in debate at the dinner table made me feel important, special—well-heard and well-fed intellectually. Everyone talking at once in heated conversation made me feel safe. Visiting friends commented, "You all interrupt one another like crazy!" But in my family words were love.

Did the Immaculate Hearts have dinner-table debates? I wondered. Baby Tom crawled over my lap after his Tinker Toys on Montecito's grass. France was probably reading Descartes over there under the Sacred Heart of Jesus statue. Mom and Dad must still be wandering the orchard looking for strays.

17

Everyone seemed nonchalant about my imminent departure behind the iron door. But then again, it was no surprise to anyone. For a decade my siblings had told their friends, "Jeanne's not going to be anything when she grows up. She's going into the convent."

I was born a predetermined soul, despite my parents' theological protestations about such things. From birth I had a sense of my own destiny, as if the news had already gone to print. I was incarnated treading a road already marked, searching for the fork not yet illuminated. The signposts were shrouded, but my intuition told me I was destined to find some Holy Grail.

At the instant of my conception, my parents were taking a nocturnal break from helping C.A.R.E. rebuild postwar Germany. For their honeymoon, they had sailed off, not into the sunset but to a devastated Europe. They landed after the V-E Day soldiers, not on Normandy's beaches, but at the American embassy in Paris, where France was born. In Europe my parents had almost as many children, myself included, as there were countries on the Western Front. Six years later, we flew to the opposite side of the world, West Covina, California, where I started school.

St. Christopher's was one of those baby-boom Catholic grammar schools built in the early fifties. Surrounded by cactus and orange groves, the school was continually adding new classrooms to accommodate the fruits of paternal ardor following World War II. I don't know why it was named after St. Christopher, the traveler's saint. Once you got to West Covina, you never left. It was a suburb in L.A.'s San Gabriel Valley utterly devoid of character or ambience, filled with tumbleweeds and twentieth-century pioneers whose American Dream was to replace the weeds with supermarkets.

At the age of seven I was old enough to play softball and old enough to make a solemn vow. The dirt in Southern California sweltered in the muggy spring morning. My headband kept the sweat from my eyes. I was leading my second-grade team to victory over the fourth-grade girls. The bottom of the seventh, the last inning, loomed now with two outs and runners on first and second. My bat wobbled for a moment as I strode to the plate. "Please, God," I whispered, "Gimme a win, and I'm yours for the rest of my life!" The pitch came in a little high and wide, but that was my specialty. I smacked it solidly to right center. As I watched the right fielder scramble through the orange fields after the ball, I knew God had answered me.

My teammates rushed to greet my return and swept me into the cactus in back of home plate. "Ow!" I yelled, pulling the painful needles out of my thighs. Glowing with victory, I pulled away from my squad. "A deal is a deal," I called back to their questioning faces, "I've got to go thank God!"

Bounding into the church, I removed my headband and kneeled solemnly on the pew in front of the statue of Baby Jesus. In the mammoth structure there were several side altars depicting images of the saints in their various poses. Passing them daily en route to Holy Communion I felt I'd never make the in-crowd. I couldn't be a saint. In order to be canonized, a lengthy Vatican ritual that proclaimed to the world you had positively gone to heaven, you had to be swallowed by lions, get crucified, or die a hermit in the desert after praying a thousand years. West Covina had no lions, and the orange groves didn't qualify as desert. I'd probably have to go to Russia to get crucified. Falling into cactus and suffering in silence wasn't nearly enough to get canonized.

I lit a votive candle on the altar. "Hi, Jesus, it's me, Jeanne. We just won the game. I heard you tell me, 'Take the third pitch, it's the one.' And it was!"

I let my presence sink in and awaited His reply. This morning when Mom was helping me find my other shoe, she had said it was time to "have priorities." I think she meant cleaning out my closet was more important than oiling my glove, but it had started me thinking.

Since I couldn't be a saint, I would have settled for becoming a priest, a Jesuit to be exact. St. Ignatius of Loyola was the founder of the Jesuits and, according to Mom, one of the smartest saints who ever lived. Chances were I'd grow up to be the smartest girl priest who ever lived if I got to study with the Jesuits. I also wanted to be a major league baseball player and a race car driver. Having my picture on a green baseball card with all my home runs, like Milwaukee Braves outfielder Hank Aaron, would be about the next best thing to being a Jesuit. Besides I could do both! Baseball players had to retire when they got old, so I could be a Jesuit as a second career. But I couldn't really be a Jesuit, or win the Grand Prix, or even be a miserable Dodger, because I was a girl. So, I was going to be a nun; it was the next best thing.

"And what have you decided?" Jesus added, breaking into my reverie sweetly. I appreciated His eternal patience.

"What I want to do is be with You all the time. And pray and love You. And have You love me too, of course!"

"I will always love you, Jeanne."

"That's why I want to be with You. I want to help others know how much You love them also. So I want to be a nun for the rest of my life. Will You take me as a nun? I know I get into trouble a lot. It's so hard to stop in the middle of a pitch when the recess bell rings, but that's small potatoes."

There was a long silence as I closed my eyes, hoping for a favorable response. "Becoming a nun is about the little things in life as well as the big things, Jeanne."

Jesus was like Mom, He never missed a thing. "Is this what you really want, Jeanne? To love Me, and serve Me alone, forsaking all others?"

"Jesus, I really do love You. I'm happiest when we talk. I've spoken with God the Father and Mary also. I can't imagine being anything else except a nun because that is the closest I can get to You. I promise You forever, Jesus, as soon as I get out of high school, if I ever get that far, I'm Yours."

20

CHAPTER 3

My Holy Family

The sun was touching down on the Santa Barbara ocean two miles to the west. Tomorrow my life would change. I turned slowly, trying to absorb Montecito. I began to panic; my stomach knotted. I wanted to vomit. Had I made the right decision? I'd never really be part of my family again. Childhood was permanently slipping away. Emotions churned as I made my way back to the picnic blanket where my mother was gathering toys.

"Mom?" I whispered softly as I watched her bent over, hands darting, picking up Bill's discarded playing deck, Kathy's dolls, Vincent's marbles.

"Yes, Jeanne. What is it? Where is everyone? I haven't seen the boys in almost an hour."

"They ran into the orchard after the dog." I didn't know to which of my brothers she was referring, but it hardly mattered. "I really need to talk with you, I feel . . . "

She straightened up and twisted the lids back on the mayonnaise and mustard jars. "I'm too busy now, Jeanne. Perhaps we can talk just before we leave. I must go find everyone, so we can get out of here on time. Tell your father I went collecting." I watched her bustle an armful out to the cars. Then she turned into the orchard.

Sitting on the blanket, I let my tears out. Mom never had time. Too many kids, too much Church work. For as long as I could remember my parents had been "too busy." Luckily, I'd found Someone who did have time, all the time in the world.

Jesus was always with me. *Don't cry*, I could almost feel His hand around my shoulders as I wept. *I know you're frightened. But you will see them again. They will come to visit, or you will go to see them. Marrying Me does not mean you must leave them entirely.*

"But it will never be the same again," I mumbled half-aloud.

No, it will never be the same. I too left my parents' house and went out to do My Father's work.

"Were you afraid even though you were God?"

I was also human, like you, Jeanne. Of course, I was afraid. I was afraid at Gethsemane also, remember? Comparing my venturing into a new life to the end of His, I laughed. I had so little about which to complain. My Best Friend had such a gentle but wry sense of humor. He knew just how to bring me out of my doldrums. I smiled my thanks. Talking with Christ for the rest of my life I'd never be lonely.

I'd returned to St. Christopher's this last summer and renewed my commitment in front of the Infant of Prague. I wasn't only playing games when I hit the home run in the second grade and made that promise with the simple clear consciousness of a seven-year-old. I'd never changed my mind, but somewhere in high school the simplicity had deepened. I'd fallen in love with Jesus Christ. Our long contemplative tete-a-tetes in the little wooden chapel at Amat during recesses, lunch hours, and after school had bewitched my heart. God, the Blessed Virgin, and especially Jesus, had always been there for me. Never too busy. To them I was very special and there was always enough time to talk, to weep, to console, to joke.

22

I took my concerns about the future to God the Father. In chapel, on my knees, I'd feel His benevolence fall over me in paternal warmth. I was convinced He had a huge rocking chair where He'd sit just outside the gates of Heaven upon a summer evening and watch me cavort through my earthly dramas. He was always telling me to worry less about grades and college. Once He paraphrased one of His Son's speeches, "Blessed are the stupid, Jeanne, for they shall know My name has only one syllable. I'm an easy kind of guy." He was always easy and kind with me.

For better or for worse, Mary was the recipient of my heart's confusion. And there was always plenty of that. To me, the Blessed Virgin always wore blue so she could float forever camouflaged in the sky, seeing to this and that little matter of the hearts of we who loved her. And oh, how I did! She had known great love and great sorrow. Who but She had ever been asked to gestate the very physical body of the Son of God in her womb, only to watch that same body being torn apart in a gruesome death He never deserved. I could trust my heart's longings to her heart's depth. When I squabbled with, or was rejected by, friends, she was my Holy Mother who held my broken heart. "I love you, Jeanne," she told me. "I'll take care of you. You don't need to be so attached to earthly love."

Jesus was my best friend, my confidant, my groom-to-be. He was my constant companion. Whether in chapel, driving home from school, fighting with a teacher, or in the middle of a football rally, my inner life was filled with sharing everything with Him. "What do you make of that?" I asked Him as we sat together at lunch. "Mom forgot to put in the sandwich!" Or I'd kick stones across left field in some dull inning. "Tell me again, Jesus, about the mystery of the Trinity. How is it that You and God the Father and the Holy Ghost are one?"

No matter what the subject, Jesus listened to my feelings. And often lectured at the end. I told Him everything and still He knew more about me than I could ever reveal. This was our love. All that I was, was inside of Him because I gave it all. He wanted everything from me. My only sorrow was that I'd probably never be a pure enough vessel to know all He was. My soul ached with the longing to know and love Him more deeply. Through all the petty distractions of childhood traumas and adolescent romances, it was always Jesus, the Christ of my soul, who was my future.

I affixed Tommy on my hip and set out to comb the novitiate grounds. It was getting late and I wanted time to say good-bye. Tommy's diaper was wet. I wondered if he'd grow up to be a ladies' man like Bill, a jock like little Fred, or some sort of intellectual hybrid. I wouldn't be around to watch him develop his roots. I spotted Vincent and Fred III off in the distance. They were playing with the convent dog. Where was Snow White and Rose Red, as Mom called the blue-eyed, fair, and freckled Kathy and brown-complected Zoe? They were probably all romping through the sacred orchard venerated by Sister Veronica Mary in her poem. Zoe, Mom's ninth child, was supposed to be the last Córdova, hence we named her after the last saint in the Book of Saints.

Obviously, Zoe wasn't the last, but today she was probably the last of the chaos I had come to know and love as my family. Convent life would be different. Mother Caritas hadn't mentioned it, but I knew Grand Silence was part of the Holy Rule. Silence meant no talking—to anyone, for any reason. It was for communing, for soul searching, for discipline over the senses. There would be periods of time each day, and on feast days perhaps the whole day, where I might hear only the sound of my breathing, the whisper of my missal's pages turning in my hands. Would I be able to concentrate without the dishwasher, the dryer, the radio, and the TV going? How strange!

I flipped Tom over to my other hip and turned to gaze again at the impenetrable main house. All those years of research and studying and I'd never asked, do nuns celebrate birthdays? Surely we wouldn't go prancing through the cells on Halloween singing, "When the Córdovas come marching in." What would they, I, do on Christmas Eve? Would we sit by the fire making up new verses to songs that fit each kid's personality? Nuns aren't supposed to have

24

personalities. *The Imitation of Christ,* our postulant mini-Bible, read, "personality is vanity . . . all then is vanity but to love God, and serve Him alone."

"How long did Silence last?" I asked Tommy rhetorically. If I didn't speak for days on end, would it change the way I think? Would I change? Maybe that was the idea. Who was I supposed to become? Silence had come to mean God to me. It was in chapel, and in the mountains at summer camp, the only two quiet places I'd ever known, that I'd heard Jesus most clearly. When I was camping this last summer, the wilderness' solitude amplified the wind-song of the high pines. Away from the mundanity of life, caught in the sunrise of a sleepless night in the San Jacinto Mountains, I wrote in my diary:

"Oh, peaks of foreign majesty
White clouds pierce thy summits,
Skies of blue shine glorious,
Resplendent sun, your subjects offer,
Reflections of silence for all to see."

There was something hidden in silence, something I loved. Yet I feared the stillness. I'd grown up in the Tower of Babble, and now the monastic desert lay before me.

The babble was suddenly approaching. Mom had herded them into the parking lot and had pressured the Middle Kingdom into repacking the picnic supplies. Dad, keys in hand, was idling against the Cadillac with France, presumably lecturing her about her return to Stanford next week.

My whole family would probably forget me in a week. "Out of sight, out of mind" was another family saying. My parents were always forgetting us. Marianne, always too opaque for her own good, had been overlooked sitting on a stump in Arizona's Petrified Forest. At the age of four, Vince had spent a night lost under a surfboard in a sand dune at Newport Beach.

Today, however, everyone was present and accounted for. Watching France get in behind the wheel of the Cordovan, I wondered if they'd sing the family song on the way home and count off aloud in chronological order as Dad had insisted ever since the Colorado Highway Patrol found Leslie in the Rocky Mountains before he did. What would they think when there was a big silence after France screamed out her name? They couldn't turn around and come back after me in the convent, even if I became lost within it. One was supposed to lose oneself here.

"Well, Pal, lots of luck." My father had left the Cadillac running to come over and clasp a firm hand on my shoulder. Dad never had much to say about my vocation, or my life, for that matter. His domains were discipline and education. Whatever other sentiments he wished to communicate were done through his mouthpiece, my mother. Dad wasn't big on emotional displays, but at least I knew he was talking to me because he used our private nickname. While away in the Italian mountains marble shopping, he'd write us each a post card. Mine was always the one addressed, "Dear Pal." Occasionally, when he stayed somewhere long enough, I'd write back, "Dear Pop."

When I was young, this intimacy also extended to the softball field. He was so proud the day I hit a homer at the eighth grade championship. He didn't write much from Europe anymore, I guess twelve postcards were just too much, and he stopped coming to my games after I went to high school. He didn't think a teenaged girl should be playing sports. Mom told me later Latin fathers don't know how to relate to teenaged daughters. Today, however, for a moment, he was all mine.

"Thanks, Pop. After hearing Mother Caritas' speech, I may need some skill as well as luck."

"Just remember you're a Córdova, and you can accomplish anything you want to. Haven't I always told you . . . "

"Yeah, I know, Córdovas can conquer the world, right?" I said, joking.

"Well, yes. But 'conquer' is probably not the right word in God's house, Jeanne." Dad seemed to ponder the issue. "'Faith' is, I would say."

"Right, Pop."

"No matter what happens, at least your college education

26

won't be interrupted. These nuns have the right priorities."

"Right, Pop!"

"We're counting on you, Pal." Dad squeezed my other shoulder as he pulled away. It was almost an embrace. "Your mother will write."

"Thanks, Pop," I called as he came to attention and marched back to the car.

In a proper Catholic household it was considered a blessing to have a child called to religious life. Yet Mom was enigmatic about my vocation. I could never pin her down on this subject or most others, especially if the confrontation or opinion involved emotions. My mother was ever-present and totally distant, comprehensive in her surveillance of our bodies and souls, yet curiously uninvolved. Like my siblings, I received my share of accolades and scoldings, but I often wondered if I existed outside of my identity as her child, her duty, her responsibility. I remained an undifferentiated soul in a house of many souls, all precious in the eyes of God and Mom, yet never particularly precious to anyone, save Bill, my closest brother, my Lancelot comrade-in-arms and laughter.

When I spoke to Mom about my vocation, she listened intently and nodded. She was eternally noncommittal. She'd sit in the room as we talked, yet it was as though she was in some different dimension holding her own conversation with God about her second daughter. She and He were comparing notes.

Driving me home from summer camp a month ago we shared our last dialogue on the subject. In a lengthy soliloquy about how much there was to do, what with buying, labeling, and packing my special convent wardrobe, she turned from the wheel to ask, "Jeanne, are you sure this is what you want?"

"Of course I'm sure, Mom. You know there's never been any other serious thought in my head. Is it OK with you?"

"It's not a matter of what I want, or even really what you want, what is important is what's God's will for you."

"I know God's will for me!" I replied brashly.

Mom concluded with some comment about humility.

27

Sufficiently assured that everyone and everything was packed for the drive home, Mom came toward me. She took my hand and led me back to the cars. "Now, Jeanne, I think you've got all that you need. There are two of everything, all labeled with your name as they instructed: towels, soap dish, slips, those ugly sets of special shoes. I put a second rosary in your suitcase. It's the one my mother gave me. I know how you lose things. Don't lose that one."

"Yes, Mom. No, Mom," I mumbled as we approached the passenger seat. I was mildly panicked. I wished I had learned to look after myself better. I just never paid attention. It never occurred to me Mom wouldn't always be there to help me find my shoes.

"Just remember that we love you, Jeanne," she said, offering up the rarity as she slid into the car beside Dad. "And that God knows what He's doing even when we don't."

CHAPTER 4

Brides of Christ

"You're late, as usual, Jeanne!" Marlene Camp smacked me on the shoulder with her missal as she sashayed down the summer house classroom aisle. After being at Montecito only two weeks I'd found I was most content in the school room. Learning was familiar, safe. "We have to be in our cells before Caritas comes to ring the bells," my postulant mate continued.

The evening had passed quickly, study time was almost over, and the other postulants had just left the summer house also. "I just need another five minutes to get his explanation into my brain," I mumbled, absorbed in Thomas à Kempis' treatise on the Eucharist. The transubstantiation of the Body and Blood of Christ was supposed to be a Mystery, a matter of faith, so why were we metaphysically dissecting it? Still, it was great exercise for my hungry mind.

"You've got about as much crammed in that exaggerated brain

29

of yours as is ever going to fit. Give it up. Offer it up. Get up. Let's go," Camp curtly yelled from the door in her monitor pose.

Marlene Camp tormented me constantly and relished the process. She was shaping up to be my antagonist, the enemy with all its properties. I didn't relish walking back to St. Joseph's with her. "I don't want to make you late, Camp. Go on without me. I'll be there soon." I remained ostensibly engrossed in my book. A few moments later I dared a glance. The doorway was empty. What a relief!

I'd come to love the grounds of Montecito. I settled back into the easy peace of the summer house. The building, situated in an idyllic setting overlooking the pool and tennis courts, was dubbed the summer house for obvious reasons. Located a hundred yards east of the main house, it must have served as the Dupont's summer pleasure center. I'd seen a few nuns playing tennis last weekend, but so far I'd seen no one in the pool. Sisters in bathing suits struck me as blasphemous. Perhaps the pool was reserved for the visiting priests and other dignitaries.

The summer house was a good fifteen-minute walk from our postulant dorm. It could take as long as an hour if you stopped to chat with someone on the cozy orchard path that lay between it and the main house or got lost in the myriad other gardens that wound between the main house and our classroom site.

The brick courtyard in back of the main house dropped off into cobblestone pathways. The southern-most path took me down through an oak and eucalyptus grove that sheltered the Stations of the Cross, the sacred ritual of Jesus' journey up Mount Calvary. Farther on was La Casa de María, a retreat complex with its own chapel, dorms, and kitchen. We had been told not to socialize with the lay Catholics who came from the cities for weekends of spiritual renewal.

My favorite walk to the summer house was the center path, the one most trodden by the novices and professed. En route was my coveted meditation spot, the Poet's Boulder, as I had named it. The boulder was actually a beautiful pile of large rocks surrounding a gurgling fish pond. Alone, I'd make my way to a small ledge overlooking the fish. Hidden from view, the gently breaking bubbles of the spring assuaged my mind, and my pen spoke my heart. I wasn't the only budding e. e. cummings. Several times I'd seen a cloaked figure lost in thought on my ledge. I would leave as quietly as I had arrived.

On that first Monday afternoon, the day after our parents had departed, the sun-filled summer house was atwitter with the forced comraderie of self-introduction. The Mistress of Postulants had corralled all fifteen of us into the second floor of the summer house to meet our fellow brides of Christ. Mother Caritas would pass out our postulant uniforms and assign us cellmates for the year.

Her rigid iron-rail form glided into the room and stood silently before us. A hush fell, as though she had given an order.

"Now I know who she reminds me of!" The voice next to me came from Michelle Callahan, the postulant who had intrigued me so mysteriously during Mother Caritas' orientation speech. I'd bumped into her this morning in the refectory after breakfast. She was washing the dishes, and as I dropped my plate into the sink, a staining splash fell on her blue polyester blouse. Curtailing my apology she winked at me and joked, "This is yet another reason you shouldn't wear those dark sunglasses so much. Don't worry about the stain, as long as you don't make a habit of it! They're giving us our mini-habits this afternoon, so I'll probably never see this blouse again!"

Michelle's muffled laughter brought me back to the summer house.

"Reminds you of who?" I whispered conspiratorially.

"The butler."

"What butler?"

"On TV, the Addams Family, what's his name?" Michelle Callahan's smile was urgent with mischief.

"You mean the tall Frankenstein character? Lurch?"

"Yeah, look at her, Caritas is Lurch!"

I turned back to look at Lurch. Yes, there she stood, as if to say,

"And *who* may I say is calling?"

"Great take!" I laughed with Michelle under my breath; finally, a spirit whose mind ran in my own sardonic groove. That's why she was staring at me that first day! She had quickly recognized a kindred irreverent spirit.

Caritas raised an angular forearm as if to bless us, but instead she pulled lint off her veil. "I will now pass out your uniforms," she began, "and give you your cell assignments. You might get to know one another as I call out your names." She spoke solemnly as if she were passing out jail sentences. Caritas rapidly called roll. We were all back in our desks without so much as a smile or even a glance at one another. Lurch was no Emily Post.

"It's a cinch she'll never be asked to do the Johnny Carson show!" Michelle quipped.

Abruptly, Lurch announced she would leave us to change and mingle. She would return in an hour for cell assignments.

"This thing doesn't fit." My co-conspirator had taken off her stained blue blouse and wrapped the new white one around herself.

"It's just a little big on you. Lurch probably thinks everyone should be as tall as she. Or is it he?" I joked. "Here, try mine." I pushed my clothing pile over onto her desk. "I like baggy shirts."

"I really appreciate it, thanks. I hate wearing clothes that don't fit perfectly. I'm Michelle Callahan, from Long Beach. Sorry, I must have sneezed during the lavish introduction and missed your name." The girl looked right into my eyes again the way she had on Entrance Day. This time however she was much closer.

Giving Michelle Callahan a cursory appraisal from afar, I hadn't noticed anything special about her. Like her hometown, she was basically nondescript. Long Beach was West Covina's sister city in anonymity. I had once heard about it on the news—there had been an oil spill. Michelle was average in height, weight, and coloring; basic white, the freckled Irish look. Her stringy brown hair fell to her shoulders in unspectacular curls. There was nothing extraordinary, nothing dramatic—that is, until I looked into her eyes. The afternoon definitely slowed right then. Michelle Callahan's eyes were extraterrestrial, haunting, aqua-marine. They had an alluring vulnerability, a Bambi-caught-in-the-brambles, come-rescue-me plea. Staring into them was slightly hypnotic.

Michelle was still waiting for me to speak. "Ah . . . I'm Jeanne. I'm sorry . . . your eyes." Michelle continued to stare at me. Somehow my name didn't seem important.

"Oh, right. My eyes. Don't pay any attention to them." The girl continued staring, making a lie out of her words. "My eyes are my Waterloo. They've gotten me in trouble all my life. I can't imagine why, can you?" She pronounced each word slowly, as though she were giving directions to heaven.

"Have you been to an optometrist?" I offered.

Michelle was still looking at me quizzically.

"I'm sure they'll take us to any kind of specialist we need. The IHM's are first-rate about medical needs."

"What about other needs?" Michelle seemed to be trying to read my face or communicate something above the din of the room.

"Like what other needs?" I pressed for clarification. I found the drift of our conversation perplexing. Michelle seemed to be speaking on a different level of reality.

Suddenly she blushed and turned away. She handed me her blouse in exchange for my own. "You still haven't told me your whole name," she laughed now, more casually, buttoning my shirt, now hers. "Ah, this fits much better, thanks again."

"My name is Jeanne Córdova. I'm from West Covina."

Michelle looked blank.

"I went to Bishop Amat High School? Home of the Lancers?" I offered.

"Oh sure, I've heard of Amat. I'm from St. Anthony's in Long Beach. We're in the southern league so we never got to play Amat."

"Sorry we didn't meet before now. It would have been fun to smack you a home run. What position did you play?"

"Position? Oh, right, position on the field you mean. I'm no jock," Michelle said dryly. "I was on the team, but mostly in the dugout with the coach. You might say I spent high school on the bench." Michelle laughed as though she'd told me a joke.

"Were you the bat girl or something?"

"Something like that. I wouldn't pick up any bats though, too heavy. I kept score for our coach."

"It's a shame you didn't get to play."

"I wouldn't be caught dead standing at home plate about to get hit by a ball. I got placed exactly where I wanted to be—in the shadows."

I nodded, distracted with turning my postulant skirt around, searching for the zipper. Well, I thought, that lets Michelle out as my jock-buddy. I thought of my brother Bill. She'd be no replacement. The girl is afraid of a pitched ball. But for some reason I still wanted to continue talking with her. I liked her mind, which seemed to understand mine, and her wit and . . . and those eyes were something supernatural.

"So . . . who's the coach that had you benched and keeping score for her all the time?"

"An IHM named Sister Paul Emanuelle."

"No kidding?" I was green. "So, Paul got sent to St. Anthony's. I'd never heard from her again."

"Did you know her?" Michelle seemed shocked.

"Sure, she was my sophomore political science teacher."

Michelle stared, expecting me to go on.

"She was very special, very bright also," I continued. "I guess that's why I liked her. She was a real role model. The day Kennedy got shot, she fainted . . . in my arms."

"Fainted in your arms?"

"Yeah, it was a big shock. Weren't you totally blown away?"

"By her fainting in your arms? Yeah, I'm absolutely shocked!" Michelle was being sarcastic again.

"No, by the president being shot!" I was surprised at my short-tempered retort. Paul Emanuelle had never written me as she promised.

"Of course. I'm not big on politics. But Kennedy was an Irish Catholic. I cried for days."

"What exactly *are* you big on?"

"Well . . . I specialize in thinking and planning. I was a great organizer at St. Anthony's. A lot of dances and affairs . . . and keeping score. I was president of the Girl's Athletic Association."

"That's amazing since you don't even like sports," I was beginning to suspect Michelle spoke and existed on paradoxical levels. "Were you close friends with Paul Emanuelle?"

"Yes." Michelle's voice dropped. She was having difficulty getting her blazer sleeves over her blouse. "We were very close."

"That must have been fun." My tone was still hostile. "Paul never mentioned she was good at softball while she was at Amat."

"Well, since we lost all of our games, I guess she probably wasn't all that good . . . as a coach." Michelle was looking through me as if I'd vanished in the haze of her past.

"Is my collar crooked?"

"What? Ah, yes. It's all bent out of shape." She came out of her dream state and stretched her arms around my neck. "I'll fix it."

Michelle's fingers were warmer than the late summer sun now toasting the classroom.

"There, you look perfect now. See if you can stay that way. By the way, now that we share a common background, call me Micki."

Micki and I walked around together meeting the rest of our class. There was Donna, a robust Italian from "Pedro" via New York, who attached herself to Michelle and slapped her small shoulders with Latin gusto every time she peeled out a laugh. And there was Janis.

"Micki, check out the music." I motioned her toward a neatly groomed girl sitting with a guitar softly playing, "Puff, the Magic Dragon."

"You check out the music. I'm trying to bring Donna up to par here, and besides . . ."

"I know. You're not big on music." I shook my head, making my way over to the aspiring singing nun. What would Micki be good for?

35

Janis Engleton was a very proper young woman of English descent who would make the perfect nun. She had completed her change before the rest of us and looked as though she had been primly born in postulant uniform. She responded warmly to my request for her to teach me to play guitar.

"I would be delighted," Janis answered graciously, "as soon as they allow us free time."

Warm memories of nights around the campfire last summer returned. I'd seen several guitars in the main house lobby. If I knew how to play, I reasoned, I'd have more social opportunities here in the convent. Perhaps Janis and I would get to be friends and I'd help her open up and relax a bit, I reflected, slouched on the couch listening, my feet on the coffee table next to her guitar. Janis was a little too proper for her own good. Certainly too proper for me.

"And what village do you come from?" The voice hissed ever so slowly, like the death gasp of the snake I'd run over with my bike on my tenth birthday. "Nuns don't sprawl all over the furniture. Ladies certainly know better."

Marlene Camp was a regimented rat. I could have hated her even before I saw her, just based on her voice. But I didn't have to. I saw her. She was squashed together, her head and shoulders interrupted only by several inches of a squat neck. I know it's not charitable to think of people as animals, but her pasty pink pouting mouth and snorting nose really did look like a pig's. Her face seemed to be in perpetual agony. My agony. And yet it wasn't really how she looked that so disturbed me. It was who she was as a human being. Or maybe who she wasn't.

I kept my feet on the table, my nose in the air. Drawing upon what was left from Mom's New York highbrow accent, I snooted back to Camp, "I was bred in an environment in which individual style and casual deportment take precedence over middle-class affectation."

"I'd rather have good manners than your uncouth so-called individual style." Camp would not back off.

"A shame you don't have either," I retorted.

"I suppose even the convent has a quota system!"

I sprang to my feet at her racial slur. I'd put the fear of God into Marlene Camp!

"Now, girls . . . " Janis sought to placate Camp and me before the quarrel became public. Caritas' hand came out of nowhere to rest on my shoulder. "Come, girls," the butler, Lurch, said solemnly. "Time enough for more socializing and playing music later. I know you want to hear your cell assignments."

There were eight small rooms in St. Joseph's dorm. I'd counted them the night before as we were instructed to choose any bed for our first night. Lurch took to her podium. "Your cells are not large," she began, "but we trust you will find them adequate for praying, sleeping, and studying. Anna Martin will room with Dorothy Travers. Jacqueline Lunch will share a cell with Michelle Callahan. Donna Stallone will be with Louise Rodriguez, and Janis Engleton and Judith Saunders will be assigned to cell number seven."

Darn! I groaned inside. There go Micki and Janis. It would have been interesting to room with Micki and stay up talking all night, or even Janis. Then we'd have a lot more time to practice guitar, and I'd become proficient and be assigned to play with the black-haired novice I'd seen yesterday. But no. Even Donna was taken. Now I'd get stuck with someone I didn't even know.

"Jeanne Córdova will share cell number three on the ground floor," Lurch continued, "with Marlene Camp. And lastly . . . "

"Sweet Jesus!" I heard Camp's snake hiss from across the room.

"Micki," I implored, tugging my new friend's blazer, "tell me I misheard Lurch, please tell me?"

"She said that Camp girl was your cellmate. What's wrong Jeanne?"

I was mute.

It was after dusk by the time Caritas dismissed us. I clumped woefully through the orchard toward St. Joseph's in a depressed daze. I was in no hurry to get to cell three and encounter Camp again. What were the odds, I wondered? There were fifteen of us. I could have had any one of the thirteen others for a cellmate. Why did I get the one who seemed to hate me the most? Caritas had said the cell assignments were made randomly; she couldn't have overheard Camp and me fighting. Yet Lurch was too supernaturally clever to allow such a terrible cross to befall me without reason. It couldn't be an accident. It must be a sign from God—or a bad omen. I had a nauseous feeling God had not spun the wheel.

Suddenly a lumpy form appeared in the shadows, blocking the orchard path in front of me. "Excuse me!" I blurted, backing away.

"Oh, thank God, someone has come to rescue me!" a small voice chirped. The girl's tiny body bounded up from her perch on the bulky suitcase. "Do you have a light?"

"Who are you?" I whispered into the darkness.

"It's Louise. Louise Rodriguez . . . Donna's roommate, remember? Are you Jeanne? I think I recognize your voice. I need some help. Do you have a match or light or something?"

"Yes, I have the matches I used for lighting my votive candles. Wait a minute. Why are you sitting on your suitcase out here in the middle of the orchard?" I struck a match and held it above us so I could see her. Louise Rodriguez didn't even clear five feet and wouldn't have tipped the scales at one hundred pounds. She had on makeup and red nail polish.

She smiled matter of factly. "I ran out of breath because my suitcases are too big for me. So I set them down and broke a nail. See, it just fell off?" Louise Rodriguez held out her right hand. The nail of the fourth finger was considerably shorter than the others. "Help me look for it, won't you?"

I began laughing, I couldn't take her seriously. But there we were, a couple of Brides of Christ, down on our stocking postulant knees looking for a red polished nail in an orchard, in the middle of the night, in a convent.

"Can't you grow another one or something?" I winced as another sharp stone dug into my shredded stockings. "I really think Caritas will be coming down the path any moment!"

"Oh dear, oh dear," Louisa moaned. "No, you don't just grow them. I suppose you're right. I'll have to send for another." She took my hand. "You don't have any nails at all!"

"Not on your life." I bent to help her with her luggage. "Ugh! What have you got in this suitcase?"

"Oh, thank you. You're so sweet," Louisa cooed sincerely as she grabbed the other bag and we crept toward St. Joseph's. "Perhaps I packed too many pairs of heels. I just don't know how I can walk around here in heels; all the paths are rocks!"

"I packed my softball glove too, just in case."

"You play baseball? I don't think they will allow baseball here."

"No, I think you're right. And Louise, you haven't seen any nuns in makeup have you? I think you're going to have to forget your heels, and even the nails."

"*Ay qué lástima!* I am afraid this is so!" The tiny lady froze in the middle of the orchard. Louise Marie Delgado Rodriguez was outrageously feminine. Only the Latins glorify the differences between the sexes like it was a lost art. Louise would bring medieval culture to our postulant class. She stretched both hands, nine nails, toward the stars. A sacrificial offering, they glimmered against the moonlight.

"I'm sorry, Louise." I set her suitcase down again as we hugged and exchanged sorrows. I liked Louise from that moment on. Not because of the bond our Latin last names implied. I was half Mexican, or Spanish as Dad insisted, and proud of my heritage, but I didn't know what to make of it. I was raised white. Louise was authentically Mexican-American from East L.A. I liked Louise because in her ultra-feminine ways and anguish over her abandoned boyfriend, Alfredo, she seemed hopelessly miscast as a Bride of Christ. I decided instantly I would be there to help her in any way I could. The novitiate was going to be a tough metamorphosis for Louise.

We crossed the threshold of St. Joseph's and I went on alone to search for cell three.

Camp filled the doorway. "Well. I suppose it will do."

"What will do?" I tried to peer around her titan shoulders. I couldn't get a glimpse of our new home.

Camp clasped her arms behind her back and strode forward like General Patton inspecting the barracks. Wordlessly she reconnoitered: two desks, two chairs, two reading lamps, two crucifixes hanging over two beds, two dressers, one closet, and one window.

"Córdova," Camp said, pointing toward the floor, "see this line?"

"I don't see any line," I said softly. Perhaps Camp was imagining things already. I'd heard gossip this morning at breakfast that one of the novices had to leave because she had started seeing things. Still, on our second day, it seemed a bit early for such a high level of stress.

"This particular line, which I am now marking in red." Camp got down on the ground, on all fours, drawing a thin, almost imperceptible, red pencil line over the junction of lineoleum squares in the dead center of our room.

"Now that you've messed up our floor, yeah, I see it. What about it?"

Camp got up and faced me. "This side of the room is yours, Córdova." She pointed to the inner side, the one with no window. "Stay on it."

Camp moved toward the window wall. "This side is mine. I will live here. Unfortunately, we have to share the closet. I'll keep my habits on the right, you keep your junk on the left. And they'd better not touch each other!"

For an instant I was devastated by Camp's outrageous welcome home. Then I detached. Watching her slam her clothes into her dresser, I knew she was serious about her line. Trying to erase it from our floor, or from our lives, would take the patience of a saint or the humility of a true nun. I was neither, yet.

Lights went out as Mother Mary Lurch Caritas glided down the corridor rhythmically swinging the brass bell that heralded absolute Silence.

The pebbles bounced gently against the window signaling Micki was ready to walk home with me. I hadn't wanted to tell Camp I'd already arranged to walk home to St. Joseph's with Michelle. Micki was very late. I wondered how her perfectionist attention to detail kept her dusting the library shelves until almost ten. Especially since her chore mate, novice Dominic Anne, was helping. Micki probably recatalogued the Holy Rule.

I slapped à Kempis shut. Caritas' admonishment to me on the day of my interview, "individual sensitivity has no place," was more immediately important than metaphysical gymnastics or Michelle's compulsions. I thought of Camp lying in her bed waiting to say good-night by criticizing me for something. No way I'm going to let that witch harass me out of my vocation, I thought. If she's going to be a nun, so am I! There's got to be something morally redeeming even about Marlene Camp. I'm gonna find it and love and respect her as my sister. Even if it kills one of us!

CHAPTER 5

She's Got Personality

"Kyrie eleison (Lord have mercy)"
"Christe eleison (Christ have mercy)"
"Kyrie eleison."
"Christe eleison."

It was a gothic night in the drafty chapel chamber; the nuns were at mass. The cloud-knit moonlight cast shadows through the stained-glass windows filtering across our prayers. Our private chapel in the main house was intimate and strictly off limits to visitors. The postulant dorm, earlier silhouetted against the deep orange tones of the Santa Barbara sunset, now sat in fog across the orchard. The ocean's mist shrouded Montecito, transforming it into a conquistador's castle. Actually, the Duponts had given the Hispanic heirloom to the Church as a tax write-off. But to the holy daughters of Christ, and to me, a sanctified aspirant of one month, the castle was a retreat from the material entanglements of the world. We were in the world but not *of* it. The real world I'd never known had ceased to exist. We heard neither traffic nor television, only God and other voices from inside.

As we kneeled to chant the *Kyrie,* I studied Father Bonaventure at the altar. He was a Franciscan, an import from the Santa Barbara mission in town. The three large knots in the rope belt hanging from his cassock were adopted by Francis of Assisi himself. According to Canonical Code, Church law governing religious life, they symbolized his commitment to poverty, chastity, and obedience. The twelve apostles were sworn to the vows of poverty and obedience by St. Peter, and chastity became mandatory for men and women of the cloth in the second century. Despite the twentieth century, the vows had never been modernized; they were still the cornerstone of religious life.

In unison with my sisters, I stood for the offeratory of the Mass and choired in Latin, "Lamb of God, Who taketh away the sins of the world, have mercy on us." I felt at peace knowing I wouldn't have any trouble with the vows I was scheduled to make in one year.

Raised by Dad on a dollar-a-week allowance, I wouldn't have much to give up in terms of poverty. Even in high school, I'd had to iron thirty uniform shirts every Saturday afternoon for my dollar. Slave labor was good preparation for the convent. I never had any money in my pocket. My parents had taken care of my physical needs, and now the Church would.

Father Bonaventure was preparing the Body and Blood of Christ for Holy Communion. I fell to my knees. Chastity seemed a bit more vague. I'd been educated by nuns and priests all my life; Catholic schools never heard of sex education. When friends in high school made risque references I went along as though I understood what they were talking about. I knew chastity alluded to marriage and, as Dad said, "the sexual contract therein." I knew that Mom and Dad never had impure thoughts about other people. And I knew going all the way with a boy was definitely not chaste.

43

Mary Lulan was the only girl at Amat who did that. Denny and I hadn't done much more than kiss . . . well, not a lot more. To hear my girlfriends talk, I thought it was much ado about nothing. I was chaste in body and spirit, I was almost positive. Here, too, there didn't seem to be much to give up.

Obedience? Now that could be problematic. I was never good at keeping rules. Mom said I was born stubborn. "You have your father's will," she said, and she wasn't talking about God the Father.

Others were lining up to receive Holy Communion, so I rose to exit my pew. A damp palm clamped my shoulder, yanking me to a halt. Marlene Camp nodded sternly toward the pew in front of us. Mother Caritas was emerging from it. Postulants were supposed to be last in line to receive Holy Communion. Heeding her, I slid back to my knees hoping my premature rise and fall would be viewed by Mother Caritas as merely a holy hiccup.

Sitting, tensely awaiting my turn for Communion, I remembered the last time I waited for Mother Caritas three months ago outside her office at the IHM's Los Angeles Motherhouse. The lobby was elegantly furnished in old wood and original oil paintings. It was somber; so was I. I'd spent the entire afternoon sweating out the *Minnesota Multiple Personality Inventory,* the psychological test required of all IHM candidates. I felt like my whole life was riding on this interview. Would I pass?

I knew I usually did well at exams, but I'd never taken such a screwball test. One of the questions, "Do you ever feel as though there is a tight band around your head?" made me nervous. I rubbed my temples trying to remember if I'd ever felt a tight band. Only when I had my softball headband on, I recalled. I didn't think that's what they meant. I checked "no."

Then there was the most confusing question, "Did you hate your father?" I was convinced this was an essay, not a yes or no, question. Sure I hated him, I remembered, when he'd come after us with his belt and beat us, or yelled at us to leave the dinner table. I

44

knew if I checked off "yes," they'd think I hated him always, which I didn't. If I said "no," the interpreter would think I lied, because all children hate their fathers sometimes. Obviously this was a trick question. I cleverly wrote in the margin, "It depends."

Going through almost four hundred of those questions, I felt ready for someone's couch. I was sure I would be rejected for having a subnormal I.Q. The IHM's had an elitist reputation for admitting only *smart* brides of Christ. Religious life must have gotten very complicated while I sojourned through childhood reading the medieval writings of the desert monastics. Nowadays it appeared more important to be declared sane than holy.

Mother Mary Caritas opened her office door. The good Mistress of Postulants was awesome, the top of her headdress seemed to touch the ceiling. "Come in, my child," her ghostly voice reverberated in the darkly paneled foyer.

Noiselessly, she glided back into her office toward a magnificent black marble desk with the letters JMJ (Jesus, Mary & Joseph) etched into the side facing me. Sitting, she opened a folder. "It is Jeannie, is it not?"

"Actually not, Mother," I choked out the words. I felt like there was a tight band around my throat. "It's Jeanne. Jeanne Robert Córdova."

"Ah, yes," she reviewed my file. "You mean Roberta?"

"Actually not, Mother. It is Robert."

"This is somewhat unusual, isn't it my dear? Did your father give you this particular middle name?"

"Actually not, Mother." I slammed my right oxford against my left. *Quit saying "actually not," Jeanne,* I scolded myself, *she'll think you are a disagreeable illiterate. The IHM's only want smart nuns.*

"My mother named me Jeanne, Mother, after St. Jeanne d'Arc, the soldier general of France. My mother's name is Joan. They were in France when I was . . . conceived. Robert is for my Uncle Bob, her brother. He had just left the Maryknoll Seminary when I was born, and he was really bent out of shape."

45

"He was what?"

"Upset, Mother." *Speak properly, Jeanne,* the scolding voice inside corrected. "He was very disheartened about not getting to be a priest as he'd planned. So I was his consolation prize . . . a niece."

"Yes, I see. Córdova, this is Italian, correct?"

I bit my lip. I didn't want to have to correct Mother Superior again. Christ in a bucket, I thought, the IHM's were supposed to be ethnically sophisticated. "Córdova is about as Spanish as O'Malley is Irish, Mother." The good Mother's eyes got smaller as she paused to consider me more closely. Perhaps she was grateful for the small piece of new knowledge. Perhaps I had been a smart mouth.

"Yes, of course. It is always nice to have sisters from different races and backgrounds. It gives us a deeper cultural perspective with which to go out and be of service to God's children."

"Christ!" I caught my breath, jumping out of my chair. "I mean, halleluja! Does that mean I'm accepted into the convent?"

"Yes, Jeanne. The Sisters of the Immaculate Heart of Mary are happy to welcome you into our postulant class of 1966. *However . . .*" Mother Caritas cut short the good news, " . . . it is my duty to counsel you on one or two matters that came to light in your test."

I shrank back into my chair.

"Some of your answers, Jeanne Robert Córdova, demonstrate that you might have some difficulty with authority figures, and that you are given to oversensitivity."

Well! my inner voice harumphed, *the IHM's couldn't be faulted for pulling punches!*

"Our vow of obedience protects us from the pitfalls of false pride and arrogance. Obedience is among the most treasured gifts we can give to our Lord and Master. Convent life is in large part built upon our dedication to living God's will as his obedient children. Remember when Jesus called out in Gethsemane, 'Father, not My will but Thine be done'?"

"Oh, yes, Mother."

"You will learn that living communally behooves each of us to be self-sacrificing for our sisters. Personal sensitivity is often a

46

manifestation of a false sense of self-importance or inferiority."

I wondered which I had.

"As a religious, you must learn the individual ego has no place in collective life, much less a life given over to our Lord Jesus Christ."

Remembering Mom's chastisements about humility, I nodded my silent understanding and made the sign of the cross.

Mother Caritas followed suit and dismissed me.

Father Bonaventure was wrapping it up on the altar. *"Ite, Missa est,"* his husky voice bade us. "Go, the Mass has ended."

"Deo gracias," I chimed, keeping beat with my collective. I reined in my volume, being careful to blend my humble voice with the others. As my stately robed sisters rose to depart, I stayed behind to meditate. The rules allowed an optional half hour of contemplation after Mass.

Suddenly I felt chilled. The cloaked bodies pressing against me from all sides had cut the draft. I pulled my postulant blazer around my neck and chest and studied the pleats in my shirt. It was a simple matter, my abbreviated habit. Mother Caritas had passed them out the day after we arrived and since that moment and forever until I donned the habit, I would wear this uniform only. I pitied any of my postulant mates who might be steeped in feminine vanity. The starch in the white blouse and blazer gave a boxy appearance to even the most shapely of us. I had never been able to work up an interest in anything I wore.

Donning the royal blue of the postulant habit had given me pause, however. I was now different. When we had been taken to visit the Franciscan Seminary at the Santa Barbara Mission this week, seculars on the street had accorded us respect. For the first time, I was treated like a nun: no one spoke to me. As we passed through the Mission gates, a few monks bowed, "Good afternoon, Sisters." I was cloaked in a new anonymity. Even our abridged habit was a symbol of nascent godliness. I felt dignified, sanctified—also a bit fraudulent. I wasn't yet a nun inside. Like the ground after an earthquake, it would take time for my new persona to settle. You didn't become a nun in a few weeks or months. You didn't transcend your material self by sliding into a uniform that made you *look* like one of God's chosen. The shifts had begun inside, but I hadn't felt the earthquake yet. I knew it would come eventually.

Rattled by thoughts of my future, I got up off my knees, sat in my pew, and stared at the multicolored Corita tapestry adorning the back of the altar. I shifted my contemplation to the past. Choosing the right order to join was tantamount to picking the right college. I recalled my selection process. You don't apply to Harvard to pursue mechanics. Entering the wrong order could spell a similar disaster. You could tell a person's religion by how he or she addressed your announcement to enter the convent. Non-Catholics would say, "Oh, you don't *look* like a nun!" or "Not *you!* I don't believe it." The first thing a Catholic would say was, "What order?"

At St. Christopher's the only nuns were Benedictine. Followers of the fifth-century Italian monk Benedict, they were covered from toe to forehead in black. They were a somber, stodgy lot. And I was convinced by Sister Mary Vincent that the Benedictines had not completed the transition out of the Dark Ages. Sister Mary Vincent must have stood six-foot-one in her black stockings. She was a nasty soul! Being appointed principal gave Sister Mary Vincent great latitude for her sadism. The first time she told me to stretch out my knuckles and cracked her wooden ruler over them, I was bruised so badly I couldn't write for a week. The second time she concluded her discipline, slapping my face and breaking another ruler, she instructed me, "Now go home, Jeanne, and tell your mother you broke my ruler and have her give you twenty-five cents to replace it." The ogre developed a predilection for picking on Córdovas, none of whom got A's in conduct. She haunted my favorite brother, Bill, and me in particular. By the time I left grammar school I had eliminated the Benedictines from my future.

Mom favored the Dominicans because her mother's sister had joined them a half million years ago. Her real name was Sister Mary

Annunciata, but we called her "Dear Aunt Sister" because that's how Mom had us address our annual Christmas cards to her. We were supposed to worship Dear Aunt Sister from afar because she was very old and had spent her entire life consecrated to God. But it was hard to get any true sense of *whom* we were adoring. Dear Aunt Sister wrote only religious poems in her cards to us. Poems that made Hallmark seem *deep* by comparison. I was convinced becoming a Dominican would forever stunt my budding aspiration to be a second Edna St. Vincent Millay.

At Bishop Amat Memorial High School, an academic artifact that added another set of nondescript buildings to the listless face of the San Gabriel Valley, I was offered a close view of other orders. I cringe to admit my vocation might have been influenced by fashion or color scheme, but the habit of my future lifestyle was terribly important. I'd have to wear it until I dropped dead.

Death was likely to come soon, I thought, if I became a St. Louis of France nun, like Sister Declan Frances, the girls' dean. Sister Dec was a robust, delightfully intelligent sparkle in my adolescence. Her magnitudinous Irish brogue wasn't enough, however, to overcome the archaic, large scrolled box that surrounded her head. The square coif was starched so that it resembled concrete and made her face look as if it were in a French provincial picture frame—permanently. Catholic asceticism never made it across the Pyrenees. I'm sure it was a Parisian who painted gilt on the pearly gates. King (and Saint) Louis of France must have wanted his religious to look like the jesters of his thirteenth-century court. But I didn't want to spend the rest of my life with a eight-inch coif boxed around my jawbone. The St. Louies, as we called them, were out.

Now the Carmelites, dressed in tunics of soft browns and black with a small oval coif that gently framed the face, were not a bad choice. My religion teachers at Amat were always Carmelites. They had a holy demeanor. Taking a research trip to aid my decision, I visited the Carmelites' Sacred Heart Retreat House in Alhambra. Though nowhere near as grand as Montecito, the Carmelite novitiate was well-appointed and felt sacred. I was impressed with the solitude and devotion of the order. As such, they emerged at Amat just long enough to sow a few spiritual thoughts . . . just long enough for me to give them serious consideration.

Fully cloistered orders, like the Trappist monks, *never* ventured outside the monastery or convent perimeters. Most of our best saints were cloistered religious—fewer distractions. But since I probably wasn't going to make saint, I was highly ambivalent about choosing to pay the cloistered price—eternal solitude.

The IHM's had myriad plus points. Their habit, designed by Katherine Crosby, wife of Bing, was stunningly austere yet beautiful. The under tunic, which draped from neck to toe, was a serene royal blue, and the crisp black scapular lowered over the head and fell down one's front and back. The simple white coif held the face proudly, crowned with a veil of fine crepe. What I most loved about the IHM habit was the three-inch sterling silver heart worn by each nun directly over her bosom. The heart was encircled by a ring of thorns and pierced ever so delicately by a miniature sterling sword, the handle and tip protruding from either side. The symbol, of course, represented the Immaculate Heart of Mary—broken by watching her Son's crucifixion. To me, the heart was a long-sought-after badge of distinction.

The IHM's had another distinction—Sister Paul Emanuelle. I could understand why Michelle had wanted to be close to her and do anything for her. Her very name sounded holy, romantic. I found her in sophomore political science. I was sitting in the first seat, fourth row, right in front of her, that twenty-second day of November in 1963. I'd been listening in rapt attention to everything she said—for three months. Paul Emanuelle was also short. Coming from a family of very short people, Dad had to stretch his backbone to make the military minimum. I felt safest around people my size. Just clearing five feet, Paul Emanuelle was slim and her fine-boned arms gracefully circulated the air as she spoke, always in a hushed voice, as if she were revealing the word of God.

She gave the IHM habit majesty. Her royal blue tunic, half-covered by the black scapular, flowed like silk when she walked. Her reed-thin coif encircled her face and lifted her chin ever so proudly. A few strands of black hair from above her forehead peeped out from her veil to lay gently against her pale Irish complexion. While countries rose and fell in political science, I remained preoccupied with Paul Emanuelle's health. She was so white, I wondered if she had some rare blood disease. Yet her hollowed cheeks glowed bright rose whenever she lost herself in the rise and fall of nations. To me, an objective bystander, Paul Emanuelle was the embodiment of the lovely little sterling heart worn over her own most immaculate heart.

"Today, class, we are exploring the religious undertones of World War I and how they influenced the political climate in northern Europe." Paul Emanuelle smiled at me as I leaned out of my chair to retrieve her chalk. She was always waving it about and dropping it.

"I interrupt you all for an important message," the overhead intercom blasted from out of nowhere. It was Father Clifford, Amat's principal. "I regret to inform you that the president of the United States, John Fitzgerald Kennedy, has been shot." I jerked upright in my chair—it was not April Fool's Day. People don't shoot the president, not in the United States! I must have misheard. The intercom was usually garbled by static and often out of order.

The voice continued, "Please pray with me, everyone. Again, the news is that our president was assassinated one hour ago in Dallas, Texas, during a motor-car parade there. Please bow your head and ask God to rest his soul."

Even in my own disbelief I saw Paul Emanuelle's shock. As Father Clifford repeated the incredible announcement, she clutched her desk corner and began to sink. She swooned ever so gracefully. The seconds stretched out like slow-motion film as I leapt effortlessly out of my desk. My arms laid a blanket inches from the floor as she crumbled into my support. I cradled her unconscious head to keep her veil from falling off; it seemed like hours.

A year later, in my junior year, Paul Emanuelle held me as she said good-bye. "I've been transferred down south," she explained. "Hey, that's no reason to cry." Her thumb brushed under my eye gently.

"Can't you tell them you won't go?" I pleaded.

"That's not what you do when you're a nun, Jeanne. You know that. Someday you'll also have to leave when you don't want to." During those years Paul had become the confidante of my future plans.

"What's the good of making friends in one place, only to have to leave?" I sobbed. I didn't understand this part of religious life.

"That's part of the Rule of Detachment. God is your total focus, not people, Jeanne."

"I guess this means you'll forget about me."

"You're a hard case to forget! I love you, kiddo."

She'd never said those words to me before. Now that she had, it was over. I covered my grief with anger. "What the hell good does it do if you love me then leave?"

"Love has no geography, no limits, kiddo. I can love you from wherever I am!" She smiled and squeezed my hand.

I was pissed for months and had nothing good to say about the IHM's. When I pulled out of my hurt months later, I was still convinced there was something special about this breed of nun.

I'd never seen a fully habited nun roll up her tunic, sling her scapular over her shoulder and play softball like our IHM varsity coach, Sister Veronica Mary. Besides writing the poetry that inspired me, she pitched batting practice with a vengeance. Her veil flying in the wind, she was a winner who wanted the best from us. The IHM's were all compelled to be the best at whatever they touched. And I wanted that for myself.

By my senior year I had to make a decision. I had boiled it down to the Carmelites or the IHM's. Part of me was deeply, and inexplicably, attracted to isolation. I was just shy of eighteen, but already found life exhausting. With their soft nature, the Carmelites appealed to my contemplative soul. There was much to be said for quieting my volatile spirit. Would a lifetime behind walls do it? I was also afraid. My mind and body wanted more of the world than praying.

The IHM's had a zip and a zest for life—a zeal to know, to experience, an intensity of spirit that somehow felt akin to my own! They also seemed to be more worldly and knowledgeable about political events. Here was an order that had integrated its participation in the worlds of both the spirit and the flesh. I didn't understand much about their private political discussions but I liked the way they debated Church dogma and doctrine just like we did at the family dinner table. This would suit me just fine, I finally decided—even if I didn't know a lot of things about the Immaculate Heart nuns, or myself.

CHAPTER 6

The Disobedient Pies

I got my inspiration one evening while scrubbing pots and pans. The kitchen of the main house was brightly lit and well-appointed. I much preferred it to the medieval dining hall where we had taken the evening meal in silence. I'd spent my silence wondering what kind of desserts Mom would be making for the Thanksgiving Day table this year.

Cataloguing the mound of remaining pots, I was surprised to see a large tray of leftover slices of apple pie on the shelf. Chief Cook Sister Agnes Marie must have expected more visitors this weekend. Montecito was a spiritual drop-in center. I could never determine exactly who was arriving, or for what purpose, but there were many extraneous priests, nuns from other orders, and even lay people coming for special meetings every weekend. They stayed in the rooms on the ground floor of the summer house or in La Casa de María's retreat dorms.

"Do you think the visitors will be needing this leftover pie?" I whispered to my k.p. mate. Arching her eyebrows because I'd broken silence, the stoic novice retorted, "No. They've left."

Waltzing around solemnly in her white veil, Sister Lauren David was a tall, aristocratic, attractive nun-to-be. I'd tried to engage her in conversation several times, but this was one novice for whom Thou Shalt Not Fraternize with the Postulants was a welcome respite. There were novices and postulants who were rule-stickers, and some, like myself, who interpreted things loosely. Camp and Lauren David were among those striving to internalize the Holy Rule.

I persisted. "It's not right that the pie should go to waste." Lauren David kept scrubbing. "Think of the starving children in China. Why don't they let us have seconds here when there's leftovers?"

"Gluttony," the stoic offered.

"It'd be difficult to commit the sin of gluttony around here. We never see food except at meals, and not much of it then, either!"

Lauren David gave me her drop-dead, sisterly, silent good-night, and hung up her towel.

I eyed the slices. There's an exception to every rule, I thought, and leaders dare to break rules. Of course, Dad used to complete this maxim with the warning: "True genius demands you know *which* rules to break."

I hoisted the pie tray, turned off the kitchen lights, and gingerly maneuvered through the dark refectory, through the main house parlor, and down the dimly lit orchard path toward St. Joseph's. I wasn't sure if pie-lifting was genius or gall—I got the two confused. But I was sure my dormmates would be delighted with my surprise.

I wanted to do something that would make Camp happy and bring us all closer together. Thanksgiving was approaching; it would be our first holiday away from home.

The routine of the last two months had been pretty much as Lurch had described: pray, work, study, pray, work, study, sleep. Each dawn I stumbled across the orchard, attempting to arrive in chapel with my eyes open so I could chant Matins with my sisters:

"Come, let us sing to the Lord; let us shout for joy to the Rock of our salvation. Let us come before His presence with thanksgiving."

Thanksgiving was more than I could muster these damp dawns of November. I loved my classes and our frequent meditations. Once a week we had recreation; most often a communal song fest with guitars and flutes. My guitar lessons with Janis were proceeding well. I could now play "Puff, the Magic Dragon" and "The Sounds of Silence." Huddled in the corridors outside our cells, Micki, Janis, Louise, Donna, and I would sing folk songs, churning memories from earlier days. They were kind, allowing me time to muddle through my repertoire of two.

Mostly we listened to Janis' sweet voice. We dubbed her the Singing Postulant of the Class of '66. Janis was good enough to evoke authentic homesickness. Perhaps that is why I decided to invoke the role of resident therapist and surprise them with the pie. Happy postulants meant happy workers in the Lord's vineyard!

I quickly stored the pie in a safe place and rushed to tell Michelle of my feat. "Guess what Micki!" We bumped into each other in her cell doorway.

"We don't have time for games!" My confidante rushed past me heading for the bathrooms, tucking in her blouse. "We're supposed to be at the summer house listening to some radical priest from Germany. Didn't you hear the announcement? Come on, Jeanne."

Michelle Callahan and I had grown close over the last two months; her job was helping me interpret the Holy Rule. She mimed holy allegiance to humility and sisterly love. She glorified obedience. Michelle was adroitly manipulative—in other words, charming. My job was to coach her through classes. It wasn't that she was stupid. Michelle just had priorities that didn't include studying.

"What's he talking about?" I was thrilled by the late-evening surprise and urgently rearranged in my own disheveled habit.

"Probably the theology of paganism. Around here that would qualify as 'new thought.'"

"Micki, there's no such thing as the theology of paganism. Of course, if you looked at culture from a pagan perspective . . . "

"Come on, Aquinas, he's giving the lecture, not you. I was just kidding. I have no idea what kind of theological lunacy they're pushing around here these days. But we're supposed to go and adore everything he says." Michelle buttoned my blouse sleeves, and scooted me out the door.

"That was a drag!" Camp fell onto her bed. "Three hours of 'Vat's zis?' and 'Vat's zat?' I didn't understand a vord of vat he said!"

I plopped down on my side of the line. "I found a fascinating book where I was sitting, Camp. Look, it's called *The Phenomenon of Man* by Pierre Tielhard de Chardin. I think the novices are studying it. It's about the nature of man in relation to First Cause, and . . . "

"Jeanne, at this hour of the night, you are the only phenomenon I have to cope with. If you don't put that book down and turn off the light, you're gonna relate to First Cause real soon!"

In the outline of her night light, I watched Camp get ready for bed, neatly stacking blouse on top of blazer, on top of skirt, on top of socks. I wondered what Freudian stage Mother Caritas had talked to Camp about the day of her *MMPI* entrance test. My cellmate knelt and stretched her arm underneath her bed looking for her slippers.

"Eeeeegads!" The girl leapt across the room, landing on my bed, her face ashen.

I reached to calm her. "What's the matter with you, Camp?"

"Oh my God! Oh God!" Camp was hyperventilating. "There's rats! Under my bed! I touched a rat. Maybe I've been bitten, maybe I have rabies. Oh God! Am I going to die?"

Oh rats, I uttered a silent pun. Rats had gotten to the tray of pies I left under Camp's bed.

"Call someone! Do something!" Camp continued her attack on my mattress, flouncing hysterically.

I dashed to confirm the horror. The tray was undisturbed—the little slices lying peacefully exactly as I'd left them! Camp must have run her finger tips across the flaky crusts. "It's OK, Camp. Look!" I

57

held up her bedspread. "There aren't any rats. It's just the pie. Calm down."

"Pie! What pie?" I'd never seen anyone transition from terror to righteousness in one breath.

"The apple pies from dinner," I quickly explained. "I put them under your bed because I couldn't stuff another thing under my bed. It's crammed with my guitar case, my poem books, and those flower pots I'm gluing back together. So I thought . . . "

"Jeanne, you're nuts. Certifiably nuts!" Camp had abandoned my bed, my side of the room, and me. "I can't live like this. I'm going to tell Mother Caritas, you can't just go around stealing food. And you had no right to put them under *my* bed!" Camp was now pouncing on her own mattress. "I work hard to keep this place neat and dustproof. If I hadn't found this tray tonight . . . get this thing out from under my bed. Now, Jeanne! If I hadn't found it, there could have been rats by morning. Rats. . . do you hear me? Rats! In all my life, I've never lived in such filth. Why don't you put your pots and junk in the garage sheds where they belong? Your refuse is just collecting dust and dirt, and rats."

"You know what, Camp?" I sat composed on the edge of my bed, balancing my pies on my lap. If she was going to turn me in to Caritas, I was going to have the last word. "You, my disinfectant cellmate, are an anal compulsive. Lie down on your bed and let me give you some therapy."

"Lord in purgatory! What did I ever do to deserve such a cross?" Camp was ironing the creases in her bedspread with her palm.

"Now . . . now." I laid the tray on my bed, clasped my hands behind my back and thoughtfully paced my side of our cell. "There will be no charge. It's my duty as your sister in love and mercy to tell you you are not alone in this disease. Anal compulsion was documented by Sigmund Freud years ago. It's not necessarily terminal. It only reflects the superego's maniacal absorption with law and order. Most prominent dictators have the same problem as well as a lot of would-be-saints like yourself, and Mother Superiors."

"I'm telling Caritas; you said she's sick too, with that, whatever you're talking about . . . "

"Now, Camp. There is a cure. And once cured, my friend, you will no longer suffer an anxiety attack like you just did when your retentive little world of boxes and schedules suffers an interruption in order to save a life or . . . "

"No one is talking about saving a life. I don't have to listen to this garbage." A hysterical Camp sprang out of bed and screamed down the corridor. " You don't belong here. I'll see to that!"

"Sit down, Jeanne." Mother Mary Lurch Caritas was seated sternly in her Mistress chair. After Camp's threat last night, I'd fallen asleep praying to St. Jude, patron saint of lost causes. Apparently Jude had also been sleeping.

"Good morning, Mother Caritas!" I gave Lurch my best early morning charm. What punishment could be so bad? I tried to comfort myself. Sackcloth shirts or sleeping on a bed of nails was entirely too primitive for this modern order. Still, I'd certainly rather sleep on rocks than be kicked out.

Court was in session. "Marlene tells me you had a little trouble in the postulant dorm last night." Lurch came to the point.

"Yes, I heard we did."

"Trouble in *your* room, that is."

"Ah."

"You stole some pie from the refectory, Jeanne? This is a serious matter."

"Oh, no, Mother! I didn't steal them." I seethed. Camp didn't have to put it that way.

"Did you have someone's permission to help yourself to extra food, Jeanne ?"

"They weren't for me Mother; I took them for the others to make us feel better because . . . "

"It behooves you to listen, my child!" Lurch straightened her steel spine and crossed her elbows. She looked as though she expected the lions to enter the coliseum at any moment. "Where sin

59

is involved, the good Lord deserves better than our paltry excuses. Disobedience is always against the Holy Rule, Jeanne."

All was lost, I figured. Humility was my only salvation. "Yes, Mother."

"Would you repeat the vows to me, Jeanne?"

"Poverty, chastity, and obedience are the vows, Mother."

"Yes, obedience. Now we realize you have less than a year before you make your First Vows. The novitiate is a training ground to prepare for such a commitment. Obedience is self-discipline and is best learned by rigorous attention to even the smallest rule." My lips had begun to move in time with Caritas'.

Lurch hadn't been to West Point but she looked the same age as Dad and it sounded as though they had shared the Great Depression together. "Discipline is character," Dad would intone to the small characters gathered in front of him for punitive action. We were instructed to always repeat the West Point dictum, "No excuse, sir!"

" . . . So there is no exception. Do you understand, Jeanne?"

"No excuse, sir!" I whispered automatically.

"Tomorrow you will go see Father Hansen and make a special confession. In addition to the penance he gives you, you will make the Stations of the Cross every night after Compline for the next two weeks."

Crushed and confused, I whimpered out of Lurch's office. My road to sainthood had been blemished by an innocent act. Charity and sisterly love had been compromised by the dispassionate dictate of obedience. Why wasn't love one of the vows? Jesus said, "Above all else, love thy neighbor." I guess that was back in B.C.—Before Caritas.

CHAPTER 7

Pebbles on the Highway to Hell

Even the Stations were preferable to Camp's company. Protestants call the Stations of the Cross the epitome of Catholic masochism. This gruesome journey took more than three hours to complete. That is, if you did it right and suffered properly. I rather liked the trip.

The Stations were composed of fourteen prayer stops in a sequence that commemorated Christ's last days on earth. An inlaid plaque of gold or plaster, depending on the parish treasury, depicted each significant moment along the journey of redemption. At each stop you paused for fifteen or twenty minutes to say a series of prayers, kneeling, then standing, then kneeling again. It was an arduous process if you had bad kneecaps. The episodes of Jesus' torture were organized into a liturgy in the fourth century by Pope

Paul II. Beginning with the Last Supper and ending with the Resurrection, saying the Stations was almost like trekking up Mount Calvary yourself. They made good penance.

I don't think the Stations were originally meant to be said by children. Nevertheless, the Stations were an institutionalized part of Lent at Catholic grammar schools. Lent, in Southern California, brought its own penance: heat. The nuns at St. Christopher's would pack all eight hundred little grammar school bodies into our church's one-hundred-plus-degrees temperature. Suffering with Christ became more than symbolic as every few minutes you'd hear a little thud as another child fainted from heat prostration. A nun-to-be, I never fainted. If Jesus allowed himself to be crucified, the least I could do was stay conscious, breathe, and suffer.

At Montecito, saying the Stations was like touring the Garden of Eden. The journey was outdoors. The fourteen handsomely carved wooden plaques, posted on birch and eucalyptus trees, were scattered alongside a creek bed in grottoes overgrown with foliage now turned wet and scented in the twilight.

I paused, in habit and overcoat, before the first carving depicting Jesus at the Last Supper. They all looked so happy, only Christ knew it was the last time. "Help me, Lord," I bowed before Him, "not to miss my home so much. You had to leave Your brothers and mother. Help me find a new family here with You."

In the shallows of the creek, with water eroding his carved feet, Saint Peter stood, betraying his Master. "I never met the man," he denied to the tiny Roman soldier threatening him on the wooden plaque. I wondered if Camp, my betrayer, had descended from Peter. "And yet You loved him," I said to Christ as I knelt in the wet leaves. "After he redeemed himself by begging Your forgiveness, You even made him Pope. Your ways are strange and difficult for me to understand." Perhaps Camp would apologize when I returned.

My Savior fell twice on His way up Calvary. The cross was too heavy, He too weak. But He always got up. I rethought my own troubles, light by comparison. In the middle of my journey I found Mary Magdalene bent over, washing her Savior's blood-caked feet; Mary, the biblical whore brought to salvation by the Son of God. Magdalene reminded me of Louise and her red-painted fingernails. Louise, who still spent most of her free time writing to Alfredo. If Mary Magdalene could effect such a lifestyle change, there was hope for Louise . . . and me.

Late in the night, Mary the Blessed Virgin stepped out of the crowd following her Son up Calvary to wipe the tears and blood off His face. The stones cut into my knees. The Romans could have killed her. Would I have her courage? "Will you send me someone to stand by me, Holy Mother?" I prayed. I thought of Michelle, but doubted she had the courage I sought. Perhaps that friend would have to be myself.

Buttoning my heavy blue overcoat, I made one of the last stations. Jesus laid in His tomb alone, friendless, physically dead. Those nights were empty and alone. I knew how He felt. At least He had His family waiting outside the tomb. No one was waiting for me back at St. Joseph's. Although, secretly I hoped Michelle was.

Mom told us so many times, "Everyone has his dark night of the soul." I must be having mine, I thought. This must be the *detachment* Mother Caritas talked about, Merton's "emptying out," forsaking all people, places, and things for the love of God. The love of God felt chilly tonight, and I wasn't sure if I was forsaking or forsaken.

Stark silence had long since fallen by the time I was ready to lay myself in my tomb, my cell. Silence was precious and peculiar in Montecito. I never had enough of it when I needed it the most, and there was far too much when I wanted it least. For most of my life I'd had to fight to find silence. Now I had a life of it—to be with God and myself. I'd never experienced myself so much! Maybe this is what *The Imitation of Christ,* our daily meditation book, meant by "he who speaks to God, speaks not to man." Caritas had lectured us repeatedly, "The silence will enable you to develop your inner life and self in relation to God." What self in me stood apart from God? From others? Such a self I didn't yet know. Such a self I would have to find. How? I wondered. And even more significantly, how would I feel, who would I be, when I found it?

I plucked the pine needles out of my overcoat as I thought about Caritas' sermon from Isaiah this morning: "The Lord shall be unto thee an everlasting light." I headed through the darkness toward the lights of St. Joseph's.

Camp had used my two-week absence from dorm night life to villainize me.

"Hi, Dorothy." I was in the bathroom preparing for Matins. "Can I borrow your toothpaste?"

"What happened to your own?" Her tone shocked me. Dorothy was one of the many postulants with whom I enjoyed a casual, friendly acquaintance.

"I don't know. I guess I must have misplaced it."

"You can't do things like misplace your things and expect to use others'." With her finger Dorothy removed a quarter inch of paste from her tube and wiped it off on my finger.

"Thanks."

Later that afternoon in class I tried to get Donna's attention. "Shhhh," she responded to my whisper. "I can't talk to you now."

"Why not?"

"We're not supposed to talk in class."

"We always have!"

"I don't want to get in trouble with you." Donna turned her back.

During common prayers in chapel I thought some of the novices peered at me curiously. Had some notorious rumor about me flown through Montecito on the wings of an Unholy Ghost?

Janis was also withdrawn. "I've missed you!" I said as I caught her just after dinner. "Why don't I come to your cell this evening and let's do another lesson?"

"We can only do lessons on Saturdays from now on," Janis replied stiffly. "We're not supposed to be singing in the dorm at night."

"Who came up with that rule?" I pinned my arms around each other tightly and leaned back on my heels.

"Marlene told me while you were gone. And I asked novice Sister Antonia Marie, whom I play with."

"Oh, Janis, Camp's just making trouble." I envied Janis her common interest with Antonia Marie, the black-haired novice I was still trying to meet. "What did Antonia say?"

"That technically Marlene is right. They only play when the Mistress of Novices has gone for the evening."

"We can do that. Caritas goes to a lot of meetings at night."

"I just don't think we should do it anymore, Jeanne. Saturdays will have to do. And besides, next week we start taking our class on vows in the evenings so there'll be much less time"

While I'd been gone Janis had become Mother Caritas' favorite. Lurch had seen her vocal potential and had Janis singing with the novice choir, which took her away from St. Joseph's much of the time. I knew I had no voice, but I'd developed a penchant for writing lyrics and for the sweetness of Janis' company.

Only Michelle seemed genuinely happy at my return. "Your first mistake was lifting the pie!" She collared me affectionately in her cell that night. "I'm so glad you're not mad at me too, Micki. What is going on around here? No one seems to want to talk to me anymore."

"Camp spread the news that you're a petty thief and a troublemaker."

"Damn. That's all I need."

"You scare people. You do the things we all think of, you say things in class we might want to."

"You're saying others don't like to see themselves in me?"

"No one here wants to see her own rough edges."

"What was really so wrong about taking the pie, Micki? You know I wasn't going to horde and eat the slices all myself." I sat on her desk chair, she on her bed.

"I know you're unsophisticated when it comes to pie-theft. It requires common sense, which you don't have. And also an awareness of the consequences. You never think about consequences, Jeanne! Your spontaneity makes you vulnerable, regardless of your good intentions. Face it, Camp will never give you the benefit of the doubt. You really should quit trying to do things for people they don't appreciate. You have enough trouble taking care of yourself. I have enough trouble taking care of you trying to take care of yourself. Do me a favor and save us both some aggravation?"

"Anything, Micki."

"Don't parade your vulnerability, mask it! Then you can use it to your advantage."

"I'm not sure I can do that, Micki. That sounds too emotionally convoluted to me. I don't even know what that sentence means! I was simply bringing dessert to everyone."

"And that's your second mistake. Thinking. You don't. You've got no strategy. You never should have admitted to Marlene Camp that *you* put the pies there. It could have been anyone, don't you see?"

"It never occurred to me to lie."

"That's not lying, Jeanne. Keeping your mouth shut would have stopped you from volunteering for the slaughter! Omission is neither a lie nor a sin. Camp is a tight-ass neurotic," my private sage continued. "She doesn't like you and you should have assessed this before 'the night of the pie.' You set yourself up for the fall. She doesn't deserve to hear your truth. So why do you trust her with it?"

"Micki, I know you often have the same opinion about people, places, and things that I do!"

"Maybe yes, and maybe no," Michelle smiled coyly. "But you don't hear me blabbing my feelings to just any holy habit that saunters across my path."

My feelings were apparently hung out to dry, fresh and real, available for assault by any passing ill wind. "I guess I'm an idealist," I offered weakly .

"'Naive' is a less sophisticated but more accurate word."

Michelle put her arm around me as she pulled me out of her chair, and we sat side by side on the edge of her bed. "Just remember, Jeanne, before you make it past the pearly gates, you've got fifty years ahead of you that will make Camp and Lurch look like pebbles on the highway to hell."

I felt Michelle was wise. It surprised me that she was only a year older than me. I wondered how she had managed to pack so much worldliness into her one year in between high school and the convent. I took to heart every social inequity and personal hypocrisy I stumbled over. But somewhere in life, it often seemed to me, Michelle had accepted the fact that she wasn't in control of her destiny. Perhaps having to grow up with what she described as an "Irish drinking father and a neurotic mother," made it imperative for her to develop more subtle ways of holding her own. No one knew the Michelle Callahan I knew.

On the face of things, I think our postulant mates must have thought us an unlikely pair. I was genetically impulsive; Michelle was born circumspect. I was tempermental and emotional, while Michelle hid her mind and heart, a master of the covert, James Bond in a habit. I upset people, Michelle said, by mirroring their fears, by being different without even daring. And Caritas and others saw Michelle as the acquiescent, model postulant. Popular, if only by guile, Michelle made sure everyone liked her.

Some, like her new novice friend, Sister Dominic Anne, seemed to like her a great deal.

CHAPTER 8

Chastity and Me

Lurch had already struck bells for the evening. It was after Silence. St. Joseph's corridor was a river of blackness as I crept toward Michelle's cell.

"Micki, you in there?" I bent to call softly under the door. Seconds passed. I let myself in and felt Michelle's bed. Empty. Strange she wasn't home yet. Class ended two hours ago. I flipped on Michelle's small night light and flopped on her bed, my legs scattering a pile of books tossed at the foot. The other bed was also empty. Michelle's cellmate, Jackie Lunch, had left a week ago, the day before Thanksgiving. Caritas had said something about "bad health." It was not customary to call a press conference when someone left. You went so much more rapidly than you came—silently, overnight.

Odd. Michelle's clothes for tomorrow were neatly hung outside her closet, as if she'd already been here and prepared. Her pajamas were folded on the dresser. I sat on her bed. Where could she be? I really wanted to ask her about the vow of chastity tonight. I was thoroughly confused about Father O'Leary's lecture this evening.

"The role of . . . of . . . chastity is obsolete . . . I mean ancient . . . in monastic life," Father O'Leary had begun. Flipping nervously through the book on his podium, the sixty-year-old cleric looked more ancient than the vow of chastity. He seemed flustered with his role of teaching young women a subject he obviously didn't remember.

"That's what I hate about the Catholic Church," Michelle whispered to Louise and me. "They never throw anything out. No matter how old it is." Was she referring to the good Father O'Leary or chastity, I wondered?

"I don't want to hear about chastity," Louise returned.

I disagreed. "I'm so up to here with obedience, I don't care what the new subject matter is. Besides, I don't know a lot about this vow."

"You don't know a lot about obedience either. If obedience eluded you, God knows chastity will!" Michelle whispered to me, but laughed with Louise.

"What's that supposed to mean?" I demanded.

O'Leary interrupted. "The virtue of chastity is exemplified by Christ's conception. The Blessed Virgin conceived by the intercession of the Holy Ghost rather than by her husband, Joseph, so the patrimony of the Son of God could be clearly understood.

"We receive our next example of chastity from the life of Christ himself. If Jesus had married, His holy destiny might have been aborted. Christ, the first priest, set the example of the religious' total commitment—body, soul, and heart—to God. Some of the apostles were married, but they chose to leave their families and follow the Lord in celibacy. Mary Magdalene, the . . . ah . . . prostitute . . . also gave up . . . ah . . . and did likewise."

"Father," Louise's hand shot up, "what about love and sex?"

"Love and . . . ? Yes. Love. The Church recognizes the need for procreation and therefore sanctifies marriage and intimacy between

69

husband and wife. There is no real love outside the bonds of marriage, my child. Within the spiritual union of matrimony, wives give their husbands the commitment of lifelong love, obedience, and faithfulness. These are the same commitments nuns and priests make to Christ.

"Now . . . Mother Noreen, the Mistress of Novices, will go into more depth with you about this vow next year." O'Leary slapped his textbook shut on chastity. "Good-night, class."

It was the shortest and most oblique lecture I'd heard in my last three months at Montecito.

I tore back Michelle's bedspread and grabbed a pillow for my head. Chastity, I knew, had to do with sex. Sex meaning Mom's two-minute lecture about the "birds and the bees" to France and me five years ago. Like Father O'Leary's, her speech had been so short we didn't even sit down at our formal dining room table in West Covina. As Mom stood, we leaned against the chairs eagerly. At the end of her disgusting description I looked at France and said, "Who'd want to do *that?*" Mom blushed and left.

I also knew there were some pleasurable aspects to being unchaste. Mom seemed embarrassed but pleased when she was doing dishes and Dad would come up and pat her on the rear or try to steal a kiss; she'd blush and whisper, "Not in front of the kids, Fred." Non-chastity never happened in front of the kids, so, of course, it became interesting. Hidden in our home, and only surreptitiously referred to in the bathrooms at school, a lot of people thought chastity was a big deal. The very subject upset Louise to no end, and Michelle, like Mom, never wanted to talk about it.

The door creaked open. "Micki, how would you write . . . ?"

"Louise." I recognized her voice. "It's Jeanne. Micki's not here, I'm waiting for her too." Miss Rodriguez, in her flannel nightgown with red hearts, flounced on the bed beside me. "Maybe I can help. What are you writing?"

"I'm writing to Alfredo. Micki helps me . . . "

"You shouldn't be writing to your boyfriend, Louise! He can't write back, so what's the point?"

"He does write back."

"Sure, and Mother Caritas hands you his letters every day."

"Remember, Jeanne, I'm the one who volunteered to go to the post office downtown everyday and pick up the mail!"

"So you get his letters *before* you bring home the mail, and you leave yours there! Louise, you can't keep doing this. Why are you still writing to a boy? Are you sure you want to be a nun? The two don't go together you know."

"Alfredo understood I was going into the convent. I didn't think I was in love with him. I thought I was only in love with Christ. I thought I understood what that meant. Now I think I'm in love both on earth and in heaven! I just don't know who I love more . . . I guess." Louise's shoulders sagged as she sighed deeply. She slid off the bed, and as her matching red-heart slippers slipped through Michelle's door, she called back to me, "Didn't you ever have a boyfriend, Jeanne?"

Sure I had boyfriends. I just couldn't recall their names as well as Louise. Of course I remembered Denny, who had thrown me a good-bye party the week before I left for the convent. And then there was Jesse in the eighth grade.

Rosemary Megan was the real reason I got involved with Jesse LaCañada at the bowling alley on Wednesday afternoons. I hated bowling. It was a low-skill game. Even totally uncoordinated Rosemary could knock some of the pins down if she let go of the ball and allowed it to meander down the alley. But I liked watching Rosemary watching David. And Jesse, David's best friend, was there watching me, I suppose.

I was still watching Rosemary Megan, and Adrienne Gary, and Sally Dougherty stick bobby pins into their curlers late that slumber party night a week before we graduated.

"Oh, God! I can hardly wait for the last dance of our grammar school careers." Adrienne Gary, a very developed thirteen, was assiduously boy crazy. "I just hope Michael doesn't do anything dumb like wear a pink shirt. I'd just die. Rosemary, do you think I should tell him what to wear? You know football players are not used to wearing anything but a helmet!"

"Just be glad a nice guy like Mike asked you. Let him decide how to dress." Rosemary Megan had a grace and poise that made her Miss Eighth Grade Popularity.

A week later, Rosemary and I double-dated at the graduation dance—she with David, I with Jesse. My formal was yellow. Jesse's tux was Tijuana royal blue. We were garish; I was bored. But Rosemary and I spent the rest of the summer reading and gossiping, trying to decide if Jesse and David were mature enough for us. Rosemary's mother settled the issue by eloping with St. Christopher's assistant pastor, Father Cagan. In disgrace, Rosemary's father took his daughter away. I never saw her, or Jesse LaCañada, again.

I sat at my desk staring dumbly for months. I missed Rosemary. Not even finally arriving at high school buoyed me. I slid my pencil through the silky chestnut hair that draped the front of my desk. Maybe I could weave it, I thought, pulling strands around a second pencil now.

"Owww! That's my hair!" My woven rug jerked apart, my pencil flew across the room.

Sharon Calloway and I, introduced by her hair, had a friendship made in heaven. She loved biology and math, which I hated. Cutting up the poor little frogs made me cry, and the rotten smell of formaldehyde knocked me out. Dad said I had a "fine abstract mind," but it was apparently too coarse to comprehend absolute x's and y's meeting together in some predefined, nonexistent point in the ethers. Sharon was poised and gorgeous, her lustrous mane charmed. She was everyone's best listener and friend. But she couldn't put a sentence together on paper without a dictionary, so it was simple: I played campaign manager for her climb to student body vice-president, and she cast herself well as my emotional inner guide. I wrote her papers and she solved my problems. She also caused me a few.

I picked my way down the bleachers to the front row where Sharon always sat. "Why do we have to go to all of Alan's basketball games? This is a bore!" Hanging around Sharon while she hung around her boyfriends was more trouble than she was worth at times.

"Ah . . . the price of popularity!" Miss Something-for-Everyone replied. "Alan likes it when I'm here. You don't have to come if you don't want to."

"*Well!* Someday I won't."

"Oh, Cordy, don't be that way." She resorted to her nickname for me. "Who would I talk to then?"

"Alan, Alan, Alan."

"You can't have a conversation with a guy when he's on the court."

"If you ask me, you can't have a conversation with a boy, period."

"Jeanne, why don't you get a boyfriend and then we could double-date and see each other on Saturday nights?"

"I'm thrilled," I replied, opening my binder to complete my book report on *Wuthering Heights.* Romance sounded better on paper than in reality. At least Catherine Earnshaw got to stand on her wind-swept cliffs and author a few good poems to her fortuitously missing Heathcliff. I wondered why Sharon didn't come to my softball games. Maybe I'd ask her.

"Hey, you, the writer!" The male voice felt directed toward me, but I didn't look up. "Are you writing about my hook shot for the *L.A. Times?*"

Sophisticated line, I thought. He insults me and compliments me in the same breath. I hardly looked like a *Times* reporter, but as junior editor of the school's *Lance,* I wished I was. Besides, his voice was more playful than egotistical. I looked up. "I haven't even seen your hook shot, but I doubt it merits a paragraph in the *Times!*"

"You haven't been paying attention. How would you know if you haven't seen it?" Denny Crawford's muscular frame was now directly in front of me, leaning against the steel bars separating the front row bleachers from the court. He was short for a basketball player, hardly four inches taller than I. His crew-cut red head topped an earthy smile that complemented a pair of piercing blue eyes.

"Now that you've become a complete distraction, what do you want?"

"I have what I want now." Denny's Irish joviality housed a spirit older than his years. "Your complete and undivided attention!"

Very smooth, I thought. "Are you winning or losing?"

"Oh, winning. Don't you think?"

I blushed. "I meant the game."

"The game? Oh, right . . . I'd better go back, quarter break is over." Denny started for the court, walking backward, still facing me, smiling. By this time, I was too. He looked so silly walking backwards.

"*Whoooo* is that?" Sharon reappeared at my shoulder.

"I have no idea." I leaned into her, laughing. "I never saw him before!" I shouted this last sentence loud enough for Denny to hear.

Denny reversed his stride. "Hey, you. I forgot something."

"Hey, yourself. I have a name."

"I know, I've known it for weeks."

"You forgot to use it."

"I didn't forget. I just haven't gotten that far . . . yet."

Yet? This boy was entirely too forward. I tried to work up some anger; he was being rude. Or something.

"Do you have a steady or anything? I don't see you at the dances." The crew cut had poked itself through the bars.

"I don't go to dances. I don't have a boyfriend, and I don't want one."

"That's great! So why don't you keep this thing for me. It keeps hitting me in the mouth when I'm trying to be a jock." Crawford's bare freckled arms lifted the silver varsity basketball and chain from around his neck and tossed it into Bronte's prose.

I was flabbergasted. "I don't want this. You can't do this!" I was on my feet now, swinging Denny's gift in my outstretched arm like a priest's censer at benediction. My laughter belied my words. I couldn't help admiring his clarity of purpose, his audacity and charm.

Denny began his backwards amble toward the court once more. "It goes better with black hair than with red!" he yelled, his face beaming a private smile as though we were alone in the gym. I thought of running after him or throwing the basketball back at him. But I wanted to hold the moment, hold his smile. Darnation! My body wanted to hold him too, I thought.

Sharon grabbed my shoulder with one hand and Alan's basketball chain she wore around her neck with her other hand. "Gosh O'Malley!" she said, staring at me.

High school is a strange cultural phenomenon; a lesson in identity, not education. The classes are background music to keep us occupied while we decide who we are. I didn't like the options. By default I fell into the the girl-jock-brain category, which was fine with me. Only there was no such category. Girls who liked sports were relegated to the weirdo category, but I was also V.P. of the California Scholarship Federation, "the brain trust." And . . . I was number-one sidekick to Miss Poise & Pom-pom Queen Calloway. I clunked around in tennies with rolled up socks and never participated in the pin-cushion hair-curling rituals Sharon and her girlfriends held as sacred. I hated the harness Mom called a bra and conformed perfectly to the rule: "good girls don't wear makeup." I combed my hair like a normal person—once a day, when I got out of bed. So what did Mr. "Jock" Crawford see in me?

"I think you're very cute pretending that you're not," he told me one Saturday night months later at the drive-in. "You've got gorgeous wavy black hair and bedrooom eyes! Besides, I like talking to you, you understand me."

"Talk, talk . . . why don't you shut up and kiss me!" I traced his lips with my fingers. I liked Denny's mouth for other reasons. He was a fast talker on the social scene, but his brainwaves stopped when applied to more serious pursuits.

"I got my papers from the Peace Corps," Denny persisted.

"When I'm a senior next fall, do you think I should apply to go to Africa or to Latin America? Do you think you could join the Maryknoll nuns and come to Argentina with me?" Denny knew I was going into the convent, but I could tell he didn't grasp the whole idea.

"Let's talk about it Monday at school, OK?" I reached to turn off his dash board lights.

Johnny Mathis' warmth stirred the chilly Mulholland night air as I leaned against the tree waiting for Denny to unpack the blanket from his car. It was Senior Prom night—an end and a beginning, I thought, looking north over the lights of the smoggy San Fernando Valley. I'd never been to Los Angeles.

"It's really sweet that you brought the radio," I called to Denny's bustling form rummaging in the trunk. My sweetheart's infectious enjoyment of life had been a tonic to my intense nature these last two years.

"I think I brought everything!"

What's "everything" I wondered? Was I crazy staying out all night with a guy? Sharon Calloway and I had both told our mothers we were spending the night at each other's house. Despite his playful sexiness, Denny had always been safe—a too-perfect gentleman, in my opinion! I knew nothing would get out of hand unless *I* wanted it to. I did, just a little! It was Prom Night, a night to break rules.

"The blanket, the radio, the flashlight, two pillows, the ice chest, two wind candles, whiskey for me, Pepsi for you, a box of chocolate kisses for your sweet tooth, a book of that Whitman guy's poems you can read me, and *you!*" He grinned from the blanket now open on the cliff side. "Come now, madam, all is prepared!"

"I didn't know you drank whiskey!" I sat crosslegged beside him.

"I don't much. But this is a special night. Isn't it terrific?" Denny's arm gestured toward the Valley lights below.

I leaned into his lap and watched the Hollywood Freeway

winding its way north. Denny's tongue slid against mine.

"Hmmm . . . yes," I mumbled. "This is the kind of special I like."

Denny stopped to look at me. "I know you do. That's why I can't believe that you're going off to be a nun."

"Let's not get started on that one again. As they say, 'Shut up and kiss me, you fool.'"

Denny drew back and opened his Jack Daniels bottle. "Nuns aren't even supposed to like guys, let alone kiss with their mouths open."

"What do you know about nuns? Anyway, I'm not a nun, yet. When I am, I won't like kissing you. Satisfied? Furthermore, I only graduate from high school once in my life, so pass me a sip of your whiskey, please."

"Here's a capful only. Drink it very slowly."

"Besides, I think I should be a mature nun and know what I'm giving up. Jesus said, 'Give unto God's the things that are God's, and to Caesar the things that are Caesar's.' It's still your turn, Caesar!"

Denny's mouth was on mine again, his hands on my neck and shoulders. The moon basked other couples parked below and above us. I blew out the candles. His hands slid to my blouse, his palm played with my breasts. "Something new tonight?" My breathing was heavier as I pressed into his shoulders.

"You know how special you are to me, Jeanne. It's been a wonderful two years. I don't want it to end."

"Don't get mushy on me, Carrot Top." My voice was husky as I used his favorite nickname. I ran my fingers through his brick-red stubs and pulled him closer. The stars seemed looser, brighter now. His fingers pulled at my blouse buttons. I laughed a little nervously. The feeling of Denny's rough callouses on my back and chest was new, stimulating. "Should I take off my shirt, sweetheart?"

"Hell, no, Jeanne. What do you take me for?"

"I thought you were trying to open the buttons. I take you for my romantic sweetheart, what should I take you for?"

"Keep your blouse on, Jeanne."

"Then keep your hand there . . . minus a few snaps." I reached and tugged the familiar snaps open. Denny lay me back on the pillow. His hand covered my breast; his mouth bent to follow it.

The jolt was entirely unfamiliar but thrilling. The exquisite shock ran down my entire body. I forgot about the blanket and Mulholland Drive; the night would last as long as my body could feel. He broke away from my side and looked at me strangely, as he took a sip of whiskey.

"What's the matter?" I was disoriented and sorry he'd stopped.

"Nothing. I'm fine." Denny seemed fine as he changed positions and came to lay on top of me. The weight of his chest pinned mine into the warm earth that cushioned my shoulders. Slowly, he began to move against me. I moved with him; our kisses were slower, deeper. My body glided with the clouds, yearned for the pine tops surrounding us. It seemed like hours. Mathis' voice seemed louder, faster, as my tongue found his, my body rose to meet him with a strange pulsing tension. I gasped for air.

"God, this is wonderful!" I laughed aloud.

"I'm glad." Denny wasn't very talkative. He was lost in his own movement. His body was moving in a way I'd never felt before, a rhythmic rolling against mine. I was glad he was having a good time. The stars seemed glazed over, as if a film had spread over the sky. I thought of the distant whiskey. Was I drunk? Is this what the feeling was? Denny's waves were getting stronger.

"Jesus, we've got to stop!" He rolled off me and sat up, shaky.

"What's the matter?" I bolted upright myself.

Denny gave me a long, level look. His breathing was tight, raspy, his blue eyes brilliant in the night. "Sometimes I just can't believe how dumb you are!"

"I'm far from dumb!"

"I mean naive . . . about sex!"

"What about sex?"

"Shit, Jeanne. I'm going to go get some firewood . . . or something. It's getting cold. Wouldn't you like a fire?"

78

"What we were doing felt warmer than fire," I laughed, trying to ease his agitation.

"That's the problem!" Denny rose to leave. He turned his back on me, straightened out his rumpled trousers, and buttoned his shirt. "Be back in a few minutes . . . "

Two months later Denny handed me the small black leather case. It was my going-away party, and the last night we'd see each other.

"It's beautiful," I exclaimed. "I'm sure they'll let me keep it in the convent. We have to have a manicure set, it's on the list."

"I know. You showed me your list, I remembered it."

The black leather was finely wrought and warm to my touch, just like Denny. It would have to take his place.

"You know, Jeanne," he began, as we stood in the dim porch light outside the main party room, "I . . . ah . . . I love you. You probably know that by now. If you ever change your mind about being a nun, I'll be waiting, like I've always said."

I felt uncomfortable whenever Denny got serious or talked about a future between us. Like Denny, Dad also never quite understood why a girl who was going into the convent even *had* a boyfriend. He'd been confused about Denny for some time. I thought it made perfect sense. High school was Denny's time, and soon it would be my time, God's time. Besides, I wasn't quite sure Denny was really my boyfriend. I didn't feel "that" way about him. Not the way my girlfriends said they were "in looooove . . . " Not like Sharon told me she felt inside about Alan, or the way *Wuthering Heights* said you were supposed to feel if you married someone for the rest of your life. The thought of spending "forever" married to Denny, or anyone else for that matter, struck me as an outrageous waste of my potential. I had a lot to do with my life.

I probably didn't feel towards boys the way Sharon or my other girlfriends did because I had a vocation. The whole sexual matter seemed very overrated to me. It felt great physically but so did diving into the ocean on a boiling summer afternoon. Denny had never been very emotionally compelling. It would be easier to give him up than softball. I could have gone on to a promising college athletic career instead of the convent.

Denny had been wonderful. His smile, his fine athlete's body, his sweet ways had brought me a pleasure I hadn't known. But even if I had a brain tumor and couldn't be a nun, I knew I wouldn't be coming back to my high school Romeo. I felt just fine about saying good-bye to him tonight. "No, I don't want you to do anything dumb like wait for me, Carrot Top." I thanked him for his gift with a kiss. "I won't be changing my mind. And you've got to go to Africa . . . yes, I think they need you in Africa more. And when you get back, you'll meet someone who thinks you're the best thing that ever happened. You're a born family man. Find someone I like and I'll come to your wedding in full habit! You can introduce me to your friends as 'Sister Mary So & So, my former girlfriend.' How's that for a happy ending?"

"It's not the snapshot I had in mind." Denny shrugged his athlete's shoulders. A shock of his recently grown hair fell over his eyes.

Michelle's cell was cold; I was startled from my daydreaming by the night wind's rattle against her window. The moon's reflection off the stark walls gave me enough light to go searching for a sweater. As I pulled out the bottom drawer of Michelle's dresser, my hand scraped a jagged edge. I pulled the object out into the light. How strange! I held an antique picture frame. The recent black-and-white photograph was of Michelle and Sister Paul Emanuelle! They were arm-in-arm smiling at each other.

Michelle's door squeaked open slowly. Terror leapt into my throat and I quickly dashed into the closet. What if Lurch found me prowling about in the dead of night?

Through a crack I saw the shape approach the bed. "Micki, where have you been?" I screamed hoarsely, throwing open the door.

Michelle jumped off the linoleum, twirling toward me. "What the hell are you doing here?"

80

"I've been here all night waiting. I wanted to ask you about O'Leary's lecture about chastity."

"Chastity, at this hour?"

"Where have you been?"

"Been? Me? Ah . . . meditating."

"It's got to be after midnight. You've set an all-time record for praying—for you, anyway. I don't believe you."

"Well . . . I was talking too."

"Who else is up this late? Talking where?"

"In the orchard, on the pavilion up by the tennis courts. I guess I fell asleep. It's really late, Jeanne. I'm going to get ready for bed."

I'd never been to the pavilion hideaway that I'd seen from the orchard path, but I had heard others talk about it. No one played tennis on the dilapidated orchard court. The net sagged in the middle as if someone with heavy thoughts sat on it daily. Weeds grew in its cracked concrete. Above the court, up a short flight of steps, was the raised pavilion. Shrouded by pine trees and cobblestone walls on three sides, the area was hidden from view, even when walking past it on the orchard path. I'd heard it was for private meditation and conversation.

"Micki, how could you fall asleep? It's freezing outside!" Pointing to the bundle she'd dragged in with her, I continued, "Do you always take a blanket to the orchard just in case you fall asleep?"

"I took the blanket to keep us warm."

"Us who?"

"Us—me and . . . God."

"I may be a little naive, Micki, but give me a break! Why won't you tell me?"

"All right, all right. Quit interrogating me. You won't turn me in, will you?"

"Of course not; this is me, your buddy."

"All right, then. 'Us' is me and Dominic Anne." Michelle sat on her bed and folded her arms, content with her confession.

"Sister Dominic Anne, the novice?" I sat at the bed's foot, folded my arms, and demanded more.

81

"Yes. Sister Dominic Anne, the novice. We're close friends."

How could this be, I wondered? Postulants and novices were hardly to speak to one another, much less become close friends. The novices slept upstairs at the main house. Their cells, the mezzanine sick room, and the entire second floor was off-limits to postulants. I rarely saw the novices.

"Remember when I had gardening duty the first month we were here, Jeanne?"

"You told me you didn't know a rose from a tulip, that all your flowers died in the first week."

"That's how I got to know Dominic. She had gardening duty on the second-floor gardens, where the novices live. I just climbed up the balcony and asked for her help."

"You, who are too afraid of a softball to pick up a bat, climbed up a balcony?"

"She helped me."

"Sounds like you're a big help to each other. You're gonna get busted climbing up and down balconies and talking in the orchard till after midnight!"

"No one knows, Jeanne. No one. We're very careful."

Michelle must have perfected the art of subterfuge. Her skills at creating illusions were consummate. I'd known her well for over three months and apparently I still didn't know her. "How often do you meet Dominic in the orchard? What do you talk about? How do you both get back into St. Joseph's and the main house after they're locked up?"

"I'm the one who volunteered to lock up St. Joe's after Caritas leaves every night."

"You and Louise with your extracurricular chores! And I get stuck with pots and pans. How does Dominic get back in?"

"She's got the same chore assignment at the main house. She's the one who told me to volunteer."

"So this is where you get your little tips on how to get around—the Novice Information Center. Micki, you've turned into the Houdini of the convent!"

"I never change, I just adapt." In the dark, Michelle threw off her clothes, jumped into her nightgown and pulled the covers over her face. "Now, Jeanne, will you please shut up and go to bed. Sleep over there in Jackie's bed, it's safer than traipsing down the corridor and waking Camp."

But I persisted, sitting next to her on the bed. "Micki . . . since you know so much about novice life . . . do you ever see Sister Antonia Marie?"

"Who?" Michelle's voice was muffled in her blankets.

"Antonia Marie. The wonderful short one who walks so gracefully like a queen with regal bearing. She has gorgeous black hair you can see under her white veil, and that dazzling smile with those cute dimples. The one who plays guitar with Janis. My God, her incredible voice has wider range than Janis'."

"Jeanne! We're not going to discuss vocal chords at one in the morning. Go to bed and shut up; we'll get reported."

"Do you see her?" I whispered.

"No, Jeanne. I don't see Antonia Marie . . . much. Just in passing. Dominic talks about her sometimes, they're friends. I only know Antonia goes down to L.A. every weekend to teach Spanish classes at one of the mission houses. Now, get into bed."

"I've got a great idea, Micki! You could help me find a way to meet her, so she and I can read poetry to each other up on the pavilion with you and Dominic."

Michelle flipped the blankets back, sat up, and looked at me. "You're crazy, Jeanne. You don't know what you're talking about."

"Sure, I do Micki, it'd be so easy. You could think of something. Like . . . uh . . . I'd have to drive her to L.A. to her class."

"You don't drive, Jeanne. Besides, even if you learned, they wouldn't let a postulant out of here once a week. And, you don't even speak Spanish."

"So it's a lousy plan, Micki. But you could think of something really . . . sneaky. I mean, clever."

"Thanks."

"Please, Micki. Think of something."

83

"All right, all right. I need a good night's sleep if my brain is expected to be creative tomorrow." Michelle stretched out her arm, brushed her fingers through my hair, and looked at me wistfully.

"What's the matter?" I asked.

"Sometimes I just wish you were older," Michelle sighed.

"How would my being older help . . . me . . . or you?"

"Maybe it wouldn't. It's my fantasy that you'd be more mature and then be able to understand . . . things."

"Like what things?" I leaned forward.

Michelle backed away lay on her pillows. "Like how to go get in bed. It's late, Jeanne, *please* go."

I lay wide awake in Jackie's bed, fully dressed and staring out the window. I wondered about Michelle's proclivity for making close friends. I thought Dominic Anne was vacuous and superficial, but I did envy that Michelle has someone who cared. Were they closer friends than Michelle and I? Micki hadn't mentioned what they had in common, what they talked about. I wished I was Michelle's cellmate. I loved talking with her and was learning so much too. "You're quite special to me, Micki. I love you." I held my breath hoping I hadn't trespassed.

"I love you too," Michelle exhaled into the night.

CHAPTER 9

Once A Heretic

"Ze problem vit man, is man himself," Father Romanoff Bruntz, our theology teacher, preached. We were at class in the summer house. "Man is ze closest zing to imperfection God has created. I say zis to you so zat you make recognition how lowly ve are in ze great scheme of zings. Ve must struggle in faith because ve know man is part of God's majestic plan."

"Vat about vomen?" I jabbed Michelle's shoulder with my pen.

"Don't start, Jeanne."

"To make good zis imperfection, Christ left us His Church, His sacred image on earth. Ze Church, vit ze Pope, incarnates salvation for all who follow Her teachings. As nuns, you vill be important emissaries in bringing Perfection, ze Church, to imperfection, man.

"You have question on zis?" Father Bruntz peered at my raised hand through his bifocals and down his Teutonic nose.

"How do we explain some of the Church's mistakes to non-Catholics, Father?"

"Mistakes?"

"Yes. How do we rationalize that for a century after Copernicus theorized that the earth was round, the Pope maintained it was flat?"

"Ah, child, you err in your Church history. Copernicus made his zeory in ze sixteenz century. Ze College of Cardinals did not declare ze Doctrine of Infallibility of ze Pope until ze nineteenz century. You understand now?"

I looked at Michelle.

"Tell him you understand, Jeanne," she instructed.

"I guess so, Father. But how about when Galileo proved that the earth revolved around the sun by looking through his telescope? The earth was not the center of the Universe as the Church taught. It took Pope Martin II another century to agree and change his mind."

"Zis issue of ze 'Centrality of Jesus Christ' is most fundamental to our faiz. Ze pagan astronomers ver not Cazolic. Zeir discoveries questioned ze role of Christ. Zere can be no Jesus Christ on each planet, you know. So ze Pope takes time to zink of zese zings."

"I can understand that, Father, but . . . "

"Goot. Zen you zit down now, please."

"But, Father, how is it valid for a group of people, even holy Cardinals, to get together and declare someone infallible? And that was only in 1850, hardly a hundred years ago. It's not only a late decision, it seems almost blasphemous. That's like deciding you're God. The early fathers of the Church were not thrilled when Julius Caesar declared himself infallible. So it seems a tall order, even for the sacred College of Cardinals."

"You vould compare ze pagan Roman Empire vit Holy Mozer ze Church?" Father Bruntz's lenses were gyrating up and down his nose.

"John Paul Sartre, the French existentialist . . . "

"You bring to my class ze vords of a pagan? Nein! Zis Sartre is a

86

heretic. I vill tell ze Mozer Superior—you are a heretic! You vill go now to ze chapel and pray for your faith."

Departing my desk, as Michelle shook her head, I followed the direction of Father Bruntz's pointing finger.

Camp stuck her foot out in the aisle and sneered, "You had it coming, heretic."

Being expelled from religion class was not a new experience. I'd never been able to tie my tongue to the roof of my mouth. In grammar school, I'd run afoul of towering Sister Mary Vincent because I didn't think we should buy pagan babies. Once or twice a year the plastic pagan baby banks would come down the rows of little desks. We were supposed to ask our parents for nickels and dimes to "buy pagan babies." These babies allegedly lived in China, where missionaries were trying to baptize them. I was never clear as to whether we were buying food and shelter for the missionaries or actually purchasing communist babies. Nothing was ever said about the parents of these pagan babies; perhaps they were all orphans. But when I compared their religious purchase to the economics of black slavery in America, Sister Mary Vincent sent me home for a week. Dad had to donate another marble altar to get me back into school.

Years later, I didn't understand why the theological debate acceptable at my family dinner table was so shunned in high school. Bishop Amat had all the marble altars it needed, so I had to resort to other means.

Father Manfred O'Lacey must have been on sabbatical from the Dublin Seminary's Retirement Home. We called him Father O'Lazy because his mind was slower than his mouth.

"What proof is there regarding the Ascension?" asked Terry McMahon, a intellectual new student who had just enrolled at Amat. Father O'Lazy had already thrown her out of class the week before for wearing eyebrow pencil. Terry had defended herself with, "Mary Magdalene did."

I liked Terry because she, too, questioned things, but I knew O'Lazy thought she was Magdalene reincarnate. So this time, I stepped in to save her. "Father, why do we celebrate the Resurrection on Sunday and the Crucifixion on Friday? The Bible says Jesus lay in his tomb for 'three days and three nights.' There's only two nights and a day-and-a-half between Friday afternoon and Sunday morning."

"These are biblical matters of faith!" The good priest clutched at his chest.

"The scriptures are an allegorical cultural statement." The soft clear voice came from the back of the room. I turned to look at Charlotte Vogt hunched over a heavy book on her desk. She didn't even seem to be paying attention to us. Her book was definitely not the *Baltimore Catechism*.

O'Lazy stomped down the aisle toward Charlotte screaming, "Out, out, the lot of you!"

Terry and I grabbed the esoteric Charlotte by the shoulders and fled out the back door. O'Lazy slammed it on us.

"What will non-Catholics think when they find out we can't even count right?" I persisted as we walked toward the Dean's office.

"What they've always thought—that Catholics have too many unsubstantiated fantasies," Charlotte answered.

Charlotte fascinated me. She and her older brother Larry, who had taken up with my sister France, were the only self-avowed atheists in a school that said there was no such thing. I was sure Charlotte had a genius I.Q., but I couldn't figure out how a genius could be an atheist. Charlotte went to Holy Communion every morning with us anyway. She called it "sharing ritual with my friends."

"We're going to have to develop better tactics," Terry strategized, noting it was her third trip to the dean's office.

I was of the same mind. It seemed to me we had to find some strength in numbers, we had to unionize. "Listen, you two, I've got it! We should band together and get organized. Why don't we form the N.H.S., the Notorious Heretical Society?"

"And everyone will think we're referring to the N.H.S., the National Honor Society that we all belong to!" Charlotte chimed in. I never had to explain my madness to her.

"What a wonderful idea!" Terry concurred. "Perhaps we shall hold salons and other students will come."

"With debates on topics of interest," I said, excitedly. "Maybe even the faculty would drop by."

The three of us took a chair in Dean Sister Declan Frances' anteroom.

"Seems like the faculty has already dropped in," a deflated Charlotte noted our surroundings. "That's a great idea for later, but today I don't want to get expelled and have to go sit in public school with those dumbos."

In addition to regular expulsions from religion class, I was nearly flunking geometry, the subject the Dean herself taught. But I wasn't worried. I had my bases covered. "Listen you two," I lowered my voice, "Why don't you both go to the library and sit tight for a while. I'll see Sister Declan alone. She and I have an understanding."

The understanding had fallen into place so sweetly, as if God's holy timing had interceded personally on my behalf. Last Friday Sister Declan Frances herself had rushed into civics class to drag me out. "Dearest one, dearest me," she scooted me down the corridor. "Your mother just called. She's in labor. A neighbor has driven her to the hospital. Your sister is on a field trip. I must drive you to be with her at the hospital. Off with us now. Follow me, hurry!"

Sister Declan Frances was a St. Louis of France nun with a stocky frame supporting her jawbone coif. Her face held a wide Irish grin and she mouthed a brogue to match. Despite my detentions in her office, she seemed to like me. I suspect she knew I was half-Irish. She was all leprechaun. She claimed Mom was "of the saints" because she had birthed so many new souls.

This would be my first near-hands-on participation in birth. Dad was due home tomorrow from Italy, and the baby wasn't due for two more weeks. I'd never been to the hospital because Mom was never gone long enough to miss dinner. She usually timed her labor for first thing in the morning or last thing at night. She held the hospital's maternity record for speed as well as quantity. I slammed the car door on the girls' dean and bounded up the steps of Queen of Angels.

"My roses aren't blooming as they should," Mom continued. She was dictating instructions covering her garden, the dinner hour, and the evening. "It's been too dry. If I'm not home before tomorrow, be sure to water them. Tell everyone—no desserts before dinner. I left the lasagna in the freezer. Three hundred fifty degrees, one hour. Tell Frances not to burn it."

"Yes, Mom," I cringed inside as her eyes closed while she breathed through a contraction.

"Now, one more important thing. Your father and I didn't have time to look at the *Book of Saints* and decide upon a name for the baby. We're running short on good names. Do you have any ideas?"

Gazing at the crucifix above her bed, divine inspiration hit me. Sister Declan Frances had been patient with me, but I doubted her forbearance would hold out for another year until I graduated. I'd never get through senior trigonometry next year.

"How about 'Declan' for a name?"

"Declan? How strange."

"Oh, it's not strange, lots of people are named Declan."

"Do you think it's in the *Book of Saints?*"

"Oh, I know it is." Mom looked at me quizzically. "It must be, because nuns only take saint's names. You know Sister Declan, the dean at school?"

"Oh yes, of course. A very fine nun, a true soul. Irish, too, isn't she?"

Joan Frances McGuinness-McGrain Córdova was not a politically passionate woman except where the Irish were concerned. The only bumper sticker she ever put on her car was "British out of Ireland!" Once, when we were watching the news about parliament vetoing Irish demands, she turned down the volume and serenely asked Dad, "Do you suppose contributions to the IRA are tax-deductible?"

"She most certainly is Irish, Mom," I confirmed. "So Declan has got to be an Irish name. Saint Declan was a bishop. Very popular, big time. Fifth century. In Dublin, no less." I babbled on, spewing out whatever popped into my head. Some of it had to be true. Ireland was a small country. "I'll bet he was even a friend of St. Patrick's!"

"Yes. Declan might do nicely. A bit unusual. Your father likes unusual names." Mom nodded peacefully in her bed.

"We could make it more usual by making the middle name 'Frances.' Like your middle name, and Grandma's." I thought of Grandma Frances McGuiness at home baby-sitting that very hour.

"Your grandmother will be thrilled!"

Sister Declan Frances will be thrilled, I thought privately.

She was. My little brother, Declan Francis, came into the world several hours later with a mouthful to learn to pronounce.

As Terry and Charlotte amused themselves in the library, I regaled Dean Sister Declan Frances with tales of baby Declan's first week on earth. The three of us were readmitted to religion class the next day. I graduated a year and a half later with honors in English, not geometry.

Michelle slid into the chapel pew and kneeled next to me. Caritas had sent me to do penance for my heresy in Bruntz's class. Most nuns have some maternal instinct, but not Lurch. I wasn't certain I'd want one of my siblings named after Lurch even if the name Caritas was in the *Book of Saints.* "How many Stations of the Cross did Lurch give you this time?" Michelle patted my arm.

"She told me I had to stay and meditate after Compline every night until I got my faith back."

"I didn't know you lost it."

"I haven't. I didn't get my point across to her."

"You seldom do." Michelle sat back in her pew.

"I don't need another Camp, not now, Micki!" I whined and turned to face her.

"How is your old tight ass cellmate?"

"Micki, don't use bad language in chapel!"

"When are you going to wise up, Jeanne. The Eleventh Commandment is not Thou Shalt Not Swear. God doesn't care. Just don't use His name in vain, the rest is ok."

"I guess you're *damn* right." I got up off my knees and sat my ass on the pew next to her.

"I don't see how anyone can be so smart intellectually and so dumb about life."

"I'm getting a little demoralized here, Micki." Tears pushed against my eyelids as I observed the crease in her ironed anklets. What did Michelle even see in me? I was a Heathcliff, eternally rumpled in mind and body. She was Jane Eyre, cautious and fair, I, impulsive and brown. We were from opposite sides of the emotional equator. "I can't seem to do anything right. Camp hates me, Lauren David won't talk to me. I can't find a way to meet Antonia Marie. Caritas treats me like the bad seed. I'm not even sure Jesus still loves me!"

"You just don't know how to stay out of trouble, Jeanne. Rules are meant to be bent, not broken. If you keep this up you're going to get your ass kicked out of here. You're too intelligent for you own good. You've got two choices, Jeanne. You can graduate from the novitiate as a dumb nun, or get thrown out as a smart nothing. Which is it?"

Peeling at the ragged cover of my *Imitation of Christ*, I whispered through my tears, "I'm not so sure I have a choice. I am who I am, and I don't know if I can change that. Trouble is, I don't know who that is."

"Why did you come here, Jeanne? To revolutionize the Holy Rule? To make life difficult for an old priest you'll never see again after this semester?"

"Ah . . . who knows anymore!" I stared at the multicolored abstract of the Virgin Mary silk-screened on Sister Mary Corita's tapestry in back of the altar. "I came because I thought I was in love with God and the Blessed Virgin. It seemed so simple. We talk all the time, or at least we used to. She listens to me, Micki. She cares. I wanted to be with her intimately all my life, to bask in that love, to return her love. I wanted to give my life in service as a nun and a missionary and help spread the Word that she and her Son love all of us."

Michelle encircled me in her arms. "I didn't know you came because you were in love! God must be very personal to you. But isn't that so romantic, Jeanne? I read that book too. That's the idealized version of life, in or out of the convent. The real fine print reads, 'What does it profiteth a man if he gains his soul, but loses the whole world?' Life's a shit."

"Life's a . . . a shit." I got the word out. It sounded disgusting.

"That's right."

"That's the fine print?"

"God might have created perfection, Jeanne. But that was a long time ago, and in the interim, like Bruntz said, man . . . and woman . . . have succumbed to gross imperfection. Even the Church has been screwed up and distorted. Life is about coping with the distortion."

I held on to my friend's tear-stained postulant blazer. "Why did you come here, Micki? You don't seem to believe in the Catholic Church, you don't speak of God personally, sometimes I wonder if you even believe in God."

93

Michelle Callahan fell back to her knees and stared blankly at the tabernacle. "Sometimes I wonder too, Jeanne. But it was a qualification to get in! Since I was very little, everyone, I guess mostly my parents, told me I was ugly, fat, and stupid. That I'd never get to college because I didn't have the brains, that no guy would ever want me, so marriage was out. I wanted to do something to make my parents proud of me, something that was hard, but something I really could succeed at. You don't have to be smart or attractive to be a nun. You just have to be clever."

"That's ridiculous, Micki," I said, kneeling alongside her. "You're both smart and attractive. Your parents must have lied or something. That's the dumbest reason for being in the convent I've ever heard."

"Your believing in ghosts is no smart reason for being here either!"

"Are you calling God a ghost, Micki?"

"Of course not, Jeanne. Don't take things so literally. I want to be successful here no matter what it takes. I want to be the best damn nun this convent ever had."

"Me too."

CHAPTER 10

How the Pope Wrecked My Life

I'm sure Catholicism is genetic. They say you get "it" at baptism, but I suspect there's a Catholic chromosome somewhere. The Holy Roman Catholic and Apostolic Church appeared eternal. Every dogma, prayer, and liturgy was hundreds of years old. Nothing had changed in the Catholic Church since my birth, and I was sure nothing ever would, especially here in Montecito.

But it was 1966, the Age of Aquarius. No one seemed to know what planet we were on. The United States was messily involved in an obscure war in a country whose name no one could pronounce for reasons that dated back to Napoleon. College students in the northern California city of Berkeley were smoking dope, demonstrating, and being promiscuous. They called this a "revolution." President Johnson couldn't convince people he could fill Jack Kennedy's shoes. And in Rome, even the Pope was proclaiming the Shoes of the Fisherman needed to be re-soled.

"I must tell you about critical news from the Vatican," announced Mother General Humiliata of the Sisterhood of the Immaculate Heart of Mary. The stately executive of my order had come from the Motherhouse in Los Angeles to pay a rare visit to Montecito's entire congregation. Nuns and priests from orders surrounding Santa Barbara had been summoned, and were now gathered, to hear the news from Rome.

Montecito was known for many things but most widely acclaimed for La Casa de María's spectacularly designed chapel. The architect must have wanted to build the House of God around the great gnarled oak that rose in back of the altar. The oak was eternal. It had been there for hundreds of years. Since the tree couldn't be brought into the chapel, the chapel was built around the magnificent tree. The wall in back of the altar had been knocked out. Only glass stood between us and the webbed branches that beckoned the soul outward, upward into the sun. A twenty-foot crucifix hung from the ceiling over the black onyx altar. I was transfixed by a writhing, hanging Christ; His head jutted forward, His raised shoulders knotted in spasm, His knees twisted in upon themselves. The image was haunting, silencing questions even from non-Catholic visitors. Agony was universal.

Assigned to pews at the rear of the chapel, postulants were always last. Our view of Mother General was partially eclipsed, but I could hear her clearly. "In *Journal of a Soul*, the autobiography of Pope John XXIII," she began, "he issues a historical invitation. 'I put forward the idea of a Vatican Council, a diocesan Synod, and the revision of the Code of Canon Law.'"

"What's Canon Law?" Louise prodded me.

"It's the Law about how the religious must live. It's about us! Shhh . . . " Palms clenched around my pew seat and backbone straight, my attention was riveted on Mother General. This was big news.

"As most of you know, the bishops of the Church have been meeting in Rome as this Vatican Council. This is the second time in two thousand years our leaders have sat at such a council. Vatican II is changing the profile of Holy Mother the Church throughout the world, and some of the changes will affect us. Vatican II seeks ecumenical brotherhood with others . . ."

"What's ecumenical brotherhood mean?" Louise whispered again.

"It means it's not a sin anymore to go into a Baptist or Buddhist church, or to talk with them about religion."

"The Church has begun a dialogue with the Jewish community. Protestant ministers have been invited to meetings also. Vatican II has even taken up issues such as birth control and the place of women in the Catholic Church."

"What place?" Michelle muttered.

"Maybe it's finally going to change!" I was thrilled.

"Maybe we can be priests in a few years."

"B.S. We'll still be wiping up the wine long after they finish talking in Rome."

Mother General dropped Pope John's book on her lectern. The thud echoed against the chapel walls. She came forward and paused at the altar rail. "The practice of not eating meat on Fridays is being abolished. I'm sure you won't mind. Some of the other changes are much more controversial. Part of Vatican II's modernization will include saying the Mass in English. We are dropping the Latin."

No one breathed.

"Some of the churches in Los Angeles have already begun to make the Mass more accessible to lay people who don't know Latin. We have all grown up with Latin, so it is familiar to us, but using the language of the Roman Empire has never been dogma. The liturgy will now be said around the world in one's own native tongue."

"Latin *is* my native tongue!" I wailed to Michelle.

97

"What's this Church coming to?" Even Louise was paying attention now.

To me, Latin was as holy and immutable as the papacy. It was even part of our name. The *Roman* Catholic Church had survived centuries of persecution, had become the dominant religion of its persecutors, the Romans. The Church had reigned supreme in Western Europe from the Crusades to the Industrial Revolution. The Latin of Julius Caesar was the voice of civilized religion throughout the known world. All the Great Doctors of the Church had penned their doctrines in Latin. Surely Latin was dogma.

I collapsed all the way back into my pew and turned slowly to look up at the choir balcony. All those endless hours of beatific Gregorian chant, *"Tanctum ergo sacramentum . . . "* How could I pray in English?

At Bishop Amat, Charlotte Vogt and I once argued about Latin. "Hebrew, not Latin, was the language of Christ," she clarified.

I countered, "Nobody speaks Hebrew anymore."

"If you ever get out of Catholic school you'll find no one speaks Latin anymore, either!"

"That's how it should be, Charlotte. It's a sacred language used only for praying. What other language has such grace and symmetry, such complex richness yet simplicity?"

"Veni. Vidi. Vinci." Charlotte retorted.

"We haven't spent four years of school learning Latin for nothing," I persisted.

"Right. You open Latin 101 and you read, 'All Gaul is divided into three parts.' That's a very critical thing to know as we venture out into the twentieth century. No one has ever heard of Gaul; it hasn't even been a country in a million years. I'd rather learn what countries and races comprise global political reality today. Why don't we learn anything socially relevant in this school?" Charlotte was an atheist and really didn't belong at Bishop Amat.

Had Mother General secretly become an atheist? "And therefore, Sisters," Mother Humilita's booming voice jarred me back to the present, "we feel it is socially relevant for the Church to speak the language of the people. Beginning next week we'll say Mass in English, with guitar music. Your missals will be revised into English during the upcoming year."

I closed my eyes. I wanted desperately to shut out her voice. I didn't want to hear the death knell of Latin, my language of heaven-directed communication. What would the Catholic Church be like without Gregorian chant, the music of the angels? I was livid. I felt as though someone was taking away a precious friend. What right did the Pope have to wreck my life?

"Listen up, Jeanne! I think the worst is yet to come," Michelle jostled me.

"We are also changing your lives as novices and postulants here." Mother General's projected words seemed to land in my pew. She paused to fling her black veil over her shoulder. "When you came to us you were told that you would be here in Montecito for two years. But it is now our feeling that seclusion from the real world is contradictory to the spirit of Vatican II. We question the relevance of contemplative life in today's very troubled times, and we feel it's time for you to blossom more quickly and more fully into your future roles as teachers and missionaries.

"In January, you will be sent to complete your training at one of our mission houses in the cities. You will live there with professed nuns who teach at our schools. You will immediately begin to take up working with the poor. You may be sent to Los Angeles ghettos, to help in Watts, in East L.A., or San Pedro. Or you may be transferred up north to the San Joaquin Valley to bring comfort to the farm laborers in their poverty."

Mother General Humiliata turned around and walked slowly back to her lectern. As she faced us once more the silence in the chapel was so deafening that the sound of her breathing filled her microphone.

"East L.A.? I'm going home!" Louise exclaimed through clenched teeth.

"I didn't join the convent to pick grapes!" Even Michelle was starting to crack.

Janis leaned toward her. "That's where the poor really need us. It's literally the Lord's vineyard." Janis could find a silver lining in a hurricane.

"Michelle, what's the matter with Jeanne?" Louise whispered.

I heard them from a great distance. I didn't want to be in chapel anymore. My shoulders were hunched into the pew's corner crevice. Balled up like a caterpillar, I sat with closed eyes trying to disappear. When Mother General began talking about the end of our life at Montecito her voice seemed to take on a shrill, ear-splitting pitch. I couldn't listen to her anymore. I wanted to go to the Poet's Boulder were things were peaceful. My whole body felt light as the Holy Ghost's. Perhaps, any second now, my spirit would fly away through the stained-glass window donated by Countess Estelle Doheny.

"Jeanne, you look sick. Say something." Why was Michelle smacking my palms together?

Marlene Camp leaned forward from the pew in back of us. "What's the matter with Córdova? She's not asking any questions."

"Stay out of this, Camp!" Louise snapped.

Michelle was anxiously bending my fingers back and forth. "Quit that, Micki." I jerked my hands back. Humiliata was still speaking, but she sounded far away. "I'm OK. I must have been day-dreaming. I thought Mother General said we had to leave Montecito." I chuckled under my breath with the absurdity.

"You weren't day-dreaming, Jeanne. She did say we're leaving Montecito in January," Michelle said.

"Oh, you mean we'll only be here for one more year? *That's* what I misheard." I breathed more easily now.

"No, Jeanne, she said this January, *next month*."

"That can't be, Micki. We just got here. We're going to be novices here next year. It will take a long time to prepare for our

100

vows. St. Francis left his family and went to live alone with his birds for five years before he took vows. Jesus went into seclusion in the desert before He returned to begin His redemptive vocation. He was getting ready. We have to stay here. It's always been this way."

"Things change, Jeanne."

I looked into Michelle's eyes. They were doleful. If we left Montecito she'd have to leave her new assignment, taking care of the library with Dominic Anne. "Maybe the grapefields won't be so bad," she said, stroking my hand.

"Lettuce fields," Louise corrected. "I'll teach you Spanish, Jeanne."

Mother General Humiliata continued to dismantle her order for what seemed like hours. My frame of reference was shattered. Finally, a flurry of figures brushed past our pew heading for the back door. Mother General had finished.

"Come on, Jeanne. It's over." Michelle's voice interrupted my escape back to my teenage paradise in Yosemite National Forest. Tuolomne Meadows had never been so lush. I watched Michelle toss her now useless Latin missal on the pew. She reached for my arm and helped me stand up.

"I still can't believe what she said!" Camp was furious as we trodded home to St. Joseph's. The orchard path was dim in the silver moon. No one was talking on the pavilion tonight.

Michelle still had her arm around my shoulder. "Will you miss Dominic Anne?" I whispered. "Maybe you won't be friends with her when we leave here in a year." I answered for Michelle, waving my flashlight through the barren December trees.

"She didn't say *next* January, Jeanne."

"How can I get to know Antonia Marie if we're leaving in a month?"

"I'll think of a plan tonight. I promise."

"It's just not possible!" Camp was now almost screaming as she pounced over the potholes. "They can't scrap the habit."

101

"Wasn't my style anyway," Louise flung her long black locks over her shoulder and primped down the path.

I stopped, aghast. "Scrap what, Camp?"

"The habit, dummy. The one with the silver heart. The one we're never going to wear!"

"That's the part you missed while you were day-dreaming," Michelle interceded. "Mother General put the habit on the to-go list. She says it originated fourteen hundred years ago when the poor dressed in long tunics. Clerics picked that dress because it was the habit of the poor, and monks and nuns should dress like the peasants, so we wouldn't stand out from them."

"I think she's got a good point," Louise said, thoughtfully. "My people are poor, but you don't see them running through the barrios in veils."

"Does that mean we should wear zoot suits?" Camp swaggered next to Louise.

"Watch your mouth, white girl!" Louise had turned on the path to face Camp.

"This is a catastrophe for *everyone*," Janis placated. "Let's not fight among ourselves. I think our assignment for tonight could be fun."

"What assignment?" I growled at Janis. "How can there be anything left to change?"

"Mother General said we're supposed to go to our rooms and take off our habits. Of course we postulants don't have that much to take off. Then we look at ourselves in the mirror and ask, 'Who am I outside my habit?'"

St. Joseph's and our mirrors loomed close. Michelle was angry. "You guys do what you want tonight. I'm not going to stand in front of a mirror, take off my blazer, look at my white blouse, and ask, 'Who am I?' Who the hell knows around here anyway?"

As usual I agreed with Michelle. I knew who I was without the habit. I wanted to know who I was *inside* the habit! I didn't come to the convent to leave it. I didn't labor in Gaul to pray in Marlene

Camp's English. I'd spent a lifetime preparing for a religious life that was vanishing just as I stood on its threshold.

What kind of nun would I be roaming the world in my postulant blazer for the rest of my life? If I wanted to be in the "real world" I could have stayed in it. What was next? Disavowing the vows? Dropping Jesus Christ?

St. Joseph's dorm was like a wake the rest of the afternoon and evening. We were all so upset no one could sleep. We milled around in Michelle's cell sharing crackers and small talk.

"Let's bury God!" Donna's bass thundered as she ran into the room. "It's like a funeral in here anyway."

Michelle was thoughtful. "Perhaps we should bury the past with some aplomb."

"What should we bury?" Louise asked.

"I suggest God," Donna repeated.

Michelle shook her head. "We should save God, He's the sole survivor of the day."

"Let's have a wake for the habit and Latin," I ventured. "They're what died. Camp, you have linen duty. Aren't there un-used habits in the linen closet?"

"Oh no, I'm not participating in sacrilege."

"How delightful! We'll have a mock Mass for the Dead." Even Janis was with us. "I'll go get my guitar. I'll sing the Requiem Mass for the Dead in Gregorian chant."

"We can make the coffin and the altar on Jackie's empty bed," I plotted further. "She'd donate it if she were here. And we can lay the dead nun right here and offer her up."

"Up to what?" Louise wanted a role.

"Up for sacrifice. Like the Lamb of God," I proclaimed.

"Where's my missal in the Pope's now good-for-nothing Latin?" Michelle began searching her cell. "I want to be the priest, Father Michelle! Ah, what a profound ring that has!"

"You can use my missal," Louise offered. "Are we sure the Lamb of God isn't on the to-go list also?"

"Camp, go get the habits," Father Michelle ordered.

"Oh, no. I thought you were all kidding. You can't do this. I can't watch this. This is blasphemous."

"Not any more," I corrected, "The habit and Latin are no longer holy. So it's not blasphemy anymore! But you can have a part, Camp. You can be the nun. We need a dead body. We'll dress you up . . ."

"I'm not having any part of this insanity." Camp leaned against Michelle' s door and crossed her arms defiantly.

Father Michelle approached Sister Holier-than-Thou. "You report us to Caritas, Camp, and you'll be a dead nun for real—in Latin *and* English!"

Camp retired to her cell.

Donna reappeared with an armful of black and blue cloaks. Since it was her idea, we decided she should have the lead—the dead nun role. We dressed her carefully.

"Requiem . . . " Janis melodically intoned over the gracious spirit now fully robed on Jackie's altar.

"Aeternam. Dona eis Domine: et lux perpetua luceat eis," Louise and I chorused back.

"In those days, according to the Book of Dead Nuns, chapter fourteen, verses ten to twenty," Father Michelle said, climbing atop her dresser pulpit and beginning the gospel, "I heard a voice from heaven, I presume, say unto me . . . 'Happy are the dead who die in the right order. For they shall rest from their bad habits. Woe be unto those who would cling to the old way, which worked perfectly well for a thousand years, for they shall be declared obsolete. Woe be unto any of you who judge Mother Mary Lurch or the good Mother General or think your superiors know not what they do, for yours is not to reason, but to have blind . . . faith.'"

"Alleluia! Alleluia!" the Rodriguez-Córdova choir rejoined.

Father stepped down from her pulpit. "Good Father Jeanne, would you please conduct the eulogy?"

I addressed the masses: "Yea, Lord, we are met on a great battlefield of our faith, as witnessed here by the body of your dearly departed daughter, Sister Donna. We have been asked to let go of the bedrock of our youth, the fantasies of our adolescence, the teachings of our young adulthood; to cast to the wind our sacred robes, the classic notes of Gregorian Latin, and finally, the home of our very vocations.

"Today is a great turning point for Holy Mother the Church. After two thousand years of being 'in the world, but not of it,' She is now stepping out on a limb to become totally with it! God rest religious life."

"Requiem in pacem." The choir rested.

Father Michelle reverently laid a large, misshapen iron cross on the chest of dearly departed dead nun Donna. "This crucifix was made and loaned to us by novice Antonia Marie. It represents the novices, it's their funeral too."

"Dies erie, dies era," the closing requiem rang out as the congregation slid to their knees on the Sears & Roebuck linoleum.

Suddenly the ringing of the bells floated through the open window.

"Caritas is coming through the orchard. Split!" Father Michelle yanked me off my pulpit.

"What about me?" cried Donna resurrecting herself.

"There's no time to undress her. Throw her into the linen closet!" I ordered.

Seconds burned away like hours in purgatory. The chimes of Lurch stopped outside the door.

"Our Father, Who art in heaven, hallowed be Thy name," Father Jeanne led the rosary, the congregation fell to its knees, "Thy kingdom come, Thy will be done . . . "

I bowed my head and clutched the iron cross to my breast.

Lurch drifted down the corridor mumbling, "on earth as it is in heaven."

105

Later, a small delegation braved the darkness and stillness, creeping to the closet where we had cast dearly departed Donna. She sat huddled, still bent with the fear of discovery. We rescued her, but we were powerless to rescue our future.

Lying in bed that night, I knew our not-so-innocent game was also not a game. We were trying to trivialize a truth we wanted desperately to deny. The radical change was outside the parameters of my imagination. It was like watching Mom pull my baby brother Tom's little blue body out of the swimming pool the day he almost drowned; like hearing Kennedy had been shot. Someone said it was so and my mind received the information. But my heart would not allow the impossible.

CHAPTER 11

Particular Friendships

Her royal-blue-robed arm rose from her lap. The precise tip of her napkin swept the corners of her mouth; within the linen, her fingers never moved. I don't think there were even any crumbs to brush off. I couldn't see any, and I was watching. Closely.

Sister Antonia Marie must have been of noble descent. She moved regally, never in a hurry. Her black eyes, deep as a mystic's in trance, told me everything and absolutely nothing. I was supposed to divine what they meant. My whole soul was listening to who she might be, for clues as to why God had made such a face and what He wanted me to know about it.

The day she moved her napkin was December eighth, the feast of the Immaculate Conception. It was the major holy day of our order. That was why the postulants were eating dinner with the novices in the refectory; that's how I got to read Antonia's eyes all evening.

Catholics don't believe in reincarnation, but when Antonia had spoken to me last week at the Poet's Boulder, for that moment I believed the Blessed Virgin must have been reincarnated in Antonia Marie's smile. I was folded in between the rocks trying to write a sonnet in Latin, a good-bye ritual, when I heard their laughter. Peering through a crack between the boulders, I saw her and Dominic Anne skipping boulders, climbing up to the fish pond. Antonia had her guitar slung over her shoulder. I had seen Sister Antonia Marie here and there on the grounds, at prayer and at meals, but I'd never seen her up close like this. Her white veil pinned atop her headdress, her long sleeves rolled to her elbows—she was a nun in buoyant flight. They passed me in my crevice and, as they turned to climb further, Antonia looked straight at me. In a holy instant her smile came and went. Or maybe it was the red and orange filtered light playing in the fall leaves or the wind through the birch that made my heart explode.

"Hello in there!" she called out, waving with her free arm.

"Will I disturb you if I stay here?" I dared.

"Not at all. I'd be pleased if you did. I've been wanting to meet you . . . "

"Antonia! Why are you talking to yourself? There's only an hour till sunset. Hurry up," Dominic Anne called back to her lagging friend.

"Coming!" Antonia shouted. She turned back to me. "Another time?"

"Anytime," I blurted. I swallowed further brashness, but she was gone anyway. A few minutes later I heard her over the gurgling waterfalls. Turning sideways in my crevice I could see them sitting on the ledge above me, their legs dangling over the fish pond.

"I want to sing you my new song," she said to Dominic.

"I've been waiting to hear it for weeks," Dominic invited.

Antonia's chin dipped and her eyebrows lifted:

"So listen to the warmth of the children in the street

The warmth of the laughter of lovers when they meet,
And listen to the warmth of your hand in mine
And know the warmth of a love so hard to find."

My knees collapsed against each other, my writing pad fell from my lap to the rocks below. For a moment I was sure she'd sung those words to me. How did she know what was in my heart? Could I ever tell her about the warmth of her smile?

"Sister Antonia Marie!" Dominic shrieked. "You can't sing *this* song during Mass!"

"I know this is a private audience. Someday, somewhere, I'll sing it to a huge audience. Do you like it?"

Michelle announced her arrival at the dinner table loudly, "Shit a brick, Jeanne! We are in trouble!" She'd come in late as usual, but we were at a back table so no one noticed.

"Did you ever return her iron cross?" I asked.

"Whose iron cross?"

"Antonia's. You know the one we used a few days ago to bury Donna with. You said Antonia actually made it with her own hands. Just look at her, Micki."

"Look at who, Jeanne? Listen to me, we've got a problem."

"At Antonia Marie over there. Isn't she the most stunningly beautiful human being you've ever seen in your lifetime?"

"No. I think Dominic is . . . a beautiful . . . friend," Michelle stammered. "Besides, Antonia is always so intense."

"That's wonderful. What's she intense about?"

"Writing songs and poems, politics and farmworkers, and . . . life, and . . . just everything, Dominic says."

"Will Antonia be coming down to school with us in Los Angeles next semester? Or will she be missioned somewhere else?"

"How should I know? Go rent an encyclopedia on the Life and Times of the Unknown Novice. Ask her yourself."

"She said she wanted to meet me, Micki. Oh God! Oh, no, she's looking right at our table!"

Antonia's eyes had wandered from Mother Noreen to me. It

109

was a stare that registered somewhere between "I know you" and "Who are you?" Nothing moved between us.

Remember the day at the Poet's Boulder? my eyes implored.

Of course! Why do you want to know me? her eyes invited.

"Because I already do," I whispered to myself.

"No, you don't," Michelle interrupted, rudely shoving a card in front of my face. "I haven't told you yet. Caritas has summoned us! I found her calling card under my door."

"Us?" My fork clanged to my plate.

"Here's her card from under your door. I knew you'd want it as soon as possible."

My mouth went dry. "When does she want to see us?"

"Tonight, after dinner."

"Darn. Can't we have a Feast Day in peace? I've got things to do." My gaze drifted back to Antonia. Damn. I'd lost her attention.

"Right. I'll have our secretary send Lurch a raincheck." Michelle stabbed her mashed potatoes. "I'm gonna kill Camp. I warned her about telling on us. I'll feed her to the lions. Listen, Jeanne, keep your mouth shut in front of Lurch and let me do the talking, all right? Maybe I'll get us off with five years instead of ten. This is no fireside chat. Don't blow it."

"If Donna, Janis, and Louise didn't get a summons it's probably not about the Mass for the Dead Nun."

"I'm sure Camp told Lurch we were the ringleaders. What else could it be?"

Lurch was pacing as we sat facing the crucifix carved into her desk.

"She's nervous," Michelle whispered to me.

"You're projecting. It's us," I sat precariously on the chair's edge. The thick Oriental carpet was familiar. The crucifix seemed to greet me, "Oh, it 's you again!"

Caritas stopped behind her desk and let the mahogany separate us. "I suppose you two are completely unaware of why I've asked you here?"

110

"Oh, no, Mother," I began.

"Oh, yes, Mother!" Michelle all but shouted, her eyes widened in assumed innocence. Damn, she was good.

"This is a very serious matter." Lurch smoothed her scapular over her breasts. "Perhaps it's my fault. I've neglected to tell your class about this rule."

This is a good sign, I thought, relaxing back in my chair. Lurch had never started with her own admissions before. Still, Michelle and I should take responsibility. We didn't need a clarification from the Pope to know stealing holy habits and burying a not-so-dead postulant in them was sacrilegious. We must have broken a half dozen Holy Rules.

"It has been observed that you two have been spending a great deal of time together, alone." Lurch remained standing.

I looked to Michelle for contradiction. We spoke only briefly during the days; besides, most evenings when I went to her room, she wasn't there.

"There is a very important section in the *Tanquery,* our rule book on the lifestyle of religious, that speaks about 'particular friendships.' You might have heard some of the novices refer to this rubric in Canon Law that chastises us against exclusive relationships."

Lurch paused as her eyes locked into Michelle's. Micki's face had turned pale as the Holy Ghost. She looked like she'd just seen a vision. I didn't understand what Caritas was talking about. What should I say? Michele said *she'd* do the talking! But she just sat staring at her hands in her lap.

"Well?" Lurch persisted.

"I'm afraid I've never heard of this rule," I offered, "or the *Tanquery* or whatever, Mother. Since I . . . borrowed . . . the pies, very few of the novices talk to me."

"I see." Caritas relaxed into her chair. "I didn't think so. I should have instructed you. Now let me be clear. The rule against particular friendships has guided religious life for several centuries

111

and applies to both nuns and priests of all orders. After three months here as postulants I'm sure you've both come to realize how important community is."

"Yes, Mother," I nodded sincerely. Caritas should really be addressing Camp or novice Lauren David about community, I thought. *They* weren't treating me like community. I was all for being family with everyone, especially Antonia Marie. "Is something endangering our community, Mother?"

Michelle sighed. Was she relieved I was carrying on the conversation for her?

"To protect our community from divisions within we must foster a sisterhood that includes everyone equally." Lurch mouthed her words with rigid lips. "We foster emotional collectivity by showing charity toward all under all circumstances. More than charity, we encourage a genuine love for one another as spiritual daughters of Christ." Her eyes bore into me. I was back on my chair's edge.

"We *discourage* exclusive friendships that develop out of . . . out of . . . common interests with particular . . . others. These kinds of particular interests dilute and distract from one's total commitment to Christ. They may create an . . . an imbalance . . . in collective life."

Lurch paused. I leaned forward. The more she said, the less I understood. I'd have to get Michelle's translation later.

"Do you understand, girls?"

I looked at Michelle again. Why wasn't she speaking? "*I* understand about community, Mother, but not really about these peculiar friendships."

"*Particular,* Jeanne." Michelle finally said something.

Lurch's nose jutted out from her cheekbones. She peered at Michelle intently, as she spoke to me. "A particular friendship, Jeanne, is when two people spend a great deal of time together and exclude themselves from other members of the community."

"That's not very charitable, Mother," I agreed. "I didn't think we had snobs here, except Marlene Camp, my cellmate. I'd love to spend more time with more people."

"But you seem to spend most of your time with Michelle!" Lurch interjected.

"Oh no, Mother. Michelle spends most of her time at the main house with Sister . . . "

"My books and catalogs!" Michelle finished loudly. "I seldom see Jeanne, Mother. She's right. We don't *particularly* spend much time together. I'm so busy with classes, and the new catalog system Sister Dominic Anne and I are developing for the library in order to further our spiritual education. You know you can't find titles in the old system unless you already know what book you're looking for and . . . "

Michelle had a mind faster than a speeding bullet; twice as fast, if you allowed for the fact that she first had to think of the truth and then decide what to say instead.

"Michelle," Caritas interrupted the history of the library. "I understand that Jeanne visits your room regularly after dinner and that the two of you spend the evenings . . . together . . . too often." Caritas continued to me, "And that you, Jeanne, sometimes don't return to your own room until the early hours of the morning."

Michelle's upper lip was taut. She slumped in her chair. Her vulnerable eyes had turned a cold gray, a trapped fox waiting. Sometimes I didn't understand Michelle Callahan.

Maybe she was upset that I hadn't told her I'd gone to her room often since that first night we talked about chastity. I just wanted to get away from Camp and study in peace. Camp was always criticizing me: "Don't read with your feet on the bed. Don't crease the pages of your textbooks." It felt safer in Michelle's room, even though she rarely returned before I fell asleep on Jackie's bed. How could I explain Camp's most unsisterly hatred of me to Caritas? I didn't quite understand it myself.

"It's true, Mother, I go to Michelle's cell and sometimes fall asleep, but usually Michelle isn't . . . "

"There's no need to speak of these things further." Lurch had begun to pace again. "There will be no further visits by either of you, to either cell. This January all of you will be missioned down to Los Angeles as Mother General instructed. In this short month here you both have a great deal to learn from *others*. I suspect you've already learned as much from each other as enhances your vocations. Do I make myself clear, girls?"

Lurch was always as clear as a butler slamming the door in your face. I knew what she'd said, but I didn't know why.

"Very clear, Mother." Michelle rose. "Do you want us to go now, Mother?"

Caritas softened at Michelle's deference. "Yes, that will be all for now."

"Well, hot damn! It must have been Camp," I concluded as we left Caritas' office and began the hike to St. Joseph's.

Michele was still pensive.

I slung a comforting arm around her shoulder. "Camp told me she likes you, Michelle. She'd never tell on you. It had to be someone else. I tried to tell Caritas we couldn't be accused of being particular because I hardly see you because you're never there. I don't know how she could have gotten things so mixed up."

"Jeanne," Michelle spoke, slowly removing my arm, "why didn't you tell me you spend nights in my cell? I never see you when I get back."

"I wake up before you come in and go back to my cell. I never see you either. Camp is such a . . . a bitch. I can't stand it! So I go into your room."

The night air grew colder as we made our way past the Stations of the Cross.

"Jeanne, you can't do this anymore."

"Oh, Micki, I like your cell. I'll be extra careful not to wake up Camp. She'll never know."

"Somebody knows, Jeanne. Please, no more."

"Where the hell are you every night anyway? You can't spend every night out on the pavilion with Dominic Anne, it's too damn cold."

"God! Now I've created a swearing monster."

"I'm a quick study."

"That's what I'm afraid of—your potential."

"What's that supposed to mean?"

"Nothing."

"Tell me where you go, Michelle."

"I'm there at the main house in the library or in Dominic Anne's cell." She waved toward the dark building in front of us as we passed the Poet's Boulder.

"How do you get in there? Dominic can't just unlock the front door and you both saunter through the foyer in the middle of the night."

"I climb up to the mezzanine balcony. I'll show you." As we rounded the south lawn of the main house she pointed. "See where these big tree branches almost touch the wrought iron railing?"

I looked up. "I thought you were afraid of heights. You wouldn't climb a balcony to save your vocation."

Michelle muttered, "We all have our priorities." We continued toward the orchard.

"What do you do in the library . . . or in her cell?"

"Ah . . . do? We read. Poetry. Books."

"You told me you hate poetry. Even e. e. cummings."

"We read books to each other then. Long books."

"Out loud?"

"Yes, out loud. It helps one's vocabulary and pronunciation."

"What are you reading now?"

"A . . . European book. It takes place a long time ago. You wouldn't like it."

"I love European books! I thought you were the one who didn't like to read. You must be near finished with it since it's been months now. Could I read it next? What's the name of it?"

We stopped by the orchard path leading to the pavilion. It was too dark to read up there, I reflected. Michelle shivered in the cold. "It's called *The Well of Loneliness*, Jeanne. But it's superficial and not very intellectual, not something you'd like. Anyway Dominic

Anne has to return it to Antonia who has to give it back to her college friend next time she comes up, so I can't lend it to you."

"Well, it sounds a little depressing anyway. More loneliness around here I don't need. Is that where you sit with Dominic Anne, Micki?" I pointed to the cobblestone-protected enclave. "It's early; Caritas won't be passing by bell-swinging for at least a half hour. Can't we go sit there a minute or two and talk?" I dragged Michelle down the path. "Where do you and Dominic sit?"

"Oh . . . just anywhere." Michelle sat on one of the benches and looked at the stars. "Dominic's teaching me the constellations," she said wistfully.

"I didn't know you had all these hidden interests, Micki. And you're my best friend."

Michelle looked at me intently, her eyes searching mine. "Are we really best friends, Jeanne? Would we protect each other under any circumstance?"

"Of course. You're the only one who understands me. I've . . ." I stumbled for the words, " . . . always felt close to you, like we've known each other from some other time. Even though we're so different, even though you're so neat and I wear clunky oxfords, we're somehow the same."

"Yes. I think we may be . . . in some ways."

"So why are you closer with Dominic Anne than me? Why do you spend all your time with her?"

"I'd like to be closer to you, Jeanne. Ever since that first day . . ." Michelle fidgeted with her blazer, wrapping it around herself more tightly. "I mean, it's just that sometimes, Jeanne, you can only share certain things with certain people."

"Like what things?" I persisted. Michelle was as obtuse as Mother Caritas at times.

Michelle's eyes affixed again on the night's constellations. "Have you ever held hands with someone?"

"Of course. I had boyfriends in high school. Didn't everyone?"

"I mean with a girl, Jeanne."

116

"Oh. With a girl." I shifted a little closer to Michelle on the bench. "Well, yes. I had a special girlfriend in my junior year at Amat." I thought of Cathy's pale freckled arms. "I guess we held hands."

"How can you guess about something like that?"

"Then . . . yes."

"Did you love her?"

"Love her?" I sighed. "Yes, I loved her. Cathy made me feel loved in a . . . I don't know, almost sort of a romantic way. I guess it was a high school crush . . . she was a role model for me."

"That's the feeling I have with Dominic when she and I hold hands."

"You hold hands with a nun?!" My fingers wrapped themselves around the edge of the rough wood of the bench, remembering Cathy's soft white fingers.

"Dominic is not a nun, she's a novice."

"Michelle, do you suppose Antonia Marie and Dominic Anne have that special feeling for each other?"

"No, Jeanne. I don't think they're that kind of friends."

"You promised me you'd think of a plan for me to get to work with Antonia Marie. I'd bet we'd be special friends like you and Dominic. I'm sure we like the same books. I found out she sings for the retreatants down at La Casa de María on Friday nights. I could volunteer to clean the altar after mass, and fall and sprain my ankle down there on one of the cobblestone paths."

"A fake medical emergency? Now that's one even I hadn't thought of! But it wouldn't work, Jeanne. You don't have the nerve to carry it through a doctor's visit, and anyway they'd send you back to St. Joseph's for two weeks' recuperation in bed. Then you'd really never get to see her. Dumb plan, Jeanne. And so is sitting out here. It's getting late. Caritas will be along any time. Listen, Jeanne, promise me you won't come to my room, not tonight, or any other night."

"I didn't know what Caritas was talking about tonight. Did you know about this particular friendship rule before, Micki?" I remained seated. I didn't want to leave the pavilion.

"Sort of . . . yes. Paul Emanuelle mentioned it to me."

I thought of the photograph in Michelle's bottom drawer. She and Paul Emmanuelle looked fairly particular in that picture. Did Michelle and Paul hold hands? Probably not. Paul Emanuelle was a fully professed nun.

"I'm still not clear about it, Michelle. If you and I are not having a particular friendship, why can't we still keep seeing each other?"

"Because Caritas *thinks* we are."

"I'll tell her she's wrong. That's it's you and Dominic . . ."

Michelle jumped off the bench, faced me and shook my shoulders. "Jeanne, didn't you hear a word she said? *No* particular friendships. You wouldn't want to destroy my friendship with Dominic would you?"

"Of course not. Sorry, I wasn't thinking."

"That's what I'm afraid of."

Michelle tugged me off the bench and we crept down the cobblestones toward St. Joseph's.

"I don't see what's wrong with loving someone anyway. How can you feel exactly the same way about every sister you meet? It's not even possible . . . or human." I thought of Camp waiting for me in our cell. "God knows it's hard enough to love some people at all."

"My sentiments exactly. But I guess we aren't supposed to be human. I don't know how I'm going to arrange seeing Dominic Anne with Caritas and her spies monitoring my cell now."

"Good. Then you'll be there more often when I visit."

"Jeanne, those nights are *over!* Let's make a deal. It's only three weeks till we're shipped to our mission houses. Let's do exactly as Lurch says and then we'll both most likely get sent to Los Angeles and we can see each other more down there. Maybe we'll even get missioned to the same house. Promise me, Jeanne, no more visits here, OK?"

I could see Michelle's anxious face in the dorm's porch light.

118

She was actually frightened. "All right, all right, I promise. But I'll miss you. I wish we *did* have a particular friendship, Micki. Maybe then I'd be more important to you."

"You are very important to me, Jeanne. I don't know what I'd do here if I didn't have you to talk with. I'll miss you a lot also. But we'll see each other much more in Los Angeles." We hugged good-bye and disappeared down the dim corridor, each alone, to our cells.

Camp's snorting nose was snoring already as I undressed in the chilled dark. "Damn!" I caught my breath and jumped under my covers. The IHM's took poverty too seriously; there was never any heat at Montecito. I liked swearing, I smiled to myself. It felt grown up. I liked a lot of the things Michelle was teaching me. Obviously she knew a great deal more about the world than I. Perhaps I'd gone to the wrong high school, except I did meet Cathy Longtree at Bishop Amat.

CHAPTER 12

The Scarecrow
and the Beast

Sitting next to me, serving detention in the high school library, she was reading a Supergirl comic book. That was what drew my attention; juniors don't read comic books. Cathy Longtree was a little person, thin, with a pert nose full of freckles, and orange hair that popped out of her head like Phyllis Diller's. She could have doubled as a scarecrow; the birds would have gladly left. But I was a captive of my misconduct, bored and itching to be back on the softball diamond, and there was no one else to talk to.

"Are you seriously reading a comic?" I began.

"What's it to you?" She flipped a page.

"Not much. I just don't know many teenagers who own comic books."

"Well, now you still don't!" Her blue eyes flashed an end to our conversation.

I gazed through the window out at my varsity teammates playing on the diamond. I checked my watch for the fifth time. Two more hours of detention left.

"I used to collect comic books," I reopened conciliatorily. "I had thousands of them."

You, 'The Brain, Córdova'?" The freckles all over her face laughed. She had an impish, open smile, a female Huck Finn rocking mischievously on her front porch by the river.

"Sure. Mostly Superman . . ." I didn't know where to go with the conversation. Clark Kent was in the closet of my childhood memories.

"So what do you want from me?" It was the first of many times Cathy's remarkable candor would cut through my flip personality.

It took several weeks to figure out what I wanted from Cathy. She read Nancy Drew, I read Descartes. My parents were strong Catholics, well-known in parish society life. Hers were divorced. She lived on the poor side of town. But Cathy Longtree was more honest and vulnerable than all the pretentious babble that filled my days of accomplishment at Bishop Amat.

My weekends at her house were full of Cathy's simple serenity. Her mother worked, a circumstance I found odd. But it gave us a lot of privacy. At night she'd tuck her two little brothers into bed and we'd romp through the orange groves in back of her house or spend the nights on her porch, talking with the universe about feelings, people, and love.

"You're really going into the convent because of love then, Jeanne?" she asked. The night was new as we lay snuggly inside our doubled sleeping bags reading by the porch light, I, *The History of the Roman Empire*, she, her Nancy Drew, *The Secret of Larkspur Lane*.

"What brings this up?"

"I was thinking about how it feels to love."

121

"I'm not too sure myself. But yes, loving God is the primary reason I'm going to be a nun. I think love is the only thing strong enough to give your life for, or in my case, spend your life with. When I'm talking to Jesus, I feel complete inside. I feel filled up! I want the feeling to go on forever and it feels like it will. I love that feeling." I lay back wondering if a lifetime would be long enough to count the stars in my Beloved's blanket. "I know God won't let me down. There'll be hard times, but that's probably like when a friend betrays you in some small, accidental way."

"Like last week when you thought my birthday was Thursday and I spent all day Wednesday wondering why you didn't mention it?"

"Yeah, like that." My voice grew smaller. "I'm so sorry. Did you like my card a day late anyway?"

"Of course I did. I always love your cards. Didn't you see it on my dresser in the bedroom? I'll miss trading cards when you go away."

"That's not for a long time yet," I said, staring off into the orange trees. "I feel that way about you . . . sometimes." It was a quiet statement. "What way?"

"Like you said," Cathy turned to face me, "complete and wanting the time to never . . . I like being with you. Turn off the light." She rolled back on her side and said, "Let's watch the moon."

I did as she asked and crept back inside our sleeping bag. "I like these weekends at your house too, Cathy. Even if no one else can understand why we're friends, it feels right to me."

"We're friends because we love each other."

"I used to think you were friends with someone and then grew to love them if you had a lot in common. We don't have a lot in common, so I don't understand that."

"Haven't you ever met someone you just love right off the bat because of how they make you feel?" Cathy's body warmth merged with mine as the moon rose and our toes curled around each other's.

"I don't know if I've ever loved someone without having

anything in common," I responded, thinking of Janie at camp that last summer. Janie who was several years older and had already applied to join the Immaculate Heart community. We'd grown close but I assumed that was because we both loved the mountains, hiking, and shared a vocation.

"I loved you from the first moment we talked, even if you were such a louse."

"I was a creep! Why did you love me then?"

"Because underneath that sarcastic way you have I heard you saying you were bored and unhappy. I knew you were trying to reach out. And because of . . . other dumb reasons."

"Name me one dumb reason," I prodded.

"Your top lip curls up cute like a mouse when you're trying to be insulting and you really don't mean it."

"How did you know these things without knowing me?"

Cathy's hand moved across the flannel between us and took my fingers. Stubby, but smooth as river stones, her fingers lay waiting for my response. They rested against my palm as though they'd been there a very long time . . . just the way Cathy felt in my life. I couldn't even hear us breathe. My fingers closed around hers in a tight fist.

"That's the way love works, silly. Now go to sleep," she chided.

The days of my junior year slipped by caressingly, like pages passing in a book well-loved. Cathy came to my softball games but rarely said much as I romped and caroused with my teammates. We had the weekends and each other's hands to hold our bond.

On a May evening months later I was helping my mother fold diapers at the kitchen table. Mom was circumspect. "I want to talk to you after dinner tonight, Jeanne." My hands stopped folding. Mom didn't have time for capricious let's-get-together chats. "Talk" meant trouble—like the day Dad "talked" to France about her "card-carrying commie pinko, atheist boyfriend," Larry. Or the time my grades sunk—then the "talk" was, "no honor roll, no softball."

Mom followed me into my bedroom after dinner, sent France

out, sat on my bed and motioned for me to do the same.

"So?" I asked nonchalantly.

"So. What's this?" She held the card about two inches from my nose. I backed away and stared at it intently.

It wasn't like my mother had nothing to do all day. It took her almost an hour to lay out and peanut butter twenty-four pieces of bread for daily lunch. Not to mention cleaning a six-bedroom house. So I don't know where she found the time to go browsing under my mattress. That's where I hid my valuables, so none of my infant siblings could "borrow" my keepsakes. That's where she found Cathy's Valentine's Day card. The keepsake in question had a picture of a lion on the front with a ruby red nose covered with glitter. The words read, "You're a Beast!"

Mom opened the card. The inside was inscribed, "But I love you anyway!" Underneath, Cathy's signature was scrawled in matching red ink. I was relieved.

No big deal, I thought. Mom told us repeatedly not to hide things under the mattress. Mice, she said. I secretly knew she just wanted everything about us immediately accessible to her.

"Explain this, Jeanne." Her tone remained strangely severe.

"What's to explain, Mom? It's a Valentine card from Cathy Longtree. You know, my girlfriend that I spend the weekends . . ."

"I *know* which one she is," Mom replied, cutting me off.

"Oh. Good." I waited.

"Why did she give you this kind of card?"

"What kind of card is *this* kind of card? It's a Valentine card. She gave it to me for Valentine's Day. I know it's pretty juvenile with the lion and all, but I like it." I felt oddly vulnerable. It was none of Mom's business. Why couldn't I have a little adult privacy?

"Did you give her the same kind of card?"

"Of course not, Mom. I gave her a different card."

"What did it say?"

'I didn't understand. Such ado about Valentine's Day. Mom was irritating me. "Gosh, Mom, I don't remember. It had two little kids romping through a cornfield, with little hearts made out of

124

corn or something. It was months ago . . . I don't remember what it said. What's so important about my card or hers?"

Mom stared at me, knitting her brows as if she thought I was lying. I should have lied, but I didn't know what to lie about.

"I don't want you spending weekends at Cathy Longtree's anymore, Jeanne," she concluded sharply. "I don't even want you being friends with her at school."

Panicked, I jumped off the bed. I was going to throw a fit. It wasn't fair. It felt like being a teenager was all about finding out who you were and losing it. Dad didn't want me to play softball because I was too old. Paul Emanuelle had been transferred . . . and now Cathy was off-limits. "Oh, God, Mom! Why? She's my *best* friend," I half-screamed.

"Don't take the Lord's name in vain, Jeanne. This Cathy comes from a broken home, her parents are divorced, and I don't think they are even Catholic," Mom said, flatly condemning as she rose to leave.

"It's not fair blaming her because her parents got divorced! It's like someone blaming me if you and Dad . . ."

"If your father and I what, Jeanne?"

"Got divorced or something happened."

"Such thoughts. I love your father. Besides, you know that could never happen. We're Catholic."

"I just meant—maybe her parents never loved each other, or never got a chance to be Catholic. What's that got to do with my being friends with Cathy, anyway? Please . . . Mom." The tears were coming. I stood in the doorway vaguely attempting to block her exit. "I really love going over there, it means *so* much to me."

"That's why it's got to stop, Jeanne. You need to make other friends . . . better friends. She can't be *that* important."

"But she is . . . " The bedroom door slammed on my anguish.

Realizing I was crying, I turned over in bed quietly hoping not to wake Camp. There was no moon over Montecito tonight. Parents never seem to know what's important to their children, I thought.

125

Or maybe they do . . . and just use what we love as a weapon to enforce their will. Soon after we stopped spending weekends together, Cathy Longtree abruptly left Amat. I heard she went to public school and got pregnant. Somehow I felt it was all my fault. I wouldn't speak to Mom for weeks and cried myself to sleep for months. After Cathy, I tried to be more careful about letting my parents know what or who I loved.

But I was a poor student of emotional subterfuge. I'd do well to learn from a master like Michelle. I arched my neck to look at the crucifix over my bed. "Jesus, is religious life really all this complicated?" Jesus seemed to be asleep with the rest of the dorm. I wondered if Michelle was still awake—concocting a revised scheme to remain friends with Dominic Anne now that Caritas had given us the particulars about particular friendships. With only three more weeks of opportunity before we left Montecito, I knew even Michelle would be sorely pressed to come up with a solution for Dominic and herself, for Antonia and me.

"Where's Michelle?" I asked Louise as I took my seat next to her in the refectory for the noon meal. "I haven't seen her all day and she wasn't in Bruntz's theology class."

"Haven't you heard, Jeanne?" Louise was wringing her hands. "I just can't believe it! They won't let us see her, so I guess she must be really sick."

"What are you talking about, Louise? I saw her late last night. She was fine."

"Sister Dominic Anne just told me while I was setting the table. Michelle got up early this morning to work in the library. She was on the ladder reaching for a book on the top shelf when she fell. She hit her head. They found her an hour later. The doctor says she has a brain concussion!"

"Oh my God, Louise!" I leapt out of my chair. "Where is she? I've got to see her."

"Sit down, Jeanne. She's right here in the main house. There's nothing you can do. They moved her upstairs into the mezzanine

126

bedroom right next to the novice cells. She must be sleeping. The doctor said she would sleep a lot for a week. Dominic says they're not letting anyone see her. Maybe she can't think. I've never had a brain concussion, have you?"

"No, I haven't," I replied thoughtfully, resuming my seat. *So they moved her to the mezzanine, next to the novice cells. Hmm . . .* I fiddled with my silverware, rearranging my place setting. "I've fallen off ladders, trees, and fences of all kinds. This is very strange."

"Dominic Anne says the doctor doesn't want her to be moved for two or three weeks . . ."

"How come Dominic Anne knows so much? What is she, the attending nurse?"

"How did you know? Apparently Dominic Anne has nurse's training, so she volunteered to care for Michelle."

How convenient, I muttered to myself—such hidden talents out of Dominic Anne also. "So Micki won't be back to St. Joseph's to sleep for the three weeks until we leave Montecito. Is that what you're telling me, Louise?"

"Maybe she'll be having meals with us in a week or two. I wonder if she'll have to drop out of classes? Don't be upset, Jeanne, she's going to be all right."

I was upset. I was torn between worry and suspicion. Only last night Michelle had been afraid she wouldn't be able to see Dominic anymore because Caritas was monitoring her cell. Now, less than twenty-four hours later, she was lying in a coma with the novice of her nocturnal meanderings at her bedside! This was certainly the most timely brain concussion I'd ever heard of. No more balcony climbing, or late-night readings in the orchard for Michelle. No more visits to her empty cell at St. Joseph's for me. Damn Michelle, her brain concussion, and Dominic Anne! I felt abandoned.

At Montecito the weeks of Advent passed slowly. It was supposed to be a joyous time, Christ was coming. Yet for me only Lurch came and went silently with her bells each dawn and dusk.

Camp was ever present. Michelle was gone. I saw Antonia Marie from a distance once or twice. In the December mist that surrounded the novitiate, I was lonely. Somehow I was always losing the people I loved.

Yet, there was God. "After all," I spoke to my *only* particular friend, as I walked the grounds alone, "I came here to be with You." Evenings, I returned to the private chapel and prayed to the hanging Christ. "I'm hoeing a lonely row here. Stay close, please."

Continually His voice reassured, *The path is not easy. I am with you always.*

And so the day of His birth approached and this Love held me close. In Lauds I chanted with my sisters:

"For Your kindness is a greater good than life;
My lips glorify You.
Thus will I bless You while I live,
And in the shadow of Your wings I shout for joy.
My soul clings fast to You;
Your right hand upholds me."

CHAPTER 13

Antonia in the Orchard

She stopped me in the orchard. I was on my way to Christmas Eve dinner, after Vespers, when she appeared among the pines by the path leading to the pavilion.

Touching my forearm just above my wrist, she asked, "Are you in a hurry?"

I'd only heard her voice a few times. The afternoon she spoke to me and sang at the Poet's Boulder, and in two or three brief and passing conversations around the grounds. But my heart had memorized the feel of her presence, the shadows in her voice.

"Antonia?"

"Yes. I want to talk to you, Sister Jeanne. Walk with me." Her odd formality charmed me. She took my hand, leading me. Her white veil drifted in the starlight as we moved toward the pavilion benches. We were not walking, we were floating, past the tennis courts, up the steps. "We don't have much time before dinner, but I wanted to say good-bye."

She sat me down, placing herself next to me. There was no space between us. I was absorbed by her mysterious eyes.

"I know it sounds crazy, Antonia, but I feel I've always known you," I blurted.

"I feel the same way. Sister Dominic Anne told me weeks ago that you wanted to meet me. I've spent so much time down in East L.A. teaching English, there hasn't been much opportunity to talk. We don't get time with you postulants. And now I have to say good-bye."

I blinked, trying to escape her hypnotic stare long enough to listen. *Good-bye? No, that can't be. We have hardly said hello.* "Where are you going?" I asked.

Her left hand reached for a pine branch, but wavered. She brushed the hair from my eyes. "All of you are going the day after New Year's; so are most of the novices. But I'm leaving the day after tomorrow. I'm being sent north to the San Joaquin Valley to live with the farm workers."

"How do you feel about your assignment?"

"I suspect it will be hard and lonely, but I'll be with my own people. I'm not one for the classroom, so I guess it's for the best."

"I don't think I'm cut out to be a teacher either."

"I know, my little friend! I see you writing in your notebook everywhere, even during Mass. You are a poet at heart, an artist like I am."

"I'll never be able to sing like you or write poetry like your songs."

Antonia gazed at the stars. "There's Scorpio, my constellation! It's important that you stay close to writing, Jeanne."

"I wrote a poem for you that day I heard you." Embarrassed, I immediately regretted my boldness.

"Say it for me?"

My head dropped. "No way, I can't!" But you can read it. Here . . ." Shyly, I pulled the creased scrap of paper from my pocket. I had carried it for a month hoping for such a moment.

Antonia held the paper against the night and read:

"Your shadows make life
A green leafed joy
That can't
But often does
Come close to play
A gentle tune of mist

That warm and dance
On pillows of unborn youth
Who never fought
Nor ever felt
Your dazzling soft smile
Whisper
Secret storms sprung
Some summer moment
Loved by you."

"Why Jeanne, this is you and I! May I keep your gift?"

She folded and pressed it within her scapular. Part of me was now tucked next to her. I moved a little closer. "Why do you have to leave so soon?"

"Farmworkers don't get the week after Christmas off. They're expecting trouble; they might go on strike. The order wants us there before the New Year starts."

"Perhaps Caritas will send me north with you next week?"

"No, I know they're sending another postulant. You'd be useless, you don't speak Spanish! You have to finish your education at our college in Los Angeles. You're going south. No matter where you are, Jeanne, remember to follow your heart. That's the only way to truly know God's will for you. Listen inside."

"I thought God's will was manifest in Mother Caritas."

131

"Even *Lurch* is human—that is a cute name, who thought of it?" Antonia threw back her veil, her laughter opened up the stars and made them bounce with her breath. Unravelling her scapular, she tugged at one side of her tunic and pulled a heavy object from her suture belt. "I also have a gift for you, Jeanne." Her hand cradled the weight as she held it in front of me. "Ever since that day at the Poet's Boulder you've had a special place in my heart. Perhaps our love for words bonds us. I feel a sensibility in you that's familiar to mine. I want you to have a friend to carry into your future."

I was stunned. It was the iron cross we had buried with Donna! The rusted crucifix was almost a foot long with bumps of raised metal peppering its arms. The eyes of a surrealistic face peered back at me. The length of it formed an Oriental tunic for covering Christ's body.

She put it in my lap. "I made it in Corita's studio at the college in Hollywood."

"Sister Corita, the famous artist?"

"Of course. She's an IHM, you know. You'll meet her in L.A. when you take her classes. She is beyond rules and conformity—you'll like her!"

The hybrid cross lay on my knees, and I looked at it dumbly. Antonia's leaving was settling in. "I'd rather be with you than it." The words fell out.

Antonia smiled at me. I closed my eyes to hold her image. A warm gust brushed my lips. My eyes popped open. Strange . . . I hadn't felt the wind before.

Just as suddenly, Antonia Marie rose to her feet, grabbing my hand. "For now this is what is, Jeanne. We go God's way. You'd better get going or you'll be late for Christmas Eve dinner. I'll follow in a few minutes." She returned to our bench with the cross, bent over and hid it in the pine needles. "There, leave the cross here for now. Come back for it when you return from dinner."

"I want it with me!" I tugged at her other hand, afraid.

"It will always be with you, Jeanne, from now on I hope. You can't eat dinner with a crucifix of this size on your plate!"

"I'll keep it always, Antonia."

"I know. Remember me in it." Antonia blew my hair out of my eyes once more. "Remember your heart."

I looked at my heart.

"Go!" she chided, pushing me toward the steps as she shrunk back into the shadows. "I love you!"

Blind with happiness I stumbled along the potholes toward the main house lights. Christmas had come early this year. I had received a most precious gift.

I never saw Antonia again. She was gone from my life as quickly as she had entered it, but I slept with her cross underneath my pillow that long week between Christmas and New Year's. I missed her presence terribly; maybe that's why I poured myself a second glass when the wine decanter came around again at dinner on New Year's Day.

I didn't understand the spiritual significance of wine on feast days at Montecito, but this was one ritual that seemed to please everyone. I disliked the taste of sour grapes and usually didn't take more than a drop or two at the bottom of my glass. Tonight was different.

Michelle braced herself as my shoulder slid into hers. "Are you all right, Jeanne?"

"My elbow dropped off the table and I can't find it. Isn't that weird? Micki, I just said, 'I can't find my elbow.' Have you ever lost a piece of yourself?" *Quit making yourself cry,* I whimpered inside.

"Jeanne, have you been drinking?"

"You lost a piece of yourself during your brain concussion, didn't you, Micki? But you got it back. Where'd you find it?"

"I found it in the mezzanine library on the top shelf, right next to . . ."

"Sister Dominic Anne's brain! Ha!"

"Jeanne! Pipe down and sit up straight." Michelle was still leaning against me, but she shifted and bent around in front of me.

133

Her head was almost in my plate. "Louise, grab Jeanne's arm. She's had too much wine."

"Where's the pitcher?" I slurred morbidly.

"Long since emptied, thanks to you. We're supposed to *walk* out of here in a few minutes."

"'I can walk/I can talk/The pitcher made a balk.' A baseball poem by Jeanne Córdova."

"Jesus y María!" Louise whistled. "Michelle, how'd she get so drunk on two glasses of wine?"

"I am *not* drunk. Being drunk is a sin. I'll have you know I come from a very fine family where spirits of the devil were not permitted under the age of twenty-one!"

"That means she's never had wine before," Michelle translated.

"Neither grape, nor alcohol, nor putbid . . . putrid . . . taste of beer has ever soiled these consecrated lips. But this is an exceptional occasion, Micki. I had a particular friendship for one whole hour. So I'm celebrating."

Michelle screamed under her breath, "Damn it, Jeanne."

"You really must watch that foul mouth of yours, Micki. One day you'll slip and get yourself kicked out of here. Then what would I do? One less soul for the Lord, one less particular friend for me. Not that you've been around to be any kind of friend lately. I'm going to call you 'Micki-come-lately' because you're never around when I need you. No, having a brain concussion is more important! So I wind up talking to the convent dog, a dog mind you, a simple dog. That's sad. And now Antonia has gone and everyone else is going away, away . . . "

"For God's sake, Jeanne, shut up. Lurch is coming toward our table."

"Now, postulants, since tonight is our last night at Montecito, we will all go over to the summer house for a songfest to welcome in the New Year. I will meet you there shortly," Caritas said, passing down our aisle and out through the foyer.

134

"That's terrific," I bounced to my feet. "On to the social hall!" Standing made the room tilt. The black-and-blue forms rising from the table gyrated like a zebra-skin rug being vacuumed. "Sit her down until the others leave," Louise whispered. Louise was such a funny little soul. "I want to go to the summer house now . . . "

"You couldn't find the summer house if it appeared before you in a vision. You're drunk, Jeanne," Michelle said tersely.

"That's impossible! Who ever heard of a drunk nun? It's not done. God wouldn't . . . "

"You're not a nun—yet—and God's got nothing to do with this."

" . . . and I suppose God's got nothing to do with Antonia leaving."

"Louise, the coast is clear, let's get started. We'll take her to bed, she can sleep it off," Michelle said.

Standing once more, I decided Michelle and Louise really needed me. We were holding on to one another tightly because we were sisters. Louise pried open the oak-and-iron front door with her dainty fingernails, no longer painted red.

"You put her to bed, Michelle. I'll fix her clothes and the room so Camp won't know anything," said Louise.

Michelle's face was close to mine as I helped her get me under the covers. "I think she kissed me," I whispered. "I'm not sure, but I think she did."

"Who kissed you?"

"Antonia Marie!"

"You're drunk, Sister." Michelle's face fell away as my head touched the pillow.

As if in a dream, I heard Louise talking to Michelle on the other side of the room. "I heard some of the professed are laying bets the three of us don't make it to First Vows."

"The odds appear steep!" I interjected, then demanded, "Which way are you betting, Micki?"

"You know me, Jeanne, I just keep score."

The tilting would stop now that they'd departed down St. Joseph's linoleum corridor. It had been just less than four months, but it felt like four years. Montecito had been, like Veronica Mary had said, "a place apart." But its external beauty had only camouflaged a growing internal blur, an alienation I'd never known before. My pillow was familiar. Things would snap back into focus, I was sure—in Los Angeles, at my new mission house.

CHAPTER 14

Skid Row Blues

Lurch summoned us to the summer house to announce our mission-house stations. The room bubbled with anticipation—and dread.

It was the last time, until First Vows next summer, that our postulant class would be together. If we were sent to different cities, I might not see Michelle, Janis, or Louise again for seven months. Would they change much by First Vows? Would they even *be* at First Vows? In the last four months, three of the original fifteen of us had left. Louise was still writing to Alfredo. She'd told me emphatically, that if she wasn't assigned somewhere within driving distance of East L.A., she would consider leaving the convent. Chances were good Louise wouldn't get what she wanted.

Paul Emanuelle had tried to tell me, but I hadn't understood—until now—the emotional reality. The convent was

137

like the army. You went where you were told to go. Never mind personal friendships, geographical or career preferences—much less boyfriends. Come war or peace we were allowed only one commitment: obedience.

"I got a place called Cathedral Chapel!" Michelle exclaimed, jubilantly waving her assignment card in front of me. Lurch had concluded handing out her sentences and had evaporated as usual.

"That sounds wonderful," I said, picturing my best friend's future. "Gothic steeples in a quiet, grassy, walled-off estate in the heart of the L.A. jungle." Inside, my heartstrings reverberated with other fears. Where was this Cathedral Chapel in relation to where I was going? If Michelle was stationed far away, who would be my confidante? No wonder they didn't want you to make particular friends. It was too particularly painful to leave them.

"Where'd they stick you, Jeanne?" Michelle asked, taking off my sunglasses to read my eyes.

Numbly, I read her my card, "Saint Vibiana's, 210 North Main Street, downtown Los Angeles." I'd been studying it, looking for some clue about my future. "Downtown" sounded ominous—no grassy estate for me.

"I'm going to a place called Blessed Sacrament in Hollywood," Camp said with disappointment. Finally. Proof that God was still in His Heaven. I might see Marlene Camp in my college classes, but at least she would not be lying next to me at St. Vibiana's. But nothing pleased Camp. "Imagine *me* in that place," she complained. "I hear there are prostitutes and drugs on the streets!"

Even in my doleful mood, I couldn't resist a parting shot: "You could use some Valium, Camp."

I returned my attention to my own plight. "Has anyone ever heard of St. Vibiana's?" I called out to the bustling room.

In the silence, only Camp answered. "I've never even heard of a saint called Vibiana, much less a convent named after her. I'll bet she's not even a real saint." Camp, however, was a real witch.

Janis, the Singing Postulant, drew an assignment in the San Joaquin Valley, a place called Morgan Hill. I spent half the after

138

noon wondering if she'd see Antonia. *Should I send a note to Antonia with Janis?*

Louise couldn't understand why she was sent to a tiny outpost in the Mexican section of Bakersfield. Bakersfield is the belly button of California. Halfway between the head (San Francisco) and the feet (L.A.), it was a fried strip of desert filled with oil wells and the poor whose futures rose and fell with the price of gas. I thought Louise would at least be happy to be speaking Spanish again, but she cried all evening. She wouldn't be speaking Spanish to Alfredo. If Louise left before First Vows next summer, I might not ever see her again.

The descent from Santa Barbara into the Los Angeles basin felt like a transfiguration. The crisp, cold purity of Montecito dissipated into auto exhaust and endless miles of bleak asphalt highways. An exit sign finally read, "Hollywood Blvd." Ah, Camp's part of town. Eagerly, I peered down the exit looking for prostitutes. Cheap, garish signs were everywhere. I felt disquieted. Maybe this was why I'd heard urban dwellers were more confused. Too many signs and no spiritual direction. The signs were too numerous and gaudy to read. How would I find my new home? With no spiritual signposts, would I become one of the lost? I began to feel sick inside.

Seeking some distraction, I turned to my driver, whose strings of gray hair poked out from under her coifed and wizened face. Perhaps she had been around long enough to know some saintly trivia. "Sister Lawrence, have you ever heard of Saint Vibiana?"

"Of course, Sister Jeanne," she replied. "Vibiana is from the early Christian Church, third century, I believe. Not much is written about her except that she was a virgin and a martyr."

"Isn't that what Holy Mother the Church says about all the girl saints they don't know anything about?"

The old nun chuckled. "Enough is known about her to have had her declared a saint. Her tomb was found during the excavations ordered by Pope Pius IX in 1853. When the diggers made new tunnels in the catacombs underneath Rome they found a tomb sealed by a marble slab."

"My father is in the marble business—marble from Italy," I interrupted.

"How interesting." Lawrence looked at me. "The inscription in the marble wall read, 'To the innocent and pure soul of Vibiana. Deposited in peace on the first kalends of September.' But what's even more interesting is that inside the tomb the excavators found a flask of uncongealed blood. Her blood was still a dark red. There were other emblems of martyrdom, but she was canonized because of the miracle of her uncongealed blood.

"Shortly thereafter, Bishop Thaddeus Amat of California petitioned to Rome for Vibiana's relics. He promised Pope Pius he would build a cathedral in her honor."

"Bishop Amat?"

"Yes. One of our high schools is named after him."

"This is very strange, Sister Lawrence. I graduated from Bishop Amat Memorial High School."

"Well, child, that is odd. The Lord works in strange ways. Perhaps you and Vibiana have a common destiny."

My immediate destiny began as Sister Lawrence stopped the car. My fear began the moment I got out and closed the station-wagon door behind me. The stench of human sweat overwhelmed me.

I dropped my small, rust-colored suitcase, containing all my worldly possessions, on Main Street. "Skid Row," Sister Lawrence had called out, as if we had just arrived at Disneyland.

I'd always thought filth was a temporary condition—in between baths. But this was eternal dirt. The entrance to my new mission home was littered with human beings who had skidded to a permanent stop. This was real *poverty,* not some obscure vow. Standing in front of St. Vibiana's Cathedral, I read the date on the cornerstone: 1876. It smelled as if the sidewalk had not been washed in ninety years. I wrapped my blazer around me more

140

tightly. The January morning was chilled with a clarity reserved for only the very worst moments of life.

Sister Lawrence called from behind me, "Ask for Mother Theresa and give her that letter of introduction. God bless you, Jeanne."

I stretched out my arm toward her. *Don't leave me!* Sister Lawrence put the station wagon in forward and drove out of my life.

I straddled my suitcase guardedly. Eighteen years old, I didn't belong here. I came from a nice family—two color televisions, six bedrooms and a power lawn mower. There were no lawns on Skid Row. No one here even owned a suitcase. The signs, the sidewalks, the people, their clothes smelled of rotted food and urine. Old men with bent backs sat in a row under a sign that read "Union Rescue Mission—Jesus Saves!" Their knees were pulled up close to their chins. I could see that all they owned was wrapped around their shoulders.

A group of angry or despondent young black men sat and slouched against a pile of construction pipes heaped against the wall of the church. A good-looking boy my own age let the cigarette droop from his lips as he looked through me. My presence meant nothing. Again, the fear spiraled up my throat. Maybe I had no purpose here. I was the intruder, another drifter encroaching on his turf.

The lone woman leaning against the Union Rescue Mission door stared at me. Her dirt-streaked, long blond hair hid most of her face, except for her eyes, which were vacant. As I stumbled toward her, making my way to the cathedral's door, I saw her skin was young, but her face was aged by a timeless despair. She kept her hand on the mission latch as if it were a matter of life and death that she be the first one through its door. She was short and thin, like me, and her free arm tightly grasped a cracked brown purse. She wore a faded purple blouse, the sleeves rolled up revealing purple lines down her forearms. Something was very wrong with her veins. I could almost smell her crumpled scarf, once a color other

141

than gritty brown gray. A long, blue, ragged overcoat (the lining of which revealed its origins as some fine winter garb) draped her shoulders.

Why was I going into a house that had heat, family, and food, while she was doomed to stand cold and hungry for days? Where was her family, her dinner table, her God? What plan did God have in mind for her, for me? Perhaps I was supposed to save her life, perhaps she would give mine purpose. Father Bruntz hadn't talked about this kind of poverty. My vow meant choosing detachment from material possessions. All my physical needs would be provided for. On Skid Row there was nothing to be attached to, and no choice.

Tearfully, I clutched my suitcase and bolted through the entrance. Emerging from the back of the cathedral, as Lawrence had instructed, I saw a wide expanse of asphalt surrounded by a twenty-foot chain-link fence. It was a combination parking lot and school yard.

The worn paint on the ground vaguely sectioned out parking spaces, yet the poles in the middle and the lines drawn through the parking spaces suggested basketball courts and hopscotch. The super-imposed, but unrelated, lines were a symbol of my inner chaos. The only building was a five-story bile-green rectangle. *This must be the convent.* It was a walled fortress. I cringed. Stretching the entire length of the girded playground, the fortress began in ragged concrete and ended in the smudged skyline of urban grit. Welcome to St. Vibiana's. Welcome to Los Angeles. No wonder no one in Montecito had ever heard of St. Vibiana's. I wished I hadn't.

I stood, out of breath and out of words, in front of Mother Theresa, the middle-aged Mexican Mother Superior of St. Vibiana's. The convent was on the fifth floor of the concrete rectangle, with four floors of school rooms beneath it. I, my suitcase, and guitar case had just clanged up the dingy stairwell. Mother Theresa responded to my letter of introduction with a single word. *"Venga!"* she commanded, as she swept us down the hallway of cracked linoleum to my room. I wondered if the letter was in Spanish or English since Mother Theresa didn't seem to use either language much at all.

"This is your room, Sister Jeanne," she addressed me formally. Perhaps she thought I was a novice. "The dinner hour is at six. The breaking of fast is also at six. Here are your keys to all the gates. They are each with a sign." To clarify her rudimentary English, Mother Theresa pointed to each key label. "You are welcome to St. Vibiana's convent. *Dominus vobiscum.*"

My cell measured ten by six feet, walking toe to toe. It was just large enough for the single bed covered with a thin brown dingy spread, an equally dingy, antiquated dresser whose drawers creaked open and shut, and a splintered desk with one drawer missing. My cell and each of the other eighteen cells on the floor were exactly the same size and had exactly one window facing the grimy red brick McPherson Leather Company building on the corner of Los Angeles and Second streets. Butting up against McPherson's was a burnt out trucking company building and below, a view of my prison playground. I could only see the playground if I stood right next to my window—in the two feet between it and my desk—and looked straight down. As I lay in bed, however, the view included a yellow, water-stained ceiling made up of seventeen rows of pegboard squares. I counted fifty-two holes in each square. The alternate view from my bed, the blinking red light atop Los Angeles City Hall, was far more mesmerizing than the ceiling. I wondered how many years had passed since a plane had flown low enough into the gritty urban ozone to see, much less hit, the red-light steeple. Nothing had flown over City Hall since I had arrived.

Kneeling at a side altar in the church in front of the marble-entombed Vibiana three weeks later, I implored the very dead saint, "What could we possibly have in common?" I still hadn't a clue. Perhaps there was no grand esoteric commonality, perhaps it was only that neither Vibiana nor I spoke Spanish. Since the great hall of the cathedral was full of Mexican-Americans, Mass was being said in the language of the people. I mumbled under my breath in Latin. All I knew of the language of my ethnicity were useless words from high school Spanish—irrelevant phrases that did not include the translation of the gospel according to St. John or offer any explanation, in any language, of poverty according to Skid Row.

"And nothing will ever fly over godless downtown Los Angeles," I informed the entombed virgin and martyr, Vibiana. Rising from my knees to sit, I accidentally knocked my purse into my guitar case. The case thudded to the ground, strings reverberating, offering a discordant note to the Spanish sanctus. Mass was almost over. Ready to go to dinner, I searched my purse for the keychain from Mother Theresa.

One key was for the car I was to use to drive to classes at Immaculate Heart College. Never mind that no one knew I didn't know how to drive. A second key was for the wrought-iron gate on Main Street that never seemed to be locked anyway. A third let me into the chain-link parking lot, and a fourth opened the stairwell that separated the school floors from the convent dorm. Arising for the end of mass, I gave up looking for my key to the main convent door. The keys were all identical in shape and color, so every time I wanted in or out of anywhere I had to read each label. Vibiana's felt like a prison, but I wasn't sure if I was the jailer or the jailed. Perhaps it didn't matter. It would have to do. It was home.

I bade Vibiana good-night, tip-toed out of the church, and in the dusk threaded my way home through the parking lot. It was almost time for dinner and for the janitor to lock the chain-link gates, now that playground hours were over.

Crouched on the convent steps, the boy looked as forlorn as I. Some kindred empathy made me pause in front of him.

"You a nun?" His tone was belligerent, yet solicitous, as he reviewed my postulant uniform.

"Are you talking to me?"

The boy looked around the empty parking lot and came back to stare at me. "Unless you got some friends I don't see. Yeah, I'm talkin' to you. You some kind of nun?" His giant black hands clung to both knees as he sat, easily yet warily, ready to spend the night, or leap at a moment's notice.

"I'm studying to become a nun."

"Whatcha studying for? I thought nuns was born that way."

How right he was, I smiled inside. *He* didn't have to enter a novitiate to find that out. "I guess I'm studying to find out if I was born that way."

"Shit, I already know how I was born!"

"What's your name?"

"Calvin."

Calvin wasn't my idea of an animated conversationalist, but at least he spoke English. It had been weeks since I'd spoken with anyone. Besides, he looked "bummed out," as Bill would have said. I missed Bill. Maybe I could help Calvin. I sat down on the steps.

"What's in the box?"

"It's my guitar. Do you know how to play?" I opened the case.

"Shit, that's for girls and faggots."

"For what?"

"Faggots. Guys who want to be girls. Queers."

"Oh, yeah. Faggots." I uttered the word I'd only heard in swearing conversations.

"What's it worth?"

"Worth? The guitar? I don't know, my parents gave it to me, maybe a hundred dollars or so. It means a lot to me. It's my best friend."

Calvin surveyed the instrument carefully. "Man, a hundred bucks!"

"Do you have a job or a home?"

"Sure, I got a home, lady. You think I live on the streets like some kind a bum? But I ain't got no job no more, so my old lady dumped me this morning."

"Your old lady?" What kind of mother would throw her teenage son out of the house because he lost his job?

145

"Yeah, man, my chick, you know. Man, where you nuns come from?"

"Why'd she leave you?"

"She shacked up with my older brother 'cuz he's got the bread . . . a job, man!" Calvin seemed more exasperated with me than hurt about his lost love.

"She left you because of a job?"

"'Cuz, she want money. Don't mean nuthin'. She pregnant—my kid. Ain't my problem no more. Joke on Jonathan now!" Calvin slapped his thigh.

A pregnant woman passing from one brother to another because of a job? I must have misunderstood Calvin.

The lights over the convent steps flicked off suddenly, it was time for dinner. "I've got to go," I said, snapping the guitar case closed. "Maybe if you're here tomorrow I can help you find another job. I know some people up at my college, my school . . ."

Calvin got up and stood close to me as I fiddled with the key ring looking for the right label. He loomed over my short frame—he must have been six feet. "Yeah . . . that sounds good, maybe tomorrow."

I felt the case bang against my shin and my shoulder jerked backwards as my purse was torn from it. Calvin was hurling through the open gate with my possessions!

God almighty, I don't believe it. "Calvin!" My scream ripped out and smacked the concrete fortress walls.

The charred buildings of Hill Street blurred past me as I ran screeching after Calvin. "Damn you, Calvin! I'll find you if I have to look all night!"

Evening was falling in the Los Angeles Skid Row ghetto. I lost sight of Calvin turning down an alley. I heard the trash cans fall at the far end and raced toward them. *He's got to slow down sooner or later.* I felt my lungs wheezing. *I want my guitar! Shit, that's my music! What right did he have? That's my stuff! I can't believe it. We were going be friends. I was going to help him get a job.*

146

"Where are you, Calvin?" The wail leapt out of my abdomen. The sound stunned me. My voice sounded like . . . like Calvin's! As if somewhere during my chase I had become him.

I slammed the lid back on one of the trash cans. Shadows dotted the forsaken streets as I raced through them searching for the shape I knew. A black woman with a rickety stroller gave me a hostile stare as she pushed her baby past me. I must have looked like an asylum escapee. There were no name tags in this place, only ghosts, missing persons.

As I raced deeper into the ghetto, barricaded storefronts now appeared between the houses. I spied Calvin down the block as I rounded a corner. I ran into a girl leaning against a parking meter. "Watch where you're going, bitch!" she said, her face painted with more colors than I'd ever seen in a rainbow.

"Sorry, I'm so sorry," I gasped, catching my breath. *God damn, I've lost him.* I couldn't tell if he'd gone up the street past those guys drinking and slouching against the car with two wheels or down this other alley.

"Hey, you guys," I called to the slouching men, "did you see a young boy with my purse and guitar run past you?"

"Hey what, honey? Whatcha want? Come on over here, baby, and talk to us right," one of them replied with slurred speech.

They wouldn't have noticed Calvin if he'd hit them over the head with my guitar. And now I didn't want them to notice me. I took off down the alley. I could hardly run anymore. The street lamps snapped on. Night had come. Calvin was gone.

What's the matter with you, Jeanne? Calvin could outrun you in a ten-yard dash. You'll never find him. Sure. Just go up to that house with the porch light on. "Oh, excuse me, sir, I was just looking for a thief who stole my guitar and purse. Have you seen such a person, sir?" *Calvin could be his son! Perhaps he'd just come sauntering out from the back bedroom playing my guitar.*

Trash, beer bottles, broken toys strewn on dead front lawns, boarded windows surrounded by peeling paint and torn chain-link fences. Block after block of condemned housing fractured by atrophied and chipped neon signs: "Liquor," "Tires," "Sale." I'll bet anything was for sale here. Here, heaven seemed remote, purgatory endless.

What do you say, Jesus, to people with no jobs, no money, no homes, no old ladies? "Thou Shalt Not Covet"? "Thou shalt not steal"? I'd steal to get out of here. God, where are you in the lives of these people? Shall I tell them about faith, hope, and charity? Hope that life will soon be over so they'll die and go to hell for theft? The Blessed Virgin had made a lot more sense in West Covina.

I doubted there was a virgin within blocks of me. Except me and Vibiana. Perhaps that's what she and I had in common—martyrdom. But they wouldn't call it martyrdom if they found me dead for chasing a guitar and a five-dollar bill in my purse. That was called stupid.

An old lady with a patch of cropped, nappy gray hair huffed her way past me. The sweat began to crawl down my shoulder blades as my body started cooling from its hunt. My blouse was stuck to my back, my blazer soldered to it. *What are you doing here, Jeanne?* The red-splashed wall read, "Burn, Baby, Burn!". *Who cares about Calvin? What would you do if you found him? Say, "Calvin, could I please have my guitar and five dollars back?" He'd laugh in your face.*

The darkness had enveloped my gray companion, and now my danger felt palpable. *My God, I'm lost! Smart move, Córdova. Your anonymous gravesite won't even have a tombstone reading: "Young, Off-White, Dumb, Dead Nun Buried Here."*

Three men wearing long coats were coming down the alley. I crawled in between the bumpers of two cars that had no windows. Crouching, my calf muscles started locking into spasm. *Forget about your guitar, Jeanne, just try getting out of here alive.*

Waiting for the men to pass, I carefully turned up my blazer collar around my face and buttoned it over my mouth, neck, and chest. I smeared my soggy hair over my forehead. Completing my disguise, I mixed some dirt and gutter water and applied mud smears to my bare legs. I adopted the slow swaggering amble of the other figures I'd seen. Going nowhere, I ambled in fear, twisting and turning through the streets, searching for home. Somewhere in the night I became part of them, and I knew I was safe.

Hours later my hands gripped the familiar chain link of my convent fortress. I used the last of my strength to painfully hoist myself over the fence.

Sister Jose Angela greeted my pounding on the door. Perhaps she didn't know enough English to question my filthy state. Perhaps she was merely being kind. *"Quieres cenar?"* she simply asked.

"No, no supper." I answered flatly, pulling my aching skeleton up the flights of stairs. Slamming my cell door, I fell on my bed, a crying heap. No music either. I would play no music tonight. There would be no more music. Only the foggy, blinking red light, my tiny cell, and my ever-evaporating vocation.

Montecito was confusing and often lonely, and I'd left with great hope. But so far Vibiana's was a tomb. In this emotionless catacomb, I feared my blood would congeal long before its time.

The next morning I only faintly heard the prayer bells calling me. I couldn't wake up to go to daily Mass. I didn't want to wake up at all.

CHAPTER 15

Peace, Love and Brown Rice

As I drove off to Immaculate Heart College, Mother Theresa waved and called out, *"Buena suerte en la escuela!"* She hadn't, however, asked me if I could drive.

When I was five, Dad showed me how to ride a bike. "Here's the pedals. You put your feet on them. Here's the handlebars, you put your hands on them." He gave me a shove off the curb. "There's the road!" Several skinned knees later, I found I had survived.

The automobile seemed to work by the same principle, I deduced, lurching my way up Western Avenue through Hollywood. People were kind, shouting instructions I couldn't hear throughout most of my trip. By the time I reached the college's potholed entrance, I was basking in the sin of pride. That is, until one of my tires got caught in a hole and sent my auto into the immaculate curb.

Situated in the Hollywood Hills, the forty-acre hillside campus of Immaculate Heart College was an academic paradise, even with its potholes. God had scooped out a handful of the Garden of Eden and replanted it in the center of a smog-ridden metropolis.

The IHC campus was replete with grassy knolls holding garden statues of the Blessed Virgin and Christ. The slopes and gardens, bordered by giant elm and pine, climbed four levels. The first, closest to street level, held the Motherhouse. There lived Mother General Humiliata and the other IHM high command as well as the college professors. Level two was a campus hangout, the cafeteria. A three-story mansion of classrooms took up most of the third level, and the library, theater, and tennis courts crowned the IHC estate. Winding steps proceeded from this fourth level even further into the hills above the library, but I didn't know where they led. Parking next to the library earlier that afternoon, I had counted ninety-one steps as I descended to the cafeteria that was doubling as the bookstore on the first day of the semester. Returning later to deposit my books in my car, I paused on the sixty-fourth step to absorb the sunset. On the horizon to the north was a mammoth sign hanging on a hill. In giant letters it proclaimed: "Hollywood." Yet another brave new world lay before me, I had reflected. Perhaps here in academic tranquility my vocation and I would synchronize once more.

Pushing through the crush of people jamming the entrance to the auditorium that evening, I discovered IHC was about as tranquil as a political hotbed. The hall was tense with excitement. Hundreds of students were jumping in the aisles, stomping on chairs, swaying and clapping to a music I'd never heard before. The voice singing over the loudspeakers sounded vaguely male, but the figure in front of the microphone had hair down to "its" shoulder blades. It also sounded like she or he had tuberculosis, or at least laryngitis. Even so, most of the nuns, faculty, and students seemed to know the words to "his" song. As I leaned into a back corner trying to steady my nerves, they were all singing: "Come gather 'round, people, wherever you roam/And admit that the waters around you have grown/And accept it that soon you'll be drenched to the bone . . . /For the times, they are a chaaangin'."

Mother Margaret Rose, a robust, energetic, fat little nun who had replaced Lurch as our Los Angeles Mistress of Postulants, had all but demanded we attend this private concert for IHM's and their friends. She called the evening a "Sing Out for Peace."

The mood in the auditorium was anything but meditative. It felt like a championship high-school football rally. The lyrics of the long-haired figure—who, by this time, I was sure was male—were challenging and angry. I was now also convinced he was a hippie. I'd seen people matching this description in the newspapers.

Since my run-in with Calvin a few weeks ago, I'd replaced morning Mass with the ritual of sneaking out of Vibiana's to buy the *L.A. Times.* I was learning more from the paper than from going to Holy Communion. The United States was partially involved in a war in remote Southeast Asia. From the accounts of the fighting and dying, it seemed we were *fully* into military confrontation, yet Congress had not declared war. Americans were split over whether we should be fighting someone else's civil war.

It wasn't clear to me why Roman Catholic nuns were involved in a political issue. I found it even more perplexing that the IHM order had taken a side *against* the government by sponsoring this unpatriotic concert. Religious life was not turning out as I had anticipated. Every time I came to a new corner, it took another radical turn. I was left dragging faith in the center lane.

Recoiling further into my corner in the rear of the hall, I searched the crowd for Michelle's or even Camp's familiar face. I'd had no one to talk to during an interminably lonely January at St. Vibiana's except a very dead virgin and marytr.

The raspy-voiced boy on stage was now singing something called, "Blowin' in the Wind." I thought he was. Suddenly I saw a familiar face on stage behind the singer. It was Father Daniel Berrigan, the priest I'd almost knocked into the swimming pool during my hasty heretical retreat from Father Bruntz's class! Berrigan was speaking to a tiny professed nun wearing a brightly

beaded skirt and headband over her habit. I'd suspected Berrigan
was a hippie when I met him. His peace-symbol lapel pin had stuck
me in the cheek when we collided. But just because I agreed with
him about the role of women in the Church didn't mean I was a
radical like he was. What would Dad think if he knew I had joined
a convent that befriended war protestors who advocated "Peace,
Love & Brown Rice"? I was even beginning to suspect some of the
IHM's were hippies and revolutionaries!

I surveyed the auditorium. I could leave now if I wanted to.
Margaret Rose had requested attendance but it wasn't a Holy Rule. I
could simply turn around and drive home to Vibiana's contemplative chapel. The thought was not inviting. I wanted to be
where something, anything, was happening. Even the wall
supporting my backbone was pulsing here. My mind felt torn, but
here in the hall, my body gave itself over to life. I was seduced.

"Peace, my friends!" The tiny nun with the beaded skirt
addressed the crowd. A cheer broke out in the students' section,
"Corita! Corita!"

The college was teeming with avant-garde teachers, visiting
professors, and students, all of whom Margaret Rose said, were
engaged in "great social change." The college seemed to be the
womb of political reform in the IHM community. Our order was being torn asunder: the bulk of the IHM liberals led by Mother
General Humiliata and the left wing of the Pope's Vatican II Council
versus the conservative IHM's led by Cardinal McIntyre of Los
Angeles. The liberal IHM's were at war with the Cardinal over the
modified habit, whether or not nuns had a right to choose their
own careers, religious returning to their secular names, the role of
women in the Church, our prayer schedule, daily Mass, and what
the Cardinal called "the growing materialism" of the IHM's.
McIntyre must have been worried. If nuns were allowed to choose
their careers, who would teach in his Catholic schools—for *free*? At
Montecito we had overheard bits and snatches, gossip and plot-
tings. There were "secret meetings"—no one knew the names of
those attending. But I was sure that the Irish brother priests, Daniel
and Phillip Berrigan, were among the ringleaders.

Neither I nor the other postulants had been called upon to play a part in the growing civil discontent. The order hadn't become enough of a democracy to give postulants the vote. As the youngest members of the community, we were called into play mostly as guinea pigs. The changes were wrought upon our lifestyle by liberals who thought our age put us on their side.

I wasn't so sure whose side I was on—neither were the others. Despite our mock burial of Donna, most of us were very attached to the habit and the Latin. But I certainly favored a vote in my career and resented the Church's view that nuns were second-class helpmates while priests represented God. Overall, we were ambivalent, confused, and resentful.

I certainly didn't appreciate the further lack of stability wrought by religious changing their names. A nun's name was sacred. She spent years of prayer trying to choose the saint who symbolized the religious traits she most cherished. Her name often reflected her spiritual alter ego. But, in the post-Vatican modernization, many IHM's had begun to revert back to their given appellations. Our philosophy teacher, Sister Charles Borremeo, named after the saintly French scholar, was now to be addressed as Sister Margaret Smith. Other nuns took great offense if we dared shorten their names or titles. Some teachers retained both names, others insisted upon one or the other, many were trying to decide and shared their identity crisis with their students. I'd spent a good portion of my younger life researching what nun name I'd choose. I'd decided on "Sister Paul Francis." Paul, after the Roman soldier turned theologian, for his strength and passion, and Francis, who talked to the birds, for his gentleness. But I faced first vows this summer stuck with "Sister Jeanne Córdova" for the rest of my life.

Laying aside these identity dilemmas, I was having far more pragmatic problems, such as the theft of my guitar, having no friends, falling away from the Mass, and wondering if I'd ever get my B.A. I didn't have anyone to talk with anyway. Michelle never wanted to talk politics. She was more interested in the political

154

games of our order than the results. Perhaps now that I had arrived at the scene-of-things at IHC, I'd find teachers or friends to help me sort things out.

The sound system died for a few moments. I wondered if everyone in the IHM community was too busy changing the world to fix the sound system or repave the potholes in the campus' main driveway.

"Jeanne!" I heard my name above the din. "Over heeere." It was Michelle's voice! I bolted down the main aisle. "God, you look great! I've missed you," I exclaimed, reaching for my long-lost friend, who stood in the middle of a boisterous group.

"I've missed you too!" she screamed back even though we were hugging. "You're even letting your hair grow longer, good for you!"

"Oh, I've just been too depressed to find someone to cut it. It's been hard . . . "

"Where have you been?" Michelle cut me off and pulled me into the row in which she and her friends were clustered. "What are your classes?"

I yanked my schedule cards out of my shirt pocket and handed them to her.

"What's *your* schedule?"

Michelle shoved her own yellow cards into my hands.

I reviewed her curriculum. "We've got two classes together, Micki, Philosophy and Creative Writing. I didn't see you buying books today."

"I'm afraid, Jeanne. I'm still hoping to get a waiver out of Philosophy and into a cooking class or something easier."

"Ditching college before you start . . . Micki? They don't teach cooking at *this* school. You haven't changed in a month! How refreshing, everything else has. But school beats Montecito and Skid Row, so I won't complain."

"What's Skid Row? Listen, Jeanne, I hear this Philosophy with Sister Richard is the real thing, and you know I'm not given to abstracts. I'm counting on you to help me with term papers."

"Maybe you could climb that Hollywood sign and get another brain concussion and get transferred out of those classes into something more your speed, say, Manipulation 101." The words had simply fallen out.

Michelle looked shocked. "That's not nice, Jeanne. The doctor said I was very sick up at Montecito."

"I'm just kidding!" I screamed over the riot. "Don't get upset. I've really missed you a lot. Where is Cathedral Chapel? Do you have a phone? Vibiana's is a real pit. We've got a phone, but Mother Theresa doesn't allow private phone calls. Do you like your place?"

"Oh, I love it! Come meet my Mother Superior, Sister Luke Zoe, and the others."

Sister Luke Zoe was a large-boned woman with clumps of flaming red hair jutting out of her coif in all directions. She stopped singing, gave me a warm smile, and pumped my arm vigorously. "Hi there! Jeanne, isn't it? Michelle has told me so much about you. Welcome to IHC! Welcome to Hollywood!" Luke Zoe's ruddy face turned to her friends and the speaker on stage.

"Welcome to Hollywood?" I turned to Michelle. "What a thing for a Mother Superior to say. *That's* your boss?"

"She's a kick, huh? They call her a 'heavyweight.' She's the Regional Rep to the IHM Assembly on Reform. She argues for the liberal changes the young nuns want from Cardinal McIntyre. And . . . she doesn't even wear her habit in the convent, neither do a lot of the others. They wear sweat shirts and pedal pushers around the place."

Nuns in sweat shirts! I couldn't begin to picture it. Could I believe Michelle this time?

"We have a guitar Mass after dinner instead of at the crack of dawn. And then we sit around and talk, or watch TV. We even watch *Peyton Place*, you know, the sexy soap opera? And there's a Community Share every Friday night, where everyone says their feelings about their week and our communal living. There's even no lights out! You just go to bed when you're tired, like a normal

156

person."

"I don't believe you!"

"See that nun, at the end, right next to that man?" Michelle pointed to a demure middle-aged woman in a habit with no veil. Not clapping or swaying with the others, she was sitting serenely, every inch a normal nun. That is, except for her pink cat-eye sunglasses that looked like they were borrowed from an Annette Funicello beach party movie. Sitting next to her was a young man, many years her junior, clapping boisterously.

"That's Sister Constance Marie. But rumor has it she's not so constant—that's her boyfriend next to her."

"You mean a priest or a secular male friend? You don't mean a *real* boyfriend?"

"No one knows for sure. When he calls every night, she refers to him as 'John Doe,' and she goes out with him on weekends and stays out all night!"

"What kind of convent is Cathedral Chapel?"

"Haven't you heard its nickname, 'The Swinging Chapel'? I don't make the rules, but I sure like living by them! It's certainly a community, much more so than Montecito. People like and respect one another . . . some real Christian charity for a change."

Michelle was interrupted as a tall, familiar-looking novice standing down the aisle reached over and pulled her away. It was Sister Lauren David, the stoic novice who hadn't spoken to me since the night of the apple pies in the refectory.

Michelle returned. "Lauren says her friend would like to meet you, Jeanne."

Someone wants to meet me! I grinned with delight and peered around Michelle's shoulder. Lauren was engrossed in conversation with an intense-looking young woman whose eyes locked into mine. Not in a habit, the girl was casually leaning against an empty chair, watching me.

They say you know someone most completely the first instant you meet. She was lean and enigmatic, and somewhere deep inside I knew she didn't fit. And I knew she had already assessed that

157

I didn't either. Marnie Heathford was undeniably and arrestingly attractive. Staring at her knocked the wind out of my stomach as surely as Bill's punches in our childhood boxing matches. Her ash-blonde hair was cut angularly away from her face, brushing the back of her neck. Standing just over five feet, small-boned and slim-breasted, she looked like Peter Pan. Michelle twisted and pushed me through the aisle toward Lauren and the stranger.

"Marnie," the novice addressed her friend, "This is Jeanne Córdova, a postulant. Jeanne was in Montecito with us this last fall." Lauren's tone was dry and cool, but I hardly listened.

The fairy tale woman leaned across her friend, "Very happy to meet you, Jeanne Córdova. My name is Marnie Heathford." She said my full name very slowly, as if I was the most important person in the auditorium. She had a dashing, bewitching smile. And yet, as she held out her hand to shake mine, her face changed, revealing, for an instant, an elusive vulnerability. Her face searched mine softly. Her lips moved gently into amusement. Her hand grasped mine firmly. She didn't jostle or pump like Sister Luke Zoe. Her palm held mine with conviction. My body froze.

Marnie felt my rigidity. "Hey, there," she waved her other hand in front of my face, "you look like you just saw Peter Pan! Don't worry about it, everyone thinks of me that way."

I tried to shake myself, her eyes were too compelling—fathomless velvet green, strangely shrouded by heavy brooding eyebrows that looked out of place above her otherwise delicate features. If she had asked me to fly out the window with her to Never-never-land, I would have believed in our destination.

If she'd just let go of me I could concentrate, I thought, pulling my hand away. "I'm glad to . . . I. It's my pleasure . . . my name is . . ."

Marnie laughed and released my hand. "It's ok."

Now I was cold. *What's ok?*, a voice inside me spoke. *Say something, Jeanne. She'll think you're stupid. Ask her . . . are you a student here? What's your major? What do you think of all this peace and war stuff? How banal, Jeanne. Keep your mouth shut.*

"Heathford, isn't that Joan Baez?" Lauren David jerked

Marnie's attention back toward the stage.

The name seemed important to Marnie. She briefly touched me on the shoulder. "I'll help you figure things out around here, Jeanne. We'll talk more later."

We'll talk more later, I thought. I had never met the girl before, and probably never would again. I returned to my spot in the aisle next to Michelle. "Micki, who is Marnie Heathford?"

"Lauren's new friend. Interesting, huh? It's a compliment that she wanted to meet you. She's a junior and big shot on campus."

"What kind of big shot?"

"Ah . . . what kind? I hear she's a genius, at the top of her classes, and sort of notorious. Listen to this singer, Jeanne, she's great."

The olive-skinned woman on stage, introduced by Corita, was singing a lovely ballad about "the joys of love" in French and English. She was stunningly beautiful. So was Marnie Heathford.

During the next month, I saw a great deal of Corita the artist—but nothing of Marnie the genius. I hated art. In high school, my stick-men looked like fish, and my fish looked like dogs. I requested Corita's class because Antonia Marie predicted I would find a kindred spirit in her. As Antonia had foretold, Sister Mary Corita Kent was beyond structure.

I didn't understand why so much space on the crowded campus had been allotted to this tiny little nun and her bizarre studio. The underground warehouse was called "the Catacombs," because it was the basement of the Motherhouse. Even the Roman dead would have risen had they been buried here, overwhelmed by walls of psychedelic canvases. Every inch of space, even the ceilings, was covered by huge blobs of color with inscriptions. The inscriptions, far from explaining the colored smears and superimposed shapes, only added to the madhouse atmosphere.

"The Ground Work Doesn't Show Till One Day," appeared on the ceiling running diagonally through a canvas of a Christmas pine with no needles. On my first day, a piece of clarifying heresy held

159

me transfixed:

> "You are god, and you are not
> It's good not to get the two confused
> It is one."

I was confused by the unification of what Catholicism had always billed as a duality. God was out there somewhere, Someone to supplicate from afar. Was Corita suggesting I was God?

I looked for a place to sit my humble humanity. There were no chairs in the room. Dozens of tables had been pushed together and formed a huge second floor in the middle of the Catacombs. The students, half of them secular and the other half professed and novices in various states of habit, sat cross-legged on the tabletops.

Corita descended from nowhere and began striding about on the tables. Her tiny five-foot stature made me wonder how such a small package could cause such hullabaloo in an order fraught with major political issues. Yet Corita seemed at the center of things. Literally and figuratively, she didn't appear to have either foot on the ground. Paintbrush in hand, she wafted in and out among us, jerking her manic hands about, pointing to this or that canvas, tossing out instructions like, "Let your spirit relax into your unconscious."

Her subconscious seemed to speak in stereo with her conscious mind—that is, if she had a conscious mind. Corita had yet to complete a sentence on a single topic, including the explanation of her own name. Some religious called her Sister Mary Corita, lay people referred to her as Corita Kent, she spoke of herself as Corita. We could call her "any creative thing that came to mind."

"I want you all to get up here with me, class!" Corita exhorted. "Take these paintbrushes and run along the tabletops here. Breathe deeply, *feel* your spirits, and in that feeling splash the canvases surrounding these tables. Let your brushes flow!"

"I'm not going to run on any tabletops!" Marlene Camp hissed at my cross-legged form. Unfortunately, I was the only one in Corita's class she knew, so she'd sought familiarity by coming to stand next to me. Camp was too uptight to sit on top of a table.

"Suit yourself, Camp." I jumped to my feet and flaunted my

paintbrush in the air. "If the IHM's think it's important to run on tables and let my spirit paint the ethers, I'll obediently allow them to silk-screen the canvas of my vocation anytime!"

"Up, up girls!" Corita rallied. "Don't be afraid the tables will break. Don't be afraid of your passions!"

CHAPTER 16

A Nun Grows In Watts

The lawns in Watts were mostly dead weeds. And the people there decorated their walls with blood and scorched hopes, not paintbrushes. Michelle and I drove down Imperial Boulevard slowly. "What do you think makes people angry enough to burn down their own neighborhood?" Michelle asked.

Watts had burned just two summers ago, when the race riots of nineteen sixty-five had swept the ghettos of America. The National Guard had been called out because there was murder and looting. Blacks were still angry enough to kill whites. When Camp learned that Mother Margaret Rose, our Mistress of Postulants, had missioned Michelle and me to Watts three afternoons a week, she had sarcastically warned, "Teaching ghetto kids to study would be as fruitful as making convicts say Grace before meals." Still, I felt relaxed, it was so good to be with Michelle again. Maybe now my luck would change.

"Look at this place!" I said, swerving to avoid a fender lying in the road. Imperial Boulevard resembled a reconstruction zone and reminded me of the old photographs Dad had of Berlin right after it was bombed. For blocks, storefront windows were boarded up, although doors were open for business. Trash and bottles were strewn along the sidewalks and empty lots looked like refuse dumps. But the streets were alive with people. Young kids screaming and chasing one another, older men standing on the corners, taunting passersby. Once in a while, a car would stop at a corner and a man from the sidewalk would come up to the window for a brief conversation and the exchange of a small package. I wondered what free samples he was distributing.

Michelle reached over her shoulder to lock her door. "Why don't you lock yours too, Jeanne? Do you think we're safe here?"

"I feel right at home," I said flippantly, not bothering with my lock. "It looks just like St. Vibiana's!"

"I can't believe your mission house looks like this. You're exaggerating."

"You're right. There's no burned-out buildings. We have spray paint, no char. Same landscape design. We're safe, Michelle, let's just be careful to lock the car when we leave it, and let's try to park it where we can keep an eye on it. And . . . don't bring your purse next time. Carry what you need on your person, and don't bring money."

Michelle reached across the car seat extending a package of cigarettes. "Smoke?" she said, nervously.

"Micki, I didn't know you smoked. Caritas said we weren't supposed to."

"We're in Watts now, Jeanne, not Santa Barbara. And no, I don't smoke, but everyone else does at Cathedral Chapel. I saved these because you told me you smoked at summer camp last year."

"That's real sweet, thanks!" I dropped one hand from the steering wheel and reached for Michelle's gift.

"Watch the light! Stop, Jeanne!"

My attention flew back to the road as I braked sharply for the red signal.

"God, where'd you learn to drive?" she asked, now even more nervous.

"I haven't . . . yet. I just got my Learner's Permit. Pretty good, huh?"

"Shit, Jeanne, do you always do things the hard way?"

One month out of Montecito and Michelle was swearing more than ever. And I was now the smoking postulant.

"No wonder Luke Zoe says this center really needs us."

"Oh, shit, there it is!" I spun the steering wheel and made a ninety-degree left turn, lurching finally into an unpaved, rutted parking lot. The ragged, rusty sign dangling from a post read, "Imperial Courts Development Project." I locked the car, wondering if it was a futile exercise.

Michelle bent down to lift the other side of the rusty sign off the ground. She inserted it back through the nail on the other post. "I see we've arrived in time for the early developmental stages," she said.

"This looks more like the reason for President Johnson's war-on-poverty, than the solution!" I said, sidestepping broken bicycles and debris on the cracked sidewalks. We were searching for the main office. Imperial Courts, or "the projects," as the residents called it, was a series of three-story concrete-block tenements facing one another across yards of dead weeds—the playground. The tiny holes that served as windows peered like rows of close-knit, beady eyes down blocks of gray facelessness.

"Say, ladies," a booming voice called from inside one of the buildings, "over here!"

A large black woman with a bellowing voice and dancing eyes shooed us through a doorway with a tiny "office" sign. "Lookit here, Geraldine," she said, introducing us to a girl sitting in front of a typewriter I was sure was from Dad's Berlin. "See what I found roamin' 'round the place. Must be them young nuns they're sendin' us."

164

Michelle and I remained standing for inspection. Geraldine gave us a cold stare that our hostess ignored. "Well, Lordie, you two just sit right down here. My, you all don't look a day outta high school. Are you the nuns?"

Michelle had nothing to say, just like that day in Caritas' office. She picked the strangest times to practice Silence.

"Yup, that's us," I offered. "We're really not nuns yet, we're . . . "

"Well, that's even better. Folks around here have problems with nuns and all that religion, so it's good you folks didn't come all gussied up like penguins. Now just sit tight there, and I'll go tell the boss lady you're here. If she don't grind you up and spit you out, someone else will, so might as well get started. Oh, I'm Annabelle Williams, the project coordinator. Hush now, sit."

Annabelle Williams disappeared as quickly as she had appeared, leaving us with the mute Geraldine. "What do you suppose she meant by grinding us up and spitting us out?" Michelle whispered to me.

"Oh, who knows? Just a colloquial saying most likely. I thought she was very friendly."

"A real glad-hander," Michelle said, nodding toward our nonverbal baby-sitter. "Jeanne, I think you should take off your shades for this introduction, don't you?"

"I'll decide that after we meet the boss lady," I retorted. Michelle ought to know I didn't tolerate comments about my sunglasses. I always wore them, especially on opening nights.

Annabelle returned, corralled and scooted us ahead of her down the dark hall. "First door on your left," she called out.

Michelle and I bumped into each other and the sides of the dank, narrow hallway. She seemed unnerved, I felt apprehensive. This was like auditioning before Caritas on test day. It would be humiliating to return to Hollywood and report failure on our first day.

We stood silently in the crooked door frame staring at the black-haired woman hidden behind a mass of paperwork on the desk. The harsh afternoon sun simmered the cluttered office. I watched the long second hand on the glassless clock in front of us. The boss lady remained fixed on her paperwork. Perhaps we should announce our arrival, I signaled to Michelle. I coughed.

"Sit down."

Michelle tugged at my sleeve quizzically. "I don't know," I returned under my breath, "I thought she said sit down, but . . ."

"I did say sit down . . ." The gruff voice growled from behind the paper mound. Her face lifted momentarily, her eyes shrouded by dense black sunglasses. She clarified, " . . . now."

Michelle dove into the nearest dilapidated chair. I didn't like the boss' tone of voice. I folded my arms and leaned into the doorjamb.

"Something wrong with your ass that you can't sit down?" The boss lady didn't even look up this time.

I drew myself upright, coming to full attention. "I'm more comfortable standing, thank you anyway . . ." I almost added, "sir," as if addressing my father.

The boss threw down her pencil, swept her pile of papers to one side, and leaned back in her chair. Our sunglasses met.

She seemed startled by something about me. "I see they sent one nun and one smart ass." She continued to assess me as if she recognized me.

The boss lady removed her shades, grabbing them from the bridge of her nose. Straight black hair surrounded her face like a swimming cap. She looked in her mid-thirties, eyes as ominous as her voice. She was short in stature, but solid in the shoulders. Her eyes were absorbing everything. I almost blushed under her inspection. Michelle looked down. Her black orbs looked like they had been born on the street—like Calvin's. Her presence projected, "I'm tough." I believed her.

Slowly her gaze traveled from me to Michelle and back again, and again. The silence was uncomfortable. *Perhaps the audition is for a Bogart movie,* the smartass quipped inside.

"I'm Adele Martinez, community organizer of Imperial Courts Development Center. They call me the boss here. It's short, more honest. You will call me Miss Martinez . . . only. I'm from Chicago,

166

where I worked for Jane Addams—a pioneer in social work—when I was younger than you two. Before that I had my own gang. Do you know what I mean?"

"Yes, Miss Martinez," Michelle said, staring at the woman and hanging on her every syllable. Even for Michelle, this was playing it to the hilt, I thought.

"I don't like nuns in the ghettos," Martinez continued. "You cause more problems than you solve. Unfortunately, Imperial Courts is run by the Catholic Youth Organization, so when I call for volunteers, I get nuns. We've had IHM's down here before. Other orders also. But the IHM's are the only ones who last. I don't know about you two; we've never had postulants before, but we're too short-handed. You'll have to do."

Charming welcome. I did not speak. At least we were accepted. We wouldn't be sent home in disgrace.

"I've come to believe that IHM's are different than other nuns," Martinez went on, apparently loquacious on the subject of nuns. "They have a little *backbone.*" Her last word fell on my now stiff and aching shoulders. "Willing to break a few rules, these IHM's, willing to do what's necessary in today's world. That's why your order's in trouble with the Cardinal. IHM's have balls. Do you two?"

Michelle turned red. My mortified eyes focused on their own reflection behind my shades.

"You've got three strikes against you to start with: you're young, you're stupid, and you're white." For the first time, I saw Martinez hesitate. "Córdova," she read from a letter in front of her. "Brown is worse than white down here. I ought to know. You speak Spanish?"

"Well . . . no."

"Not very brown, either. Like I said, three strikes, but maybe you're naive enough to survive what you don't understand. This letter from Mother Margaret Rose says you're down here from honky-land three afternoons a week. What can you do?"

Michelle's mouth was, as usual, frozen under stress. She couldn't seem to say or do a thing but look at Martinez and blush.

167

"I write," I blurted out. "I was the editor of my high school paper. I'm also good at sports, and I know how to coordinate social activities. But I'd really like to learn political organizing, like Cesar Chavez." I named-dropped my hero.

"You write. Well, down here we talk, we don't write. Social activities, huh? Cesar Chavez, hmmm . . . he's one of my favorite people." Martinez's attitude softened, a bit. "So you want to be a social worker?"

"A nun and a social worker, both."

"Don't know that those occupations are mutually inclusive. Maybe one is a phase . . . I wonder which?" Her monologue confused me.

Why couldn't I be both?

"I've got a group of young thugs . . . teenagers. Their leader just got sent to Youth Authority. They like 'social activities,' so I'll put you in charge of seeing that the cops don't find them, OK?"

"The cops?"

"Just an expression. The kids like to go on trips and throw dances. You know any interesting places to go to around Los Angeles?"

"Sure," I lied. *I'd lived in Los Angeles for a whole month,* I added to myself.

I'd have said "yes" to any assignment from Martinez. Not just because I didn't want to spend those afternoons at St. Vibiana's. In the last half hour I'd found myself liking the boss' blunt frankness, her toughness. I, too, would have to be tough to make it down here. She was rude as hell, but probably just to scare us into blind obedience or a quick trip home. It was easy to see she knew her stuff. She could teach me a lot about the ghetto and perhaps about a lot of other things. That is, if she didn't order me around so much. Maybe, even if she did.

"Can you do anything besides sit down?" Martinez's attention turned to Michelle. Despite its sarcasm, her voice had softened. She was teasing.

"No," Michelle whispered. "I mean, yes, maybe. I like to raise money."

"Money! You might be helpful. We need money. You any good or are we talking bake sales after Sunday school?"

"I have a lot of good ideas," Michele declared. "I can talk people into donating anything." Michelle was not exaggerating her ability to sell overcoats in Ethiopia. Martinez was still staring into Michelle's eyes.

"I'll bet you *can* sell anything with those baby blues!"

"Yes," Michelle responded, staring back, "they help sometimes . . . raising funds."

"And a mouth to match, no doubt! Very important assets . . . for fund-raising," Martinez agreed.

"I'm glad you think so." Michelle lowered her eyes to her lap and began blushing again. I wanted to kick her chair and yell at her. She wasn't making a very professional presentation.

"Michelle organized some of our convent's educational field trips," I offered, sliding into the chair beside my best friend and bragging for her. We postulants had only been to town twice, but Michelle *had* made the luncheon reservations.

"I'll bet they were *very educational* too," Martinez said softly, leaning forward. Why was she suddenly acting so friendly with Michelle, I wondered. "Well, then. Michelle, you'll work in the office with me . . . and Annabelle . . . on fund-raising ideas."

"Terrific!" Michelle seemed very pleased.

"Great!" I enthused.

"Now get out of here, both of you. Report to Annabelle."

Spring passed quickly in Watts, and I didn't see much of Miss Martinez. We communicated through her edicts left in my assignment box in the main office. She'd leave instructions as to what to do with my group, or notes like: "Hear you two lost the radio in your car. Don't bother getting another." Other times she'd leave books on social work with a scrawled introduction—"This Saul Alinsky is the best on grassroots organizing, read it." When Cardinal McIntyre was thinking of pulling nuns out of the ghettos, the convent grapevine said Adele Martinez had helped organize an IHM protest. My three afternoons each week rapidly stretched into long evenings. I had a rough debut. For weeks I endured "honky do-goody" and "stupid bitch," to name two endearments I could understand. Gradually, as I inaugurated role-playing job interviews, and made fun of the dinosaur tar pits on our ridiculous field trips to places they would never see again, we warmed to one another. Geraldine, our gloomy receptionist, clumped through Disneyland's Frontierland despondently complaining, "What good is lookin' at these dumb animals, I'll never see a real live lion or tiger anyway."

"I don't know about that," I pointed to the fake rhinoceros heaving water through his massive plastic jaw. "I think your ol' man looks a lot like that guy . . . and you see him every day." Slowly their names for me changed to "hey, girl" and "the little nun-boss." I was accepted and became a part of their lives.

I felt myself come back to life. There was little hyprocrisy or spiritual confusion in Watts. Life was rough, tough, poor, and primal. In this urgency, I discovered purpose and pride in finding clever ways to keep my roving band of teenagers off the streets and out of jail. At times this called for desperate as well as clever tactics.

At six-foot-two and weighing just under three hundred pounds, Oogie Bell was big enough to silence anyone who thought his name was a joke. But his size became the problem the night the LAPD arrested him. The liquor store clerk said the pistol-carrying robber was "over six feet and musta been three hundred pounds."

Dressed in our cleanest postulant blues, Michelle and I raced down to the Watts police station with evidence. Our evidence was our holy word—we introduced ourselves to Officer Fredericks as Sister Mary Maria and Sister Mary Jesus Maria, respectively—that Oogie was boiling black-eyed peas with us for Imperial Courts' annual potluck on the ill-fated night in question. Luckily, Imperial Courts had indeed just celebrated its anniversary with a potluck. Oogie was drunk and sacked out in the activities room that night, but cooking sounded more wholesome.

My impassioned plea, "We are sooo hopeful that Oogie might

be released in time to attend a special Mass at our Vow ceremony tomorrow morning, sir," finally prevailed. Officer Fredericks was a lapsed, but guilty, Catholic. Oogie was released that night under the recognizance of the Sisters of the Immaculate Heart of Mary. A week later the cops caught the real six-foot robber in another downtown holdup.

Michelle and I later joked about our evening as stand-up probation officers, but seeing Oogie's ashen face as he was unhandcuffed was sobering for us as well as for him. Justice was belated that night, and had almost not arrived at all. The three of us walked out of the police station knowing other innocent people remained inside.

I had never heard the term "social worker" before meeting Miss Martinez. And there certainly wasn't much "social activity," as I once understood the term in the white suburbs of West Covina. I considered my dances successful if no one got knifed or overdosed on the dance floor.

Michelle was also surprisingly effective. When it came time for the Catholic Youth Organization's annual peanut drive to send kids to camp, she persuaded the director at C.Y.O. headquarters to let her talk to white high schools to raise money. Speaking at Immaculate Heart High School on our college campus, an impassioned Michelle cried as she told her affluent, white teenagers, "These kids have never seen a pine tree, or gone swimming in a mountain lake." She created demand by telling her audience, "We have a peanut shortage. We only have enough cans for each of you to buy *one* can!" Naturally, every one of the four-hundred students bought a can. A week later, Michelle "found" a new supply of peanuts and was back selling more cans to the same altruistic student body. Michelle perfected her pitch at a dozen white high schools in greater L.A. Imperial Courts sent more kids to camp that summer than any other C.Y.O. center in Los Angeles.

I was playful but strict. I threw Dude and his sidekick, Jackhammer, out of my program because they wouldn't bend to my rule of no drugs during program hours. I never heard from

Jackhammer again, but Dude returned sober days later. I played big sister by taking up a vocabulary that would have made my Dear Aunt Sister pray for my soul. But all the while I was falling in sync, maybe a little in love, with my kids who didn't ask much from life except a boyfriend or girfriend, a job, a father who didn't beat them, and a mother who slept at home. I came to the IHM's to learn to be a nun, but in Watts I learned to care.

CHAPTER 17

A Silent Piece of Wood

My sisters at St. Vibiana's had been to Compline prayers and were now alseep in their cells. I didn't sleep much these days. I lay awake in my cell staring at the blinking red light atop Los Angeles City Hall, and trying to make sense of the seemingly disparate parts of my life.

In the last year, I'd been exposed to five wildly incongruous realities: West Covina, Montecito, Skid Row, Immaculate Heart College, and Watts. These worlds had no apparent connection to one another, yet all of them were very much alive and at war inside of me.

West Covina and the campus had a lot of grass. No one could afford to waste water on grass in Watts, and no one planted trees on Skid Row. Grass had a whole new meaning to me now. Grass meant money. Grass meant space saved for beauty, simple things I took for granted growing up.

When I was young I used to think my family was poor. We didn't have a swimming pool; we ate hamburgers on Sunday, Monday, and Wednesday and hot dogs on Tuesday, Thursday and Saturday. We had to wait until Christmas to get that special bicycle and all the toys we wanted. Yet children in Watts ran in the "sprinklers" when a fire hydrant broke and didn't eat at all when food stamps ran out before the end of the month.

Money was never mentioned at Montecito, where there was visual luxury at every turn. In religious life, money came from Mother Superior, the Cardinal, the Pope—God? There was always enough, although I had never seen much more than lunch money or been called upon to think about it. My reality about economics had been shattered. Before entering the convent, I thought the whole world was middle class.

At Immaculate Heart College, the grounds were manicured and the students and faculty—despite their radical airs—were white, right, and privileged. Everything was intellectualized, and you could find a stimulating conversation on anything from the nature of dichondra to abstract physics.

St. Vibiana's was staffed by the same IHM organization, but the lifestyle practiced there was so archaic, the Cathedral and convent might as well have been in Spain, where Mother Theresa and her flock of taciturn sisters, I suspected, had come from originally.

Sister Fabian's philosophy class raised more questions than I could answer. Fabian was a tall, intellectual woman in her forties who commanded respect from the rest of the faculty. She was thought to have been around the world and know it all. She had more than enough I.Q. points to make up for knowledge gaps about the few countries she'd missed. Fabian spoke of the other great religions of the world, the similarities in theological archetypes.

"When we study the life and teachings of Buddha," she said, "we see clearly the reflection of Christ's own life." I looked around the class to see if anyone was as shocked as I. Listening to her exposé of the common value systems and historical roots of each religion, I began to wonder how in the world Catholics had the audacity to think we had cornered the market on the True Faith. Intellectually or morally, I had never been able to accept that a fair and loving God could condemn millions in Africa or China to Hell simply because a missionary had never instructed them about Jesus Christ.

Sister Fabian thought that Vatican II wasn't going "far enough" in its ecumenical outreach. She believed the very notion of spiritual separation between God's children was "religious nationalism," anathema to the simple words of Christ: "Whatsoever you do unto the least of them, you do unto Me."

The more I listened to Fabian and other teachers at IHC, the more centered I felt. At last I'd found other religious who called themselves Catholic yet still disagreed with the more ridiculous trappings that the Church—not God—had concocted. I'd wanted to become a nun for love of Christ, not for love of an institutionalized Church. Other students and faculty at IHC also disputed the judgmental positions of the Church. They said the Church, as a collection of men, could be wrong sometimes. I'd been right all along! "Christ-like" and "Catholic" were not always synonyms.

And Fabian never threw me out of class or insinuated I hadn't read enough Church history to properly brainwash myself. Unlike the others, she welcomed my questions. "What do I tell my teenagers in Watts when they say St. Joseph must have been a queer if he never 'laid' his wife?" I asked.

"Start with a more important truth," she said. "Tell them in the name of Jesus, 'Love thy neighbor as thyself.'" But promoting a divine respect for other people and their property to a population that received no respect from others would be a formidable task.

My theology professor, Sister Frances Anne, spoke of birth control in wildly different terms than Mom and Dad. The new, liberal Catholic theology believed it was justifiable to have an abortion if pregnancy was the result of rape or incest. I found it embarrassing to discuss such matters in a classroom. I'd never heard of rape in

175

West Covina and had to ask a classmate what "incest" meant. I wished I hadn't. I wondered if Mom and Dad knew of such things and had just never mentioned them. How would they counsel Geraldine, our embittered secretary down in Watts, about the sanctity of sexual union in marriage? Geraldine had finally opened up and told me that when she was thirteen her single father had said she had to earn her room and board by hustling on the streets. She started on the pill the day after she heard about it.

I was raised in white, middle-class, Republican suburbia and had been transferred to white, upper-class, liberal Montecito. Now I woke up in the morning in a Dark Ages' Spanish convent, attended a radical intellectual oasis in Hollywood, and spent my evenings in a black ghetto. The jigsaw puzzle of my life was missing more than a few pieces.

At Vibiana's no one was available for discourse in any language. In the isolation there, my spiritual inner world chafed against my external reality. In the friction it was I who made little sense. Jesus' voice had grown dim. Mother Theresa had stopped rattling her key ring under my door in an attempt to get me up for morning mass. Occasionally, I did get up, hoping the Eucharist would speak to me as it had all my life. Jesus' sacred Body and Blood had been my heart's consolation. He had always been home for me. Kneeling in my emptiness in the back pew, I tried to talk to Him. My prayers rose as my tears fell. But the crucifix above the altar remained a silent piece of wood.

One morning, I realized it wasn't prayer, but anxiety, that constricted my throat. I was terrified that Jesus, too, had abandoned me. I couldn't hear His voice in my soul anymore. The last day I went to Mass was March 19, the Feast Day of St. Joseph the Worker. I couldn't remember what goal I was working toward. Most nights I lay in my cell, reading news magazines, social work pamphlets, and books, anti-war stories in the newspapers and textbooks by New Wave theologians. When my eyes grew too bleary I'd stare out my window and spill my sorrows onto Skid Row.

176

CHAPTER 18

Marnie: The Joys of Love

"Why the tears?"

No one was supposed to know about my private enclave high above the college. It was shrouded by trees and held a lone concrete bench, left over from some campus grotto. A weeping willow shadowed the bench, its branches draping over the hillside. This enclosure was where I went when I felt most alone, to chart the growth of Wilshire Boulevard skyscrapers in the smog below. On a clear day, I fancied I could almost see the Pacific ten miles to the West. Today was not a clear day. There were few of them lately.

The hand on my shoulder shook me firmly. In the winter's early-evening damp, I shuddered and clenched my jaw to stop crying.

"You shouldn't be afraid of your tears," the husky voice said, becoming a face as its owner rounded the bench and sat next to me. "It's Marnie Heathford, remember me?"

Little did she know how much I remembered her! I smiled with delight, my tears receding. For weeks after I'd met her that night of the concert, I'd scoured the campus for her. After a month, I finally gave up, thinking perhaps I'd misunderstood when Michelle said she was a student at IHC. She sat her lithe body next to me on the bench. Her dark eyes flashed warmly. "Of course," I managed, as tongue-tied around her as I had been before.

"You're Jeanne," she declared.

"Yes. Sorry you caught me at a bad time. Things haven't been going well."

"I'm glad I caught you at all. I've been looking for you for a week now." Marnie's arm slid around my shoulder protectively.

I felt giddy. Why did Marnie make me feel important? She was so casual about our sudden intimacy. "That's probably because I don't hang around campus much. I just zip in and out of classes and down to Watts most afternoons. But tonight I just couldn't go home. I live at St. Vibiana's on Skid Row. It's a dump. There's no one to talk to." I started crying once more. "I'm not going home to that pit, maybe I'll stay here all night and . . ."

"Slooow down, you're talking too fast, too much, too soon!" Marnie's laughter made the weeping willow's leaves dance around me. "What 'pit' are you referring to? Listen, you don't have to go home, but it's getting chilly. Come over to my place and make it home for a while. I live back in there." Marnie pointed through the dense brush that walled off the college from a set of bungalows. "Come on, I'll make you dinner."

Without waiting for my answer, she hauled me off the bench, pulling me up with both of her hands clasped around mine. She camouflaged her forwardness with exaggerated grunts and groans as if she were hauling an elephant. Her eyes sparkled with playful abandon. With her charm and spontaneity, Marnie transformed ordinary moments into magic.

Her home was a rough, clapboard bungalow sequestered from view on all sides by trees. She tossed me into a reclining chair while she lit the brick fireplace at the foot of her bed and went to start dinner in the corner of the room that looked like the kitchen.

"Hand me your starched little postulant blazer, Jeanne. I'll hang it in my closet so you won't get it wrinkled."

Peeling off my uniform, I felt more comfortable and began exploring as Marnie rummaged in her refrigerator. Bookshelves lined the room, covering every inch of space. Michelle must have been correct about Marnie being an intellectual. A sedate black-and-grey bedspread and dark-stained beams completed the secluded cave. I felt like I was in a sanctuary, a private world that breathed its own mysterious warmth.

"I've never seen a home that's one room. It's so tiny and cozy," I called to her in the kitchen-corner.

"It's called a studio," Marnie, said returning to my side. "I'll bet you've never had a place of your own."

The thought was novel. A place of my own . . . a whole place for me alone. What freedom! For me there was only West Covina and the convent. "I never had a *room* of my own, much less a whole house! But I do have a room now . . . my cell," I replied.

"There's a lot you haven't experienced," Marnie said, putting a cup of cocoa with marshmallows in my hands and sprawling on her bed. "The cocoa is an appetizer, I'll make dinner later. Tell me, is this cell in the home you call 'the pit'? And why don't you want to go there?"

By the time I had finished the story of my ontological identity crisis, and a fairly lengthy autobiography, Marnie and I were laughing uproariously. She picked up her guitar and introduced me to the doleful lyrics of "Eve of Destruction." She pointed out the parallels between my sad tale and the song's cynicism. Ultimately, she assured me, I wasn't losing my mind, just "growing up" and experiencing a severe case of "culture shock."

The two of us were curled on the floor in the small space between the foot of her bed and the fireplace, as Marnie revealed her own dreams to me. She wanted to be a nun and had applied for admittance into the IHM's for the coming fall class of sixty-seven.

179

Listening to her rapture as she detailed her last three years at the college with the IHM community, I held back some of the specifics of my own rude awakening. Inside me a voice screamed, "Why do you want to give up all this freedom? Your life is so perfect." But Marnie told me she already knew of and agreed with all of the liberal changes I'd found so devastating—all, that is, except not wearing the habit. She was older and far more sophisticated than I. It was unfair of me to assume she would have my same problems. I knew what it meant to dream, and I wanted Marnie's vocation to be true for her. Aloud I echoed her enthusiasm, "That's spectacular, Marnie. I hope you get accepted! Wait till you take that *MMPI* entrance exam."

"No problem, I'm a psych major, you know." Marnie began another song.

I threw another log on the fire and sat near the blaze watching Marnie sing. It was Joan Baez' "The Joys of Love," the song I'd heard in the auditorium the first night I met Marnie. My new friend seemed to know even the French verses perfectly. I couldn't understand the lyrics, but as she sang I noticed a vacant look invade her eyes, and her voice seemed to question a past that did not include me. Suddenly her words stopped, her fingers stilled the strings.

I prodded, "I thought there was another verse?"

"No," she whispered. "I mean, yes. There's more."

"Finish it for me?"

"I don't like it anymore." Marnie turned the instrument flat on her lap and brooded into the fire. "It reminds me of Lauren."

"Sister Lauren David, the novice I met you with who's your friend?"

"*Was* my friend." Marnie tossed the guitar to the floor, stood, and walked toward the kitchen. "They transferred her," she called back to me. "She was assigned as the assistant librarian here when you all came down in January. Two weeks ago, they sent her to teach eighth grade at some jerky elementary school in San Bernardino. That's a hundred miles from here," Marnie concluded, sprawling on the bed and staring into the fire once more. Her dark brows knit into a wall. Marnie was such a paradox—in one evening she acted so much the wordly intellectual about campus, yet, at other moments, she seemed the forsaken, sad tomboy waiting to be crowned king-of-the-hill once more. Aching for her unknown pain, I sometimes saw in Marnie my own longings mirrored back to me.

"Why did they send her away?" I ventured.

"Didn't they tell you about particular friendships up at Montecito, Jeanne?"

Marnie was downright hostile. What had I said to upset her? "Of course. Mother Caritas called Michelle Callahan and me in and told us exclusive friendships were antithetical to collective bonding, that we should spend equal time with everyone."

"That's *all* she told you?"

"Yeah. Pretty stupid, huh? Who'd want to spend their free time with people they have nothing in common with? There's nothing to talk about."

"So . . . are you and Michelle still particular friends?"

"I don't know how particular is particular. I do spend much more of my time with her than any of the other postulants, so I guess we are particular friends. I told you she's my mission buddy in Watts. I tell her everything that happens to me, and vice-versa. Although with Micki you never know if you're getting the whole story. Anyway, I see her less now. I work on the streets and she's always in the director's office or going to meetings after I drive home."

"What's the director's name?"

"Adele Martinez."

"Del Martinez!?"

"Yes. Do you know her too?"

"Well, what do you know about that!" Marnie seemed amused.

"What do you know about what?"

Marnie laughed aloud. "About Michelle and Martinez!"

"What about them?" I wasn't following her conversation again. Marnie brushed her fingers through my hair lightly as she made her way to the kitchen for a beer. "Nothing," she called out. "It

181

doesn't matter."

"Yes, it does. What's Michelle and Adele Martinez and Watts got to do with Lauren getting transferred?"

"Jeanne, my sweet, you really don't know much about much do you?" Marnie took my cocoa cup and replaced it with a glass of milk. "I was merely thinking that Adele Martinez really gets around the IHM community. She's involved with the politics of the order and the fighting with the Cardinal, and I've heard her name associated with one or two other nuns in particular. Maybe Michelle and Martinez are having a particular friendship."

"Well, I think you're wrong!" I protested. Marnie was so off-base; she just didn't understand things. "Miss Martinez isn't even in the convent, so it wouldn't count as a particular friendship. Besides Michelle *works* for her! Furthermore," I continued, annoyed with Marnie for making up things about Michelle, "I'd know it. Michelle tells me what's she doing . . . eventually." My last word trailed off as I thought of Michelle's still-unexplained, but timely, brain concussion.

"Anyway," I said, flinging a heavy log atop the blaze in front of me, "I don't understand why a religious order is more obsessed with friendship than with God, or the fact that people are starving in Watts. It's all a lot of bullshit."

"It sounds like you're learning vocabulary, if nothing else down there. Listen, I agree with you about particular friendships, Jeanne. I don't see anything wrong with them either. So don't get so testy with me." Marnie rejoined me at the foot of her bed, kneeling to unfold a crease in my postulant skirt. "Sometimes this worries me about joining the IHM's. I was very close to Lauren David and another novice back in my sophomore year."

"You mean you had a particular friendship with them?"

As Marnie leaned against my knees I watched her strong hands restacking the scattered wood pile. *I liked Marnie's hands.*

"I guess you'd call it a particular friendship," Marnie answered, preparing a new batch of kindling. "Although that term is so vague no one seems to know exactly what it means. A lot of the young nuns think this rule should be scrapped all together. I've heard them talk. Maybe I'll help make a shift in priorities after I'm professed."

"That'll be in five years if you're accepted. I need some changes now!" I looked at my watch. "Holy Moses, Marnie, speaking of now, it's almost midnight. Mother Theresa will have the nun patrol out searching for me if she's looked inside my cell!"

I slid back into my blazer and buttoned it against the cold air. Her arm around my shoulder, Marnie walked me through the dim starlight all the way down to my car on the cafeteria level. I drove her back up to the knoll by the library.

"I had a wonderful evening, the best in months!" I said, putting the car in park and smiling at her. I wondered when I'd see her again, tomorrow didn't seem soon enough. It might be another month before we bumped into each other.

Marnie leaned forward out of the passenger seat, and rested her arm on the wheel in front of me. She faced me closely. I think she whispered something, but I was too distracted by her proximity. In the shadowed contours of her face I thought I saw a strange destiny. Some faces are special and have been assigned important work much beyond their self-knowledge, Paul Emanuelle had once told me. Did Marnie have such a face, or was I, again, looking at myself in her? Was it me, not Marnie, who was supposed to write some book, invent a machine to reduce world hunger, spin the world on its axis just a fraction of an inch?

Paul Emanuelle said I had a "destined" face. Father Sullivan, the vice-principal at Bishop Amat, had once stopped me in the hall and asked out of nowhere, "So when are you going to become a saint, Jeanne?"

I had laughed, but promised, "Sometime just before I die, Father." But the man asked me the same question everytime we met for four years. Sainthood looked farther away from my life plan than it ever had before. So why was I searching for my future in Marnie? My brain was immobile, but my elbow wasn't. It slipped, and the horn blasted, breaking the moment.

"So what are you doing this Sunday early evening?" Marnie

asked, opening the car door.

"Probably pondering the mystery of the Holy Trinity while playing basketball with myself at St. Vibiana's. Why?"

"I'm having a few friends over for analysis and a barbeque . . ."

"That's an appetizing combination."

Heathford laughed. "Not of one another! We're doing a Freudian analysis of Dante's *Inferno* for our Developmental Psych course. You said you liked poetry. Why don't you come? The barbeque is chicken, and you'll like my friends."

My first social invitation since coming to L.A.—I could hardly contain my delight. "Sure," I accepted, politely, "I can make it." Inside I finished, *no one seems to know or care where I am most of the time.*

"Great!" Marnie reached across the car and squeezed my hand. "Plan on staying late and we'll go to that Ingrid Bergman movie I want to see. Make up some excuse for Mother Theresa!"

CHAPTER 19

Cesar Chavez No More

Like Adele Martinez, I was a female Cesar Chavez. I lived alone in a tiny cell, but three nights a week I shed my clerical persona as I took the highways south into Watts. I spent hours in my office—my cell—in urgent dialogue with Cesar or Del about solving the problems of the downtrodden. Other nights, I'd steal out and sojourn to another foreign land, Marnie's bungalow. She and I would discourse as the moon arched into morning. Or we'd attend political movies and philosophize about global injustices. Weeks passed without my thinking of my previous soulmates—God, Jesus, and the Blessed Virgin.

I wasn't the only one with fantasies. The entire IHM order was caught in a time warp, implementing a futuristic reality that Cardinal James T. McIntyre of Los Angeles found increasingly "fanciful and unbecoming to Catholic nuns." Mother General Humiliata was

185

called to his office almost as regularly as I appeared before Margaret Rose, our new Mistress of Postulants in L.A. Her sins, the sins of our order, were that the IHM's were taking the new rhetoric of Vatican II too literally. McIntyre did not like his nuns jogging through the ghettos in pedal pushers, harmonizing "Blowin' in the Wind" to the sanctus bells of the Body and Blood of Christ, or agitating against a war patriotic citizens supported. He was scandalized when activist priests Phillip and Daniel Berrigan had absconded to Montecito as a refuge from the FBI! I agreed with him about some of the excesses. I wanted the habit and the Latin back. I'd come to the convent for serenity and stability. Religious life was changing faster than I could adapt. My identity was disintegrating rapidly. Overwhelmed and depressed, I couldn't figure out whether the convent and I were going in the same direction. I was going in all directions, but spinning into nowhere just as quickly.

One April afternoon while I was waiting for my favorite hoodlums, Michelle found me daydreaming on the sawdust grass of Imperial Courts. "Mother Margaret Rose wants to see us in her office tomorrow morning, Jeanne." She collapsed beside me, clutching my arm.

"Yeah, what about?" I feigned calm.

"I think it's something about our work down here. I told you a month ago, Adele says the Cardinal doesn't like black people."

"McIntyre thinks he's still back in Ireland and there's no such thing as a black Catholic. But if it's about Watts, why doesn't Margaret Rose want to see Sister Barbara Anne also?" Another novice from Cathedral Chapel had recently been assigned to Watts with us. She'd joined Michelle in her fund-raising duties so the two of them sometimes drove home together. My teenagers often kept me at Imperial Courts until almost midnight. I wasn't pleased with Barbara Anne's arrival. Now Michelle no longer had an excuse to wait and drive home with me.

"Maybe Margaret Rose doesn't want to see Barbara because she is just in charge of us postulants." Michelle paused and flicked some dead weeds off her skirt. "I guess her sum-

186

mons isn't about particular friendships again—since it's no longer *my* cell that you visit. How is Marnie Heathford, anyway?"

Startled, I looked into Michelle's ocean eyes. I never felt she set any premium on my company. "What do you mean?"

Michelle rose to leave. "Forget I said that. I've got to go, Adele is expecting me."

"Hey, white girl!" Dude called out from the activity-room doorway. I was late to my "How to Find a Job" seminar with them. I turned to see him and Pamela hugging each other and whispering. "We're gonna start job interviews without you if you don't move your ass," he continued. "Hear you're looking for a job!" They both burst out in laughter.

"I might be!" I called back. "Micki," I turned back to see her walking away, "see you in front of the ax tomorrow."

Mother Margaret Rose was short, squat, and jolly with a great sense of humor and a perennial smile plastered on her rotund face. She could have passed for a genuine human being except that she employed the same smile to say good morning as she did to notify one of excommunication or transfer to Molakai, the leper colony.

"Good morning, girls! Do sit down." The ubiquitous smile greeted us. "How are things in . . . oh, what's the name of this tenement you two are teaching in these days?"

"Imperial Courts, Mother," I answered, going along with her pseudo-absentmindedness. Word had it Mother Rose was like the F.B.I.'s J. Edgar Hoover—she knew where every one of her citizens were, night and day.

"Ah, yes, Watts. Jeanne, how is your prayer life coming along?"

She caught me off-guard. "My prayer life, Mother? My . . . prayers . . . I. Everything is fine, Mother."

"Good. First Vows are only three months away now, and we want to make sure none of you are so caught up in your mission work that you don't have ample time to contemplate your first devotion." Margaret Rose paused, awaiting some response. Having learned a little from Michelle's M.O., I remained silent.

"I've talked to both of your Mother Superiors—that is, to Sister Luke Zoe and to Mother Theresa. I'm told everything is going well with you, Michelle, at Cathedral Chapel."

"Oh, yes, Mother. I really love it there!"

"Well, best not to get too attached. You know attachment to material persons, places, or things only separates us from God . . . but I am glad your vocation is going well."

I wanted to scream at Michelle, *What vocation?* She hadn't mentioned God or praying once since we left Montecito. All I heard from my best friend lately was Adele Martinez and excerpts from *Peyton Place*, the television soap opera that seemed to be the only real ritual at Cathedral Chapel.

"Mother Theresa tells me, Jeanne, that she doesn't see you at morning Mass often, and that you don't seem to be home there much."

I was shocked Mother Theresa knew I was coming in late so often. I left the light on and my bed covers bunched up hoping she'd think I was asleep. I continued Grand Silence before Margaret Rose.

"Mother Theresa suggested you might be going to daily Mass here at the college since she doesn't see you in Vibiana's chapel. It is a fine Mass here, don't you think?"

"Oh, yes, Mother. I like the Mass in English rather than Spanish, and I like the guitar music here." I had indeed gone to Mass at the college with Marnie—twice.

"Well, perhaps the changes I must make in your schedule will enable you to spend more time at St. Vibiana's at night studying and preparing for your vows."

"What changes, Mother?" My silence had definitely ended.

"One of our nuns in San Pedro was accosted walking home at night and was almost ra . . . almost . . . Ah. She was raped. The Cardinal is demanding we take our sisters out of dangerous mission sites. And so we must. We can no longer permit any of you to drive home or walk alone after dark in some of our . . . rougher . . . mission sites. We cannot have you driving home from Watts alone so late at night, Jeanne. So I've talked to Miss Martinez down there and told her we'd have to reassign you."

"I don't drive home alone," Michelle blurted out. "I drive with Barbara Anne who is . . . "

"I know you don't, Michelle. We've decided to let the two of you continue because you are together and you come home at dusk, but I don't know how much longer we can keep this Watts assignment. I don't know what we're going to do under pressure from the Cardinal to change so many things, and . . . "

"What about me?" My horrified voice squeaked. I was not interested in troubles with the Cardinal. I couldn't believe I was hearing the end of my social work career. I was dumbfounded.

"You will get to teach at St. Vibiana's, Jeanne. Mother Theresa says they need an after-school catechism class for the lower grades."

I slumped in my chair. I must be dreaming. I couldn't be transferred back to the place I was trying so desperately to escape! And to teach babies a faith I had begun to doubt! Shell-shocked, I pulled my sunglasses from my purse and quickly shoved them over my eyes. I was not going to cry in front of Margaret Rose.

Closing the door to Margaret Rose's office behind us, Michelle tried to soften my fury. "Sorry about the news, Jeanne." She reached out to put her arm around my shoulder. "I know what Watts means to you."

"Cut it out." I jerked away.

"Maybe it'd be good to cry, let it out."

"I'm sick of crying. That's all I've done since I got to this miserable excuse for a convent." Pausing by the grotto of our Lady of Fatima on the way back to class, I slammed my philosophy text against one of the sculpted plaster children praying in adoration. "I'm fed up with this!" I yelled.

"What's going on, Jeanne?" Marnie finally got up from the recliner and turned off the movie. "I've never seen you like this."

189

Lying on her bed watching TV, I hadn't uttered much more than a guttural "yes" or "no" all evening.

"I've got nothing to say tonight, is that all right with you? Can't we just watch this fucking movie and not talk?" I screamed. It was more than I'd said all day.

"I must be rubbing off on you too much. What's this 'fucking' business? I swear, but I don't talk this way!"

"What are you now, my mother? Give me a break, I've got Mother Theresa and Margaret Rose—I don't need another mother!"

"And I don't need your anger or your rudeness. It's way past your bedtime, after midnight. Why don't you go home?"

"And I don't give a damn what time it is. I'm not going back to that hellhole. Why the fuck should I anymore?"

"Quit swearing." Marnie came over and sat next to me on her bed. Her hands grabbed my wrists. She relaxed her grasp and slid her fingers through mine, capturing them. "Tell me what happened today. I've never seen you so upset!"

My anger melted under the warmth of her touch. Her face was close, her eyes compelling, inviting me to let go. I leaned forward and allowed my head to fall on her shoulder. "I just don't know what to do anymore, Marnie. Margaret Rose cancelled me out of Watts this morning!" I sobbed, my tears spilling all over her new blue vest.

"Oh, shit, Jeanne. Why?"

"I don't know, I guess it's the Cardinal, or the whole damn order, or me, or something. I just don't know what's happening anymore."

The months of tears welled and broke as I told Marnie about my crushed dreams of being Sister Mary Cesar Chavez, about wanting to be a social worker like Miss Martinez—and how strong and self-directed she appeared to me. Adele Martinez was the closest thing I'd ever had to a father or mother who believed in *my* goals. In her gruff way she'd said I'd might mature into "something valuable to others." I had just begun to feel a part of Dude's and Pamela's life; I was keeping Todd from selling heroin and a probable next and last trip to the California Youth Authority prison. I was just convincing Geraldine that she really could go back to high school and become a beautician. I was part of their lives down there, and they were part of mine. At Imperial Courts, I felt useful and needed, maybe even loved.

While I sobbed, Marnie's hand never left mine. Her other arm held me to her and stroked my head. Marnie's mind was so gifted, we spoke over each other's words on almost any topic and, without any spaces, understood each other perfectly. But the heart of the matter was that I'd come to love her. She was a slightly older version of me; I was her yesterday's innocence. I could feel her loneliness, so I allowed her to see mine. Sometimes it felt like we were both precocious children, digging tunnels in an adult sandbox, stalling until our parents came home.

In the last month, her secluded cave had become my haven, her friendship a rebirth into emotional intimacy. Michelle was my friend, our minds played and schemed together, but there had always been some kind of barrier between us. Not with Marnie. It had been years—since I protected Cathy in the night—that anyone had been so gentle with me, so tender with my emotions.

"It's gonna be all right," Marnie rocked me, whispering in my ear. "We'll figure out something. You need some sleep now. Come on, let me tuck us in. You'll see, it's gonna be all right. I love you, Jeanne."

Midnight fled with a pale rose moon fading over Marnie's bungalow as I drifted from tears to sleep. Somewhere near dawn, consciousness came and went. Something had awakened me briefly. But it was only Marnie turning over. Perhaps her lips had brushed my cheek. She must have been trying to pull the pillows closer.

CHAPTER 20

Apocalypse Cometh

On the first of May, Mother Caritas summoned us back to Montecito for a lengthy ritual celebrating "Mary, Queen of the May." Waiting for the cars to return us to Los Angeles, Marlene Camp grabbed my arm. "Jeanne, I've been hearing things about you around campus."

"You're always hearing things, Camp. It's probably your own recycled gossip!"

"If it was, I wouldn't be warning you," my old cellmate huffed.

"You wouldn't warn me if the Apocalypse cometh!"

"Well, it is coming, and I care about your vocation . . . as a sister, anyway."

"So what's the warning? They're cancelling First Vows? We gonna say them in Russian? Frankly, Scarlett, I don't know that I give a damn anymore."

192

"Well you should care about your reputation as a nun!" Camp's palms rested righteously on her hips.

"What do you want, Camp?"

"Talk around IHC is that you're getting real tight with that . . . girl, Marnie Heathford!"

"Yeah, so what? I'm proud of it. Marnie's got more brains than our entire postulant class put together—present company included!"

"You don't know who she is?!"

". . . Of course I know who she is." I had no idea what Camp meant. *What was she trying to say about Marnie?* I knew my friend a hell of a lot better than she did.

"Then that's what I'm talking about. If you're particular friends with her, people will think the same of you. They already do."

"That's just fine with me. I wouldn't mind being thought of like her at all! She's going to be a nun too, you know. She'll be a welcome relief from the likes of some of the hypocrites they let in here." I turned to open the car door.

"You're outrageous, Jeanne!" Camp yelled at my back. "You're stupider than you are arrogant! I don't know why I bothered. I don't care what happens to you."

"Well, now, that's an honest sentence," I called over my shoulder. "Why don't we leave our conversation at that?"

Perplexed by Camp's ominous warning, I went to Marnie's the next night. The key was under the back door planter as usual, and I flipped on the stove to heat up water for some cocoa before settling on the bed. Summer was coming, and the air was stifling inside our cave. I lifted the blinds in back of her bed and opened the window. A little beige notebook fell and flipped open on the bed.

I saw my name. It was Marnie's diary! I stared at the dog-eared pages and thought of Camp. "Talk around campus is . . . " Marnie and I had said "no secrets." Hmmm . . . perhaps she wouldn't mind if I read it . . . as long as I told her when she came home.

The page was dated March nineteenth.

"Thank God, I met her again! I saw the young postulant I'd met months ago with Lauren David. She was sitting practically right outside my bungalow today! The kid was crying and seemed lost. I asked her over and we spent a lovely evening.

"Jeanne is so out of touch with reality, so confused about her own identity and her vocation. She really needs an older friend. Well . . . it wasn't all good Samaritanism. She's bright as hell and cutely naive. Lauren's going left me heartbroken. Jeanne is lonely too. Others around campus, even her postulant mates, shun her because she looks and dresses too masculine. I'm used to that, we're very much alike."

I knelt on the bed and looked at my reflection in the mirror on Marnie's bathroom door. What did she mean "too masculine"? Arriving earlier, I'd crawled into the long overshirt and baggy jeans she'd lent me. Naturally, I didn't wear such garb around campus. What could be "too masculine" about my postulant habit? Michelle probably wore something similar in her cell at Cathedral Chapel. It's true Louise looked like Sister Mary Zsa Zsa Gabor no matter what she wore. But she got in trouble for being "too feminine." Besides, nuns were supposed to be genderless; we transcended sexuality. I stared at my no-frills haircut. I looked rather neuter to me. There were even two little curls below my ears. It was getting long. The topic of dress in the convent was silly anyway. Once under the habit I would look just like the rest of my sisters—like a spirit.

I tucked my shirt in and lay back down to re-read the last section. I was a little shocked but not displeased that I was someone else's replacement. Lucky timing on my part. But what was Camp so concerned about? I flipped the pages to the last entry.

"Jeanne came over last night pissed as hell because her Superior pulled her out of the ghetto. She spent the night crying in my arms. She needed me to hold her. She didn't brush my hand away from her hair, she didn't withdraw. I put her to bed and she snuggled right up to me the whole night. I wanted to kiss her. I did once or twice while she slept, but she seemed far too upset earlier in the evening. I didn't want to risk traumatizing her, or losing her."

194

Watching the moonlight ripple shadows on my toes, I remembered being awakened that last night I spent with Marnie. I thought I'd imagined her lips brushed my cheek. I sipped my cocoa and smiled contently.

"God, I miss that with Lauren. The nights together, sharing a kiss. Probably just as well, though. I can hardly enter the convent if I keep wanting to kiss a girl. What if they knew that Lauren and I kissed? That a few years ago Anne Francis and I did too? God, they'd never let me in! I wonder if there's a question on that MMPI test, Have you ever kissed a girl? Couldn't be. I'm not like that anyway. I loved Lauren . . . and Anne. But I need to protect Jeanne and not get her into more trouble. Just as well not to open that door with Jeanne. The past is past. I didn't understand what all that was about with Lauren anyway.

"It's hard sleeping alone. Lauren couldn't get away that much, neither can Jeanne. Shit. I wish I wouldn't get involved with these nuns and all their restrictions. But it keeps happening. Undoubtedly because I want to be a nun myself."

Marnie worried herself to death about the stupidest things, I thought, closing the book on my stomach. Nuns kissed each other hello and goodbye all the time; I'd seen it. In fact, I'd come to realize nuns were a very huggy-and-kissy species. Friends were always rushing up to each other after a few weeks' absence, exclaiming and almost fawning. It wasn't unusual to see sisters holding hands. Teachers and Superiors often took my hands, especially when I was being lectured. Michelle and I kissed goodnight sometimes. What did Marnie mean by kissing? Antonia's kiss had felt . . . well, extraordinarily special. Why is it when you kiss some people on the cheek it feels like "see you later" and others—like Cathy or Antonia—it's just more, more . . . particular. I laughed inside, pleased with myself; *that's* the "particular" in particular friendships!

Anyway, I should let Marnie know nuns kiss all the time so she won't worry. I wish I'd been awake when she kissed me. Replacing Marnie's book, I set my cocoa cup on her side of the bed and rolled over to sleep on mine.

I mumbled and tried to wake up when Marnie returned late and crawled into bed. "Warn me about what, darling? You can hardly talk!" She laughed, bringing her pillow next to mine, and threw her arm around me.

"'bout me staying with you all night . . . or something. I need to tell you I read . . ."

"Jeanne! Did someone accuse us of having a particular friendship?" Marnie sat up.

"Marlene Camp 'accuses' me of breathing her air. But yeah, maybe that's what she was getting at. Is that what we're doing?" I was secretly charmed Marnie had used the intimate phrase to refer to our friendship. She'd never commented about our relationship before.

"I suppose so, yes," she said. "Listen, wake up, this is important."

"I can't, I'm exhausted . . . talk to you tomorrow. I need to tell you not to worry." I dozed happily. Perhaps she'd kiss me in my dreams again.

"I thought you said you were being very careful about leaving Vibiana's late like Michelle said and sneaking back in?"

"I am, I am, I am," I said, half-asleep on her arm. "Also . . . I love you."

Marnie mumbled, "Me too. But maybe we should cool it for a while, spend fewer nights together. I don't want you, or me, to get in any more trouble."

April passed. Cut off from my life in Watts, I grew more depressed. In Los Angeles I could find no evidence of spring. Not a daisy grew anywhere near Skid Row. My existence at Vibiana's was as desolate as the life of the Mexican woman who waited every twilight on the corner beneath my cell. There she dutifully met her despondent husband after his vain search for work. We both waited for a job, a future, a vision that never came, some sign that fate had not forgotten us.

By rote I entoned the catechism about a God with whom I was no longer in communication to youngsters who hardly spoke

English. I felt a similar barrier between me and my sisters at Vibiana's who spoke no English. I took the evening meal with them in unmandated silence. Silence had become a welcome protector.

Marnie was showing me her world, but it wasn't mine. Her caring made religious life more tolerable for me, but it couldn't stop my growing despondence.

My mind ceased asserting signs of life in Sister Fabian's philosophy class. I wasn't asking questions anymore. It had always been easy to lose myself in mental abstraction. Debating the nature of the soul before and after embodiment seemed profoundly irrelevant now. My only reality was Marnie. My only intellectual exercise was concocting excuses to leave Vibiana's after dinner. On nights when I could find no excuse, I'd wait until my elderly sisters retired to their cells and sneak down the flights of concrete and head for Hollywood and Marnie. When Marnie was busy at classes, I'd wait in her bungalow or visit my enclave and stare at the city veiled in smog. Mother Theresa never brought up the night I hadn't returned.

One afternoon I caught Michelle in the halls at school. We picnicked on the lawn and I told her about my overnight violations of the Holy Rule.

Michelle threw her sandwich crust at me, "Silly, that happens a lot!"

"You mean professed nuns do it?" I fell on the lawn, incredulous.

"Sure. At Cathedral Chapel, I know Sister Constance Marie does, and Luke Zoe doesn't come home at night herself sometimes!"

"Where does Constance Marie go?"

"I think to see her boyfriend. John Doe, she calls him."

"Where does Luke Zoe go?"

"Mostly to weekend political conferences, I guess. She's the regional director of the IHM Reformation Committee. She's also very tight with those anti-war hippies; so, she has a lot of meetings. She talks about politics constantly, but she never has much to say about her private business."

197

"Well, I'll be a horse's ass," I said, slapping my thigh.

"Jeanne, come to think of it, you always have been a little behind."

"How come I'm the last one to know such things? And, by the way, where do *you* go?"

"I stay down at work."

"In the ghetto?"

"No, we go over to Del's house in Garden Grove, in Orange County. To work. We organize the fund-raisers late at night and do a lot of . . . of the planning at her house. Annabelle and the others come over sometimes too. You can't be an effective social worker only three afternoons a week. It takes a lot of overtime."

"So it's 'Del' now? It was always Miss Martinez to me!" I exploded.

"We've just gotten to . . . know each other better, Jeanne." Michelle sounded proud of her new familiarity. She smoothed the creases in her postulant skirt with a blade of grass.

I put my jealousy away. I wanted to talk to Michelle about other things. "Yeah, I guess I can see where it takes a lot of overtime. I couldn't get my work done during the time I was there."

I stretched my sandwich's cellophane wrapper over my fingers and began poking at it. *Should I tell Michelle that Marnie sometimes held me during the night? Marnie and I didn't talk about this. I wondered if "Del" held Michelle? Of course not. After all, she was much older and Michelle's boss! When Michelle slept over, of course they slept in separate rooms. Martinez probably had a large house with several bedrooms. They didn't have as much in common as Marnie and I, school work and such. Michelle stayed down there because it was a thirty-five mile drive home from Orange County in the middle of the night. It was the safe thing to do.* I sighed and fell back on my elbows in the soft grass. I missed Imperial Courts.

"What do you do when you spend nights at Marnie Heathford's?" Michelle broke into my thoughts.

"I didn't say I spent *every* night there!"

"And I didn't say you said you did. Why are you so defensive?

What do you do . . . in the *evenings* then?"

"Her friends come over to study sometimes. Or we study alone, or play guitar, or go to a movie. Mostly we talk."

"Oh."

"Anyway, Micki, how do you get out and back in at Cathedral Chapel with the door locked?"

"That's easy!" Michelle leaned forward. "I leave after Compline at ten and return before morning chimes and Matins at six-thirty. No one is awake during that time. I go down the fire-escape ladder next to my room and come back the same way. Besides, at Cathedral Chapel, they don't want you to feel locked up. Everyone comes and goes. Luke Zoe and Constance just leave with a 'See ya later!'"

"Right. I can just see their flowing robes tumbling down the ladder and the men with a net below yelling, 'Jump, Sisters!'"

It wasn't so easy at Vibiana's. Mother Theresa was a traditional stay-in-your-cell Superior. I hadn't thought of Michelle's escape timetable, besides, Vibiana's had no fire escape. The thought of me and my keys clanging through the iron locks and down the concrete stairwells frightened me. I didn't have Michelle's steel nerves or subtle brain machinations. I was heeding Marnie's warning; we were keeping our overnights down to a minimum.

We were too late. The morning after I talked to Michelle, Mother Theresa handed me a letter from Margaret Rose. The Mistress of Postulants had left the night before with other IHM top brass on a two-week trip to Washington, D.C., for a conference on the Church and the war. I tore off the envelope's edge. I'd never received a personal letter from the Mistress of Postulants.

"Dear Jeanne, I wanted to see you before I left, but there were too many necessary preparations for our trip. So I take this opportunity to communicate with you and will see you when I return.

"It has come to my attention that you have been seen keeping frequent company with one of the secular students at the college. I

remind you and caution you about forming exclusive friendships. I must ask you to refrain from any association with Marnie Heathford until I return. I do not think this friendship can in anyway foster your vocation. As The Imitation of Christ reminds us, Jeanne, 'Desire to be familiar only with God and His angels, and fly the acquaintance of men.'

"Please try to use your time to be especially close with Mary Immaculate and let the Blessed Virgin guide your time and thoughts as we approach First Vows.

"God bless you, dear child. Mother Margaret Rose"

CHAPTER 21

The Blinking Red Light

Distorted by the eerie neon fog, the red light atop Los Angeles City Hall blinked on and off thirty-four times per minute. My heart beat with the signal as I lay there in my cell at St. Vibiana's.

Margaret Rose had returned and summoned me. Her monologue had been succinct. She repeated her letter; I observed silence. For six weeks, cut off from Watts, Michelle, and finally Marnie, I had no one to talk to. I was slipping deeper and deeper into depression.

Marnie had been warned not to see me anymore. A week after Margaret Rose's letter she had slipped a note into my hand as she paused next to me in a classroom aisle pretending to speak to someone else. It read:

"Sweetheart, I got turned down to enter the IHM's this fall. I guess you were right, I'm not nun material after all. I'm giving up.

I'm also leaving the college and transferring to a secular school after finals next month. I don't want anything to do with nuns anymore.

"I miss you terribly, but I don't want to jeopardize your vocation any more than I have already. So I'll say good-bye this way. What else can I do?

"Go with God . . . or maybe . . . just go!

"I love you, Marnie."

Or maybe just go. Marnie had left my life. The suddenness of her departure stunned me. Rising from bed, I went to the window, my eyes drifting over the city lights—searching. Memories of Marnie's favorite song, like the drizzle on the streets below, flooded my heart: "The joys of love are but a moment long/the pain of love endures a whole life long." Sleeping alone was much harder now. I woke up fitfully in the dawn, wondering why Marnie's arms weren't around me. Was our friendship as abhorrent to God as it seemed to be to the Holy Rule? Would the void of her ever go away?

Marnie had overestimated the state of my vocation. Life in the convent itself had jeopardized my vocation. It was only further decimated by her leaving.

Months ago, before I'd been yanked out of Watts, I somehow clung to the hope that getting Camp for a cellmate and drawing Vibiana's for a mission site were just tests of my faith. I was wandering a *temporary* desert of the soul. Any week God would lean down and say, "You passed, Jeanne," and I would be reprieved. Like the blinking red light, my vocation was eternal.

But finally, I had to acknowledge something was fundamentally wrong. Each dawn I awoke wishing I hadn't. In the conscious moment before my eyes opened I knew I couldn't go on. I tossed and turned every night. My stomach was knotted. Every morning I found the blankets crammed into the crack between the wall and my bed, as if I were trying to stuff them into a space in which they wouldn't fit. But it was I who didn't fit.

My initial task of the day was arguing with myself. Should I get out of bed?

Why bother?

Surely there must be something urgent for me to do, some important piece of life that needs my attention.

No. You have no life anymore.

I could go to my classes at college. I stretched my neck to see the small clock on my desk. Was it a school day or the weekend? Why couldn't I keep track of simple things like days of the week anymore? It used to be so important to know what time it was.

When did time start slipping away, Jeanne?

Was it when I first came to Vibiana's? It was so dark in here, I couldn't tell day from night. But no, I was interested in time when I was seeing Marnie. I used to watch the clock all night until it was time for me to go visit her. Maybe time started evaporating after Margaret Rose's letter.

At first I just lost a day here and there. I noticed the weekends because I was supposed to mop the corridors of Vibiana's on Saturdays. The last time I had mopped I wondered if I had skipped a week—would there be twice as much dust? Or did dust condense so that my sisters wouldn't notice two layers, or three, or four. I stopped mopping the dust away. Time would.

I'm sure I should be *doing* something.

Perhaps you could brush your teeth.

No, there is something much more important. My chest pounded, heaving rapidly. If I don't figure out what I'm supposed to be doing I'm afraid my heart will burst. Maybe I'm suffocating! I yanked my blankets out of the crack.

Why are you so terrified?

The days preceding finals dragged by. Somehow my mind read and memorized words in my text. In spite of my mental state, finishing my freshman year seemed strangely mandatory. I no longer opened my mouth in class, but studying still came easy. Passing tests did not require my emotional presence.

203

Time washed the days away somehow, immersing me back into reality at dusk. Every night I lit my sputtering candle in the window sill and lay on my bed, staring into the night, into the blinking red light. Being a nun was all there had ever been for me. There was no other life. And yet I was contemplating leaving the convent.

What is the process of falling in love? I beseeched my blinking nocturnal companion. It seemed an inexplicable obsession. Had I spent a lifetime coming to my Lover only to find He was an illusion? Could my vocation have been a gossamer deception spun out of endless hours of childhood fantasy? I thought the habit and Gregorian chant were redemptive separations. The seclusion of the novitiate was supposed to allow me to build a foundation for my internal Church. I was promised protection by the sacred vows and solace in the sisterhood of a holy family.

What *fraudulence!* Immutable Holy Mother the Church had simply changed her mind. I had poured my faith into a sacred vessel—but found that it leaked.

In the candlelight, I wept in despair and tried to pray, *Where are You, my Lord and Savior? Please, answer me. It's only been ten months, but it feels like ten years. Tell me, Jesus, why have I lost my appetite, why can't I get out of bed?*

And why is Mass an empty chalice now? Mass was my transcendence with You. That's when we always talked. That's when You always loved me. Remember me in my softball uniform, You in your radiant magic?

I have no reason to receive Communion anymore. It was Your Body and Blood to me. But I don't feel anything now. Does this mean I've lost my faith? What have I done to fall so far from Grace? You promised—'Fear not; for I am with thee even unto the end of the world. I will never leave thee or forsake thee. Yea, if you walk through the valley of the shadow of death, I will be with thee.'"

I screamed at the blinking red light, "I've been in the valley of the shadow of death for months!

Maybe Mother Caritas had been right from the beginning. I

204

was psychologically unfit for religious life. She'd said, "Individual personality has *no* place . . ." Yet I didn't want to melt into this anonymous cauldron of collectivity. I couldn't help but feel Jeanne Córdova had a place—*some* place. I couldn't make myself believe this was the "Way, the Truth, and the Light."

I couldn't take the pariah role, people shunning me and whispering behind my back. Was I that different? Too masculine, as Marnie had suggested? What did femininity have to do with spirituality?

It seemed important, in the candle's glow each night, to watch the transients on Skid Row below. Perhaps my observation kept them alive. It kept me alive. All used up, they drifted from corner to corner.

Where do they go? Where do I go?

Of course! I blew out the candle so I could see their silhouette against the street lamps. They're waiting. Waiting for a miracle. A sign from Someone who isn't paying attention. They're in prison and they know it. At least Skid Row *looked* like a prison—paneless windows, used needles. Their prison was poverty, but what was mine?

Pulling the dingy curtains back to get a clearer view, I accidentally knocked my cob-webbed *Imitation of Christ* off the window sill. I opened the tattered bible of my religious life: "Son, see thou dispute not the hidden judgments of God. These things are above the reason of man, neither can any discourse penetrate into the judgment of God."

No reason could penetrate into the mind of God because there was nothing to penetrate. There was no reason, no judgment, no God. Oogie would wind up in jail for the rest of his life; Dude and Pamela would stand before a Justice of the Peace and he'd leave her with six kids, seven years later; Geraldine would never become a beautician. And I would not be a nun.

"It happens all the time!" I tried to shout through my window at the old Mexican woman below. On that Friday, five weeks ago, the

205

day Marnie had slipped me her note, her husband had not returned to their corner. And he had never appeared since then. Yet she still came, night after night, same as before. Her denial enraged me. I wanted to reach down from my prison, shake her desolate shoulders and scream, "Stop coming here, you fool! He's never coming back."

And neither was my past. My rage reached the core of me—and snapped. I threw the *Imitation of Christ* against the cell door.

That night I didn't watch the blinking red light. I closed the worn-out curtains on the McPherson Leather Company and crawled into bed. I felt a terrible wrenching in my shoulders; my nun atoms were splitting, the musculature of my body was restructuring. It was too late to go back.

But what did going forward mean? I sat upright in bed. Should I drop out of college and become a vagrant, a belated teenage runaway, an ex-postulant soda jerk? I used to gauge where I was going by where I had been. But my past was dead. In what direction was my future?

My feet were cold. I fell out of bed and crawled to my closet searching for socks through the rubble on the floor. Ahhh! I sat in my closet and stared at the object of my attention. Perhaps forward was my rust-colored suitcase!

I grabbed the luggage and threw it on my bed. Madly, I ripped my dresser drawers free, flipped them over my suitcase and dumped out their contents. Time enough to fold things properly when I unpacked later.

Later. Where would that be?

Don't stop, Jeanne.

I scooped all the dirty socks, my rosaries, songbooks, and spider webs from the bottom of my closet. I heaped them on top of my underwear in the suitcase.

Later doesn't matter. Now is happening. Now has to happen

206

before Margaret Rose leaves to teach her classes at 8 A.M. tomorrow morning. Now is tonight!

I grabbed the crucifix over my bed, retrieved my *Imitation of Christ* and dropped them on top of my socks and cobwebs. They were souvenirs, now.

CHAPTER 22

Silent No More

Margaret Rose's wire-rimmed spectacles slid sanctimoniously off her nose and fell into the crack of her open prayer book. "What did you say, my child?" The Mistress of Postulants blinked, trying to locate me.

"I said, 'I quit.'" I stood with my weight even on both feet and my hands clasped behind my back. "I won't be making First Vows this summer."

Margaret Rose wanted to talk. I leaned against the back of the mahogany chair and wondered how many other nuns, or postulants, had stood in this Motherhouse and announced the end of their religious lives. All the furniture in the room was old and stuffy—the set for a mystery I no longer needed to solve. I observed my former jailer coldly. She looked much older now as she droned on about vows, vocation, and volition in the love of God.

Finally the Mistress of Postulants asked, "Where will you go, Jeanne?"

"I haven't the slightest idea, Mother!" I laughed aloud with an exuberance I thought had died so many months ago. "I'll think of something. I'm not afraid anymore." I wasn't. My world, my past, had been annihilated. I had nothing more to lose. All I had left was one semester of college education and my name.

I hadn't been able to sleep all night. Just after sunrise, I'd clanked down the stairwell and jumped into the car. Gunning the motor, I'd taken off for a last good-bye to IHC before going to see Margaret Rose.

I'd passed my last final a week ago. Classes had recessed for the summer. The secular students had left only days ago, and the postulants were awaiting orders to return to Montecito for the summer to go on retreat and make First Vows.

My enclave was deserted. So was Marnie's bungalow. It was already rented to someone new for the summer session. Why hadn't I had the nerve to at least go up to Marnie and ask her for her address before she left? A month ago that seemed a futile move as well as horrendous disobedience. Now I was free, but she was gone.

Los Angeles sprawled like a rampant ground cover below the hills of Immaculate Heart. This would be my first summer in a big city. That is, it would be if I could somehow concoct a way to remain in L.A.

I curled into the bench where Marnie had first offered me her censured particular friendship. There was still a little piece of God in this particularly lovely spot. Briefly, the tears returned. I should probably go report to Father Sullivan that I wouldn't be making sainthood after all. "But I'll be back someday," I promised the guardian weeping willow, " . . . someday when it doesn't hurt so much." I swallowed my past, this was not the time for another silly adolescent vow.

I leapt off the bench and strode to the edge of the cliff. The

209

willow branch whipped across my neck, snagging my crucifix chain. Trying to free it, I broke the chain. "What the hell!" I said, laughing as I threw the cross down the cliff into the urban jungle. "I won't be needing this anymore."

Arms folded, I studied my new home. Somewhere out there in the grit and anonymity I would have to find a place to live, some clothes, money, a car, a job, and, hopefully, some friends. These were real problems.

"I won't go back home to my parents house," my words catapulted down the hillside. "I'm gonna stay in L.A. where I belong!"

Thinking of living with my parents made me depressed. The thought of having a place of my own, making friends, and being free to come and go made me breathe freely. Since I'd made my decision to leave, I'd felt a strange new confidence and clarity. I had a new way of looking at things now. My *feelings* had become my barometer.

Standing in front of Margaret Rose, I didn't want to tell her of my impractical but firm decision to forge a new life in Los Angeles. Mother Superior was no longer privy to my future plans. "Perhaps I'll see what my parents want me to do, Mother," I answered. "They'll probably send me to college somewhere."

"That's wise, Jeanne. Maybe a few years in college will give you time to hear God's will for your future."

"I finally know my own will, Mother."

Margaret Rose stared at me for some time. "I'll send for your personal belongings from Montecito, Jeanne. They should be at Vibiana's within the week. Please wait outside for a few moments while I write Mother Theresa a letter saying you are leaving."

"Yes, of course, Mother." I stopped staring at her spectacles and turned to go.

I bounced out of Margaret Rose's office and began pacing the sidewalk outside. Getting into a convent took some doing, and staying in was excruciating, but, when you were finished, the agony was suddenly lifted. *Damn, that was easy!* The simplest thing about my vocation was leaving it. There was no death ritual for a shattered dream.

I picked up the *L.A. Times* that was lying on the bench outside Rose's office. I should save it and start looking for a job! Maybe the hard part was just beginning. Maybe, as usual, I'd overestimated myself. Money would be a problem. How would I feed myself? Adele Martinez had told me Cal State L.A. offered the best Pre-Social Welfare B.A. in Southern California. How much money would I need to earn to afford three more years of college? Dad always said France's Stanford, "cost an arm and a head." He had a nasty parental habit of only paying for things he approved of, and he would not approve of the indecency of a young girl living alone in the prurient urban jungle.

Quickly, I looked in my purse and scribbled in the tiny notebook I'd been carrying around—"Call Cal State: tuition money?" My small pad had filled up rapidly overnight. There were so many things I didn't know. Where to mail a letter? How to buy a car? A studio like Marnie's must cost several weeks' salary. Where would I live until I got a job?

I stopped pacing and sat to calm myself. One agenda at a time, I reasoned. Perhaps it would be easier if I went home, just for the summer, long enough to get a job. Dad would be less than pleased when I announced I wanted to be a professional social worker. A poor boy turned millionaire, last summer he had slammed the morning paper down on the breakfast table criticizing President Johnson's CETA programs by saying, "Welfare doesn't cure poverty, it maintains it!" I also doubted my parents would approve of my new friends. Michelle certainly wouldn't drive all the way to West Covina to visit me.

No, returning to West Covina would be like falling into a coma. Trying to pretend that the last ten months hadn't happened was impossible. I was a different person now. I had to make a space in the world, to find a new reason to be alive.

My former Mother Superior rang her bell. Silently I entered her office for the last time and received her letter to Mother Theresa. Margaret Rose looked at me wistfully. "You are sure, child, you don't have a vocation?"

"I am sure, Mother, that my vocation is not here, not now."

Margaret Rose nodded. I saw the sad kindness in her affirmation. "Yes, I think you are right about that." Mother Superior always seemed to know things she wouldn't say. She had larger problems than me to worry about—her order's own dilemma, an entire way of life now caught between a past they couldn't return to and a future that was becoming present, too quickly. My struggle was over, but that of the IHM's would continue. In a moment of guilt I looked away. For better or for worse they had been my family.

"*Dominus vobiscum.*" Rose stretched out her hand and took mine.

"*Et cum spiritus tuo.*" I clasped hers. Turning to go, I strode hurriedly toward the door, smacking the *L.A. Times* against my leg. The smarting kept me from crying.

Saying good-bye always hurts, even when you're leaving of your own free will, I confided to my blinking red light that night. At long last, my light was green. I was no longer on hold, but tomorrow there was still the inescapable necessity of the pilgrimage home to tell Mom. I'd called that morning to say I was coming home for dinner and wanted to talk. In the awkward silence at her end of the line I heard Mom decide not to ask why I was coming home so abruptly for an unscheduled visit.

Would Mom be devastated or nonchalant? I'd always had the feeling my father thought nuns and priests were made of far more supernatural stuff than any of his offspring. If Mom asked the reasons I'd left how could I explain? I didn't even really know what had happened to my vocation. I only knew I wasn't in love anymore. Then too, leaving the convent was one thing. If I told them I'd stopped going to Mass, if I told them I didn't believe in God anymore, they'd drag me back home for certain.

It was late that Sunday before Mom had gotten the kids to bed and it was quiet enough for us to go into the living room alone. Other than the living room, the rest of the house was in shambles with boxes everywhere. In my depression, I had completely forgotten the main topic of Mom's recent letter. The family was moving to San Marino, a ritzy suburb south of Pasadena. Dad had bought a mansion. That evening, walking around the old West Covina kitchen, I said good-bye to the only childhood home I had ever remembered. Their move confirmed my decision. My parents' home was my past.

The living room was Limbo—the Catholic way station for souls-in-waiting. Methodically, my fingers tucked my postulant skirt down into the cracks of the living room sofa. Mom sat in her floral-patterned armchair, facing me across the marble coffee table. She hadn't turned on the light because the proper time for adult conversation was somewhere after sunset and before moonrise—twilight.

We sat in the shadows.

"It's good to have you home again with us after so long, Jeanne," she offered.

"It's nice to be back," I called vacantly to her outline. Should I turn on the light? No, perhaps it was better this way. Mom always knew best.

"How is your vocation coming along?" Mom was studied yet casual—decorum was the essence of her persona. "First Vows are this summer aren't they? Do you find collective life agreeable? Is there anything you need from us?"

"Yes, Mom, I mean no, Mom. I mean yes, First Vows are this summer. No, I really don't need anything. Actually, I need everything! My vocation isn't coming along. I'm not making vows this summer, Mom. I've decided to leave."

"The convent?" Mom's coffee saucer did not jiggle in her hand, and her other hand continued tracing the armchair pattern. Two summers ago I'd passed by the pool in our backyard and noticed my baby brother Tom floating lifelessly in the water. As I yelled, Mom walked out the back door, flung herself into the pool, grabbed Tom like a sack of wet beans, threw him to the ground, revived him with artificial respiration, and then returned to the preparation of the evening meal, telling me to snap the lock on the pool fence. A week later, she broke down in delayed hysteria.

"Yes, Mom. I am leaving the convent."

"I thought that was what you came to tell us." Mom let our climax fall on the coffee table. *I should have known she knew.*

"Oh." My shoulders drooped. "Then you're not upset, and you won't be upset later either?"

"It's not for me to be disappointed. A vocation comes from within; Grace must be given by God."

"You seemed nonchalant about my entering in the first place."

"That wasn't nonchalance. It was detachment. Your father and I were dispassionate, then as now, because we didn't want you to feel your parents encouraged you. Nor do we want you to feel like a failure if it didn't work out. There are many years between postulancy and taking final vows for a very good reason, Jeanne. It's not like encouraging France to be a physicist or go to Stanford rather than M.I.T. A vocation, a spiritual calling from God, is really none of *our* business. Besides, you don't have to be a nun or a priest to be close to God. Great saints such as Christopher were lay people.

"It would have been nice if God wanted it that way, but I've been close to Dear Aunt Sister and other religious for many years now. So I know if a vocation doesn't bring internal happiness it's an impossible life. Dear Aunt Sister's life has been filled with peace and enriching love."

"Good . . . I suppose." I didn't know whether I should feel reprieved or guilty, regarding her sermon on Dear Aunt Sister. I breathed into the stillness between us. I was dumbstruck by the exclusively spiritual interpretation of her emotions. It was my mother who should have become a nun. I also felt let down. Part of me wanted her to ask me what really happened, to ask me to explain, to show her my tears. But maybe she was right, a vocation comes from within and doesn't need an explanation. I should be grateful she wasn't calling upon me for one; no deep metaphysical exploration, no tears or ranting and raving. Mom's naivete coupled with her piety, her deep love juxtaposed with her emotionally detached demeanor, combined to present a perplexing human being.

"I'm glad you told me, Jeanne. I've been feeling you were going through something hard lately. You stopped writing. Were you hurt or angry at something? Was this a rash emotional decision?"

"No, Mom, I don't think it's rash. I've thought about it for months now. It just wasn't what I thought it would be. It took me a long time to figure things out. By the way, I told them to keep the dowry—for their troubles with me." I laughed.

"That's fine. I'm sure your father wants it that way. What did you figure out, Jeanne?" Mom was getting close. If I wasn't careful, in a moment she'd have me dropping clues about my lack of faith, the death of my prayer life, my atheism, or my particular friendships.

"A lot of it was all the changes wrought by Pope John. With the habit and the Latin gone, and religious wanting to be part of the real world, I just figured, What's the point? Why not just be part of the real world?"

"Your father and I don't approve of what is happening in Rome these days. Vatican II has been the cause of many religious' leaving."

"Yes, I know, in the IHM's, many are leaving."

"Well, I must say, I'm not surprised you didn't stay with those IHM's, as you call them. I've read about them in the paper and they seem like kooks to me!" My mother returned her coffee cup to the table. "Letting you and that friend of yours, Michelle, drive down to see us over Valentine's Day. And that day I had lunch with you at your campus, I saw a nun dressed in a veil and an orange sweat shirt and a common skirt! There's not much stability there. That's not religious life."

I wasn't comfortable with Mom insulting my order. *Revolutions are unstable sometimes, you have to give them a chance!* I muttered to myself, wanting to rally for a political argument. But I realized I hadn't discussed my growing liberalism with my parents. This evening they might attempt to decide what to do with the rest of my life. It was not the time to get caught in the West Covina trenches. "I guess they got carried away a bit," I agreed. "Or maybe it was just that I don't do well in collective life. I might be happier out on my own." I threw my shoulders back.

"I don't know what you mean by 'out on my own.' I thought you'd be coming home." "Ah, no, not really. I want to live in Los Angeles and go back to work as a social worker in Watts. I wrote you about how much I loved working there. I could be offered a job there again. Miss Martinez said she was looking for an opening for me."

"Who is this person?" Mom interrupted my slightly fabricated future. I hadn't had a chance to ask Martinez to find a way for me to go back to Watts. When I left, she had offered to help me find a job . . . if I ever needed one. One thing I'd learned from Michelle was that anything could happen, especially if you acted like it already had.

"Adele Martinez, you know. She was my boss down there. Remember, I wrote you?"

"Well I don't know, Jeanne," Mom said, reaching for her coffee cup, holding it in front of her face as if she could divine my future in the coffee grounds. "I'll have to speak to your father. You know he thinks single girls should live at home."

"Mom, that's so medieval! France lives alone at college."

"She lives in a dorm."

"Perhaps I could live in the dorms at Cal State L.A. That's where I want to get my B.A. anyway."

"That's not a private school. I don't approve of men and women living in the same dorm."

216

"I have to go to college somewhere!" I noticed the room was getting darker.

"That's the first thing you've said your father will agree with."

"Well, I'm not coming home to live!" I jerked my postulant skirt out of the sofa and crossed my legs.

"Joan!" My father slid open the living room door and poked his tired head through it. "I'm going to bed, are you coming soon?"

"Yes, Fred, very soon."

"Goodnight, Daughter," Dad called out formally to me. "Good to see you again. Tell them to let you come home more often," he joked, closing the door on us. Poor Dad, he had a communication barrier with the world and his children. Mom would interpret later. For the moment, I was relieved the difficult conversation was not including him. He might have said, "Córdovas never quit! Get back in there and try harder."

Mom had risen with her coffee cup and motioned to me to restore the chairs back to their usual positions. "Do you want to tell me any more about your decision, Jeanne?"

"No, not really, Mom. Just try to get Dad to let me go to school and live in L.A. Please!"

"I was referring to your decision about the convent."

"Oh. I don't know what else to say, Mom." Standing with coffee cups in the living room did not seem conducive to further discussion. "I guess it will take me a long time to understand it. Maybe it's like you said, I just don't have a vocation."

"Perhaps, Jeanne. Perhaps. God speaks to us in strange ways, you know. So I guess we'll leave it in His hands for now."

"No, Mom," I declared silently, following her back out into the kitchen's bright fluorescence, *this time we'll leave it in my hands!*

CHAPTER 23

Peyton Place:
The Swinging Chapel

"This time, we'll leave it in my hands!" Michelle demanded. Her enthusiasm was always at a fever pitch when she engaged in her true vocation, manipulation. "It will work, I tell you."

"It's a locomotive idea, Micki. I love it, but it's nuts." I guffawed as we scurried down Vibiana's dank hall toward my cell.

"So what? The IHM's specialize in new lifestyles for religious. Things are such a mess with the Cardinal, Mother General has more important things to do than track a missing ex-postulant."

Michelle had appeared that morning, banging on the downstairs door where months ago I had first introduced myself to Calvin. "Jeanne, let me in. This is some hell hole." Michelle was breathless as we climbed the fourth flight of stairs. I slammed the last iron gate in back of us. "It looks like the Skid Row Development Center."

"It *was* good training for the vow of poverty."

"Listen, those days are over for you. I've got a wonderful plan, the answer to all our prayers!"

"I haven't had an answer to a prayer since I entered the convent, Micki." I laughed at her excitement and my own as Michelle detailed her plan. It was wonderful to feel excited about my future.

As I shut my cell door behind us, Michelle grabbed me around the neck. "Weep no more," she exclaimed, "I've talked to Luke Zoe, my Superior. Sister Mary Bernardette left Cathedral Chapel last week."

"Why?"

"How should I know? Even the professed are dropping like flies these days. Things are in such turmoil. I think McIntyre wishes the whole order would leave the Church. Luke Zoe says that might happen someday. She's at the center of all this because she's our regional coordinator to the IHM Reformation Assembly. She says the whole order is splitting into two camps."

"What two camps?"

"I don't follow politics, Jeanne, just gossip." Michelle sat on my bed thoughtfully and crossed her knees. "Ask Luke Zoe yourself. All I know is that the Cardinal is in one camp and Cathedral Chapel is in the other. Cathedral Chapel is *your* new camp!"

"I just left the convent. I'm not in any camp."

"Even the laity is choosing sides. But I didn't come to this grizzly hole to talk politics. I'm trying to tell you that you can come live in Mary Bernadette's empty room. Luke Zoe is offering you a home. Come live at Cathedral Chapel!"

I leaned against my prison window. "You mean I, Jeanne Córdova, ex-postulant, am going to leave one convent and go live in another?"

"Yes. Except you won't be a nun there."

"What the hell would I be then? *Nuns* live in convents!"

"Luke Zoe believes in the ecumenical concept that a spiritual

219

community is for everyone. She believes nuns and lay people, and even priests, should live together. So I told her that you, my particular friend, had no particular place to live, but you wanted to stay in L.A. and be a social worker."

"Michelle, your spiritual gall is unbelievable!"

"So, start packing!"

"I'm already packed, Micki." I waved my arm toward the empty desk and bookshelf. "But this is too strange. Aren't we breaking some rule? Doesn't someone have to give permission?"

"Now is no time for *you* to start worrying about rules. What do you care about permission anymore? You're a free adult!" Michelle stood up and began pacing my cell.

"Shit, I could get used to this. I guess we have Luke Zoe's permission. I'll do it!" I jumped on my bed, arms flailing.

"Mother Theresa will never know where you went."

"What about rent? Since I'm not in the order it wouldn't be right if I didn't pay rent. What about my food?"

"I've got that covered. You get to teach Sister Bernadette's summer school shift in the afternoons, and that will pay your food and rent, Luke says."

"I hate teaching in an academic setting."

"That's the other part about being a free adult."

"I know, it's called 'get a job'"

"Do you have other big-time employment lined up?"

"Sure, Cesar Chavez called this morning. He's got a top organizing position for me!"

"Right. I'll tell Luke Zoe it's yes on teaching, yes on living."

"I'm off Skid Row." I bounced mercilessly on my dingy brown spread. "Halleluja!"

Michelle pulled me down. "First, *I'm* out of here. Unlock my way out of this pit. I'm on my way to Watts, but here's the address and directions to Cathedral Chapel. See you tonight, my sweet!"

That evening, I stood once more on Main Street with my rust-colored suitcase. I had no personal chauffeur this time. I saluted my dismal little corner of the world good-bye and hopped the bus for Hollywood.

Cathedral Chapel convent rested comfortably in a residential neighborhood of similar structures and immaculately manicured lawns. The two-story graceful adobe was formerly a large mansion. Letting myself into the unlocked back door, I stumbled into what appeared to be a family den. Seven or eight female bodies were comfortably slouched, sprawled, and huddled in sweat shirts, cotton skirts and pedal pushers. They were watching television. With large glass windows, lush green plants hanging from the ceiling, and a rich burgundy Persian rug, Cathedral Chapel felt luxurious and warm.

"Hi, Jeanne, welcome. Have a sofa," a husky voice called out.

"Hi there!" several other voiced echoed. Everyone seemed glued to the television set.

The husky call came again, "Michelle called to say she'd be home in a few minutes. Come wait for her. Join us. *Peyton Place* is on."

I finally recognized the vibrant gravel of Sister Luke Zoe's voice. The orange wisps of hair I'd seen strands of that first day at the college were now abundantly released from her veil. Mother Superior Luke Zoe was in a powder-blue bathrobe with turquoise pedal pushers.

"Where are all the professed?" I asked Michelle when she arrived moments later. "What are all these lay people doing here late at night? I thought I was the only lay person living here."

"You are," Michells whispered, trying not to distract the room's inhabitants from their TV obsession. "These *are* the professed. The blond sitting next to Marie Therese is a secular. We get to have our friends visit us here."

"Hush up on the back sofa, please, we can't hear Mia Farrow," someone chided from one of the front rows.

I couldn't hide my naivete. "They're watching *Peyton Place*, and they're serious!"

"Sometimes I think Cathedral Chapel is *Peyton Place*."

221

Michelle cradled my arm protectively in her own.

My cell was a sunny room at the front of the house overlooking the lawn. A large window was framed by yellow rose bushes. It reminded me of France's and my bedroom in West Covina. It was three times the size of my cell at Vibiana's. My single bed came with a bright yellow-and-white striped quilt. I disliked both yellow and stripes, but after the somber brown of Vibiana's, and the starch white of Montecito, stripes were a joy.

Luke Zoe, the woman to whom I owed so much, also introduced me to my first job two days later. Like most of Luke's overtures, the gift came through Michelle.

"Luke says you probably need some spending money, so here's a start." Michelle sauntered into my room and dumped seven boxes of envelopes on my bed.

"So now I'm the post office?"

"It's the Beverly Hills *Blue Book*. You hand address each envelope from this list. You get a nickel per envelope." As Michelle slammed my door with a grin I couldn't tell whether she was serious or if this was a new punch line to an old joke. Me, Miss Cesar Chavez, addressing envelopes for the rich? But she was serious.

I became serious about my envelopes, too. I was thrilled to be earning money and urgently added up thousands of nickels per week. I had responsibilities. I needed a car and money to return to college in the fall. I was happy being *in* the convent but not *of* the convent. The beautifully tiled kitchen at Cathedral Chapel was filled with boisterous chatter all evening, every evening. I never thought the sound of English would be so pleasing to my ears, the smell of baked cookies and breads so welcomed. The average age of the nuns at my new home was late twenties. In her mid-thirties, Luke Zoe's extraordinary dynamism set a jovial but responsible tone.

Two of the nuns were much older, throw backs to ancient Christendom, just like those at Vibiana's. They walked about

222

silently in full habit, and more than once I caught them shaking their heads when someone announced, "Constance Marie is not coming home tonight," or "Luke Zoe wants us to clean out this place and have a garage sale next Sunday!" The older sisters, Marie Julian and Dominic Savio, lived upstairs and were accorded a great deal of personal respect.

But Cathedral Chapel was also very much a convent. At breakfast we welcomed Christ into our day, each evening we said good-night holding hands in a circle. Ironically, my only real experience of community was at the Swinging Chapel as we rocked one another gently and sang, "We are one in the Spirit/We are one in the Lord/ . . . and they'll know we are Christians by our love/By our love . . . " I didn't know if "Christian" was still a label that applied to me, but the sisterhood warmed my nights.

As for the Holy Rule at Cathedral Chapel, I assumed Luke Zoe was rewriting it as she went along. She obviously had the almost unanimous support of her adoring cadre, myself included.

Each morning I bounced out of bed and took up my pen-and-ink contribution to Beverly Hills society life. In the afternoons, I walked across the convent's backyard into the grade school where for weeks I had my kids building the world on their desks. In papier mache, that is. I figured, what better way to find out where everything on the planet was than to have to put it there yourself? Luke Zoe was enthused about my creativity and told the janitor not to bother with my classroom.

Evenings were spent doing the dishes—my chore—playing cards, and watching *Peyton Place*. Eagerly, I awaited Michelle's return from Watts three nights a week and badgered her to tell Del Martinez I wanted a job. "Any job!" I pleaded.

One Saturday found me looking in the local paper. I had seventy-three dollars, and I wanted to buy a car. Not that I had any place to go, but the other nuns sometimes went to movies, and Michelle said we could if we had a car. My main motivation was to return to Watts. As a professional social worker, I would need my own transportation.

There was only one car in the paper within my budget: "'53 Chevy, orange and yellow, souped, lots of miles, runs good. Body needs work. $75." Orange and yellow wasn't a color scheme I'd seen around a lot, but I was thrilled my seventy-three dollars would include paint. I dialed, and after some language difficulties that required all ten of the Spanish words in my vocabulary, the young man insisted on coming right over.

I was hoping Michelle or Luke Zoe would be present at my first major financial negotiation. I hadn't told the guy I was two dollars short. When the coughing orange-and-yellow bomb pulled up in front of the convent, I was grateful no one was home.

Prudently, I walked around the car several times. "Body needs work" was obvious. I caressed the caved-in left rear bumper, no sense making more of that. The automobile was very large. That's good, I rationalized—it'll be safe. "What does 'souped' mean?" I asked Miguel Sanchez.

"See that fancy wheel?" Miguel pointed.

It was then that I noticed the miniscule, six-inch steering wheel with a cheap blue diamond in its hub. "Isn't this wheel a bit small for such a large car, Miguel?"

"No, shit. All the guys want this kind of wheel. This is where it's at, mon!"

I agreed with Miguel about the wheel's location. I surveyed it more closely. It was firmly bolted in. At least I'd get some arm exercise.

"What's that stick coming out of the wheel, Miguel?" I continued.

"What stick?"

"This piece." I sat behind the wheel and grabbed what looked like an extra large turn signal.

Miguel looked at me oddly. "That's the transmission, mon!" The house car at St. Vibiana's didn't have a transmission stick. Miguel seemed indisposed to teaching me anything further, so I moved into our final negotiation.

"It's fine, I'll take it. I have seventy-three dollars." Enthusiastically, I waved the bills in front of him.

"Oh, mon, that's no good!" Miguel was not happy. I got to take the bus home. It costs a dollar."

"I'll take you home in the car, and save you a dollar, that'll be seventy-four dollars. I'll mail you the extra dollar next week when I get paid. Here, write down your address for me."

Miguel eyed Cathedral Chapel with its crucifix hanging on the front door. "You live in this convent, you a nun?"

"Yes," I lied, hoping Holy Mother the Church would at least be useful for some material purpose.

"Oh, mon, forget the dollar. Just take me home." Miguel concluded our arrangement, grabbing my seventy-three dollars and handing me a small pink piece of paper.

"What's this for?" I asked.

"What a dumb broad!" Miguel was getting testy as he slid in behind *my* souped steering wheel and gunned the engine. "It means you own the car now." He grabbed my pink paper, opened the glove compartment and threw it in. I slid into the passenger seat and tried to close the glove compartment.

"It doesn't close," I offered as Miguel hurled us down La Brea Avenue.

"No problema. Try it later. You got money for gas?" Miguel pulled into a station.

"No, I don't." I was flustered now. "I gave you everything I had."

Somewhere, Miguel found a quarter, and somehow I figured out what to do with the transmission stick as I careened out of East L.A. and back to Hollywood. Rattled, but proud, I jerked into Cathedral Chapel's lot.

Michelle was right about Cathedral Chapel—it was the Swinging Chapel. I couldn't follow the intricacies of *Peyton Place* because I was much too absorbed with Sister Constance Marie's midnight arrivals, Michelle's increasing non-arrivals from Watts, eavesdrop-

225

ping on Luke Zoe's political friends, and the shaky cease-fire between the vociferous Dominic Savio and the liberal majority. My new bomb had trouble starting in the mornings, so I added junior mechanics to my new-found skills and spent Saturdays repairing my first adult possession. Life around me had more sub-plots than *Peyton Place.*

I'd been at Cathedral Chapel almost a month when Michelle finally brought word from Del Martinez about a real job. Del's boss, Joe Vargas, the head of the Catholic Youth Organization, had another center in East L.A. He was looking to hire a group leader. I was to start the first of July. I scribbled envelopes from dawn till dusk, listened to Michelle's gossip, and saved my nickels to buy real clothes so I wouldn't be embarassed at my first real job.

The phone rang for the ninth time that night. But no one in the room appeared to hear its insistence. It was ten after nine on a Tuesday night, *Peyton Place* night. Ryan O'Neal was about to tell Mia, his wife, he'd consorted with her best friend.

I tossed my envelopes on the sofa beside me. Mrs. Rose Waxenberg on Bel Air Drive would have to wait. I couldn't stand the phone ringing.

Using Mom's best etiquette, I slid into the tiny phone booth closet next to the kitchen, grabbed the receiver and said, "Hello, may I help you, please?"

"What a wonderfully sweet way to answer the phone. Who is this?" The woman's voice was inviting.

"This? Oh, this is me, this is Jeanne."

"Jeanne, who? I don't remember you, did we meet?"

"I don't think so. Who is this?" What a silly question, I thought. How would I know if I met someone I didn't know.

"I'm Connie O'Malley." She paused. "Sister Luke Zoe's friend?" Connie O'Malley paused some more.

"No, I don't think so."

"Well, you've probably heard Luke speak of me?" I was shocked at a lay person's familiar use of Luke Zoe's name. She

226

must be a very good friend.

"No . . . Mother Luke Zoe hasn't spoken of you to me. And . . . she's not here tonight. Should I tell her you called?"

"Mother Luke Zoe, huh!? You must be new!" Connie O'Malley was playful. "So, Jeanne, what's your last name? Where do you come from? Who are you?"

"Córdova is my last name. I used to be a postulant and live in another convent, but now I'm not . . . and now I live here."

"Now that's one for the books. How did this happen?" Briefly, I broke down my strange tale into credible segments. Connie recognized Michelle's name when I told her we were friends, and was soon grilling me about that friendship. I wondered why Michelle hadn't mentioned Connie O'Malley to me.

Peyton Place was long over and in the background I heard my sisters sauntering to and fro in the kitchen. I closed the phone booth door and sat on the bench.

"Getting stuck with that awful bitch for a cellmate sounds terrible, and then being so isolated. Are you still lonely?"

I stiffened, torn between the stranger's warmth and interest and her blatant prying into my life. Since Marnie, I hadn't been close with anyone, other than Michelle. Her reading my thoughts was annoying, yet enticing. I was lonely. "I'm just fine, thank you."

"Now we're getting touchy, huh? Do you have any friends at Cathedral Chapel?" Connie persisted.

"Yes and no. People are very nice to me. I haven't been here long enough to make any really good friends."

"How long have you been there?" There was no getting away from her! I rearranged the bench cushion underneath me.

The eleven o'clock chimes sounded. There was no offical lights out at Cathedral Chapel but Luke Zoe dutifully had the bells rung just for ritual's sake.

" . . . So then, after Watts and after Marnie got turned down, I decided to leave." I concluded to Connie.

"What a miserable story, sweetie. I'm sooo glad it's over for you."

227

Sweetie? Perhaps I had misheard the use of yet another familiarity.

"I can't believe I haven't met you in all this time. What do you look like?"

"What do I look like? What kind of question is that?" Surely this girl was pulling my leg.

"Didn't anybody ever ask you what you looked like?"

"Not in the middle of the night when I answered the phone for someone else, no!"

"Good. So tell me, in minute detail."

I started to shake. Trying to steady myself, I leaned back on the bench and propped my left foot against the wall. I jerked the booth door open. The house was still and dark except for the phone booth light. *I think this woman is flirting with you, Jeanne!* An unusual new voice from inside spoke through my free ear.

How can this be? I refuted. *This is a woman. And a stranger. And a friend of Luke Zoe's.*

"Jeanne, are you still there? Hey, I didn't mean to put you off, I'm sorry if I offended you. I'm just interested in you . . . "

"Yeah, no. I mean, it's nice. It's been nice talking, but . . . "

"I agree, I've had a wonderful evening . . . on the phone and everything, and . . . "

"It's getting real late," I said, picking up on her closing. "We've been on the phone for almost three hours."

"So?"

"Well, I've never been on the phone for almost three hours. It must be expensive . . . or something for you . . . "

"What a sweet, young thing you are!" She said. *This woman is still flirting with you, Jeanne!* the voice repeated. "Yes, this is getting expensive on the phone. I'll be right over!"

The dial tone hummed in my ear.

228

CHAPTER 24

Mutiny Over the Boundary

With the receiver still in my hand, I was startled by the door bell. Either Connie must live next door or I had gone into shock and lost ten minutes from my life. I rushed to the door to catch it before the second ring. She was mad to sound a convent bell at midnight! Even the Swinging Chapel had some boundaries; everyone was asleep.

When I opened the door, I lost another slice of time. Before Connie, I didn't know life could pivot in an instant.

Her ear-length, golden hair was iridescent in the porch light. The brilliance bounced as though delighted to accompany the most winsome blue eyes I'd ever seen. A muscled, tanned arm held her weight as she leaned against the doorjamb smiling. Connie O'Malley was radiant and not much older than I. Her smile sucked the air out of my throat. I was dazzled! The Santa Ana winds were

229

blowing off the desert that night, the hot gusts stirring something deep inside.

Let me tell you what this is, the voice inside erupted imperiously. *You are physically attracted to a woman!*

This can't be happening. I clutched my throat. *It isn't supposed to be this way. God! She's the sexiest thing I have ever seen!*

Exactly my point.

You're crazy. I gasped for air. *It just means she is an extremely attractive girl. So what? She is. Lots of men and women are attractive. So I notice.* I regained my inner composure.

"Hiya!" Connie's voice vibrated, yet caressed the space between us. "You must be Jeanne. I can tell."

"Yes." I responded.

"You have bedroom eyes to match your voice!" she said. Denny used to call me "bedroom eyes." But Connie made them, made me, feel so much more . . . erotic?

I believe I was gracious and asked her in. I believe she said, "No, thanks," and invited *me*—into her car, but I don't remember the ride.

"Can I fix you a drink?" I sat on her couch holding a guitar on my lap. Connie stood next to my knees, her belted khaki shirt tucked into bell-bottom jeans.

I nodded.

"What, hard or soft?"

"Hard or soft what?" Everything was surreal.

"Liquor, beer, wine, or what?"

"Whatever you're having."

"Haven't been around much have we?" Connie ran her index finger down my strings. The discordance brought me back to reality.

Connie's place reminded me of Marnie's. It wasn't warm or beautifully crafted like my most particular ex-friend's, but it was an intensely personal environment, I thought, pleased with the first coherent thought I'd managed since I answered the phone hours ago. Unlike Marnie's place, there was only one row of books. It was filled with volumes on nursing, death, and psychiatry. Odd. What did Connie do for a living?

The cheap, yellow walls held posters of Sister Corita's work interspersed with huge photographs of nuns and other women, none of whom I recognized. A poster of Janis Joplin, looking deranged, screaming in pain and anger, hung over the couch. Most of the posters and photographs had a plaintive quality. I shook off the depression in their faces. Muffled voices came from the walls. Must be an apartment building, I concluded, listening to Connie clink bottles in the kitchen.

Two votive candles on the coffee table to my right offered the only light except for what escaped from behind the kitchen door. Maybe Connie was trying to save on electricity. This must be Connie's guitar. I hugged the instrument closer to my chest. I didn't remember picking it up. Did everyone in the IHM circle play guitar?

"Here you go, my little nun!" The kitchen door swung open. Connie positioned my drink on the coffee table in front of me and slid to the carpet beside it. "Throw me a couple of those pillows, will you?"

"I'm not a nun. Remember? I told you I left the convent." I adamantly needed to keep my reality straight. I tossed Connie the cushions. She lay back on the floor, propping her knees next to mine against the couch, as she deftly tucked the pillows under her neck.

"I know, but you really have a nun-like innocence. I'm just playing with you." Connie's voice was teasing.

Whoosh . . . my lips pursed and I gasped, "This drink is tart. What is it?"

"A Whiskey Sour, drink it slow. It's like a fine liquor."

Whatever it was, after the initial blast it tasted just fine.

"So, what do you do?" I asked Connie. "Do you have a job?"

Connie's golden hair grew a little dimmer as the night wore on and her life story began to sound disjointed. She was now working as a nurse. She wanted to be a psychotherapist. When she told me she wanted to join the IHM's and had applied for admission, I grew pensive thinking about Marnie. Why was it that everyone I met

231

wanted to become a nun? Was I still chasing the shadows of my vocation or were Connie and Marnie looking for themselves in me? "I'd give up that ambition if I were you," I spoke up suddenly. "You aren't the nun type. Take it from me; I was at the scene of the crime."

Connie was on her feet before I finished my sentence. "How the *hell* do you know who I am?" Her words spat out with hurt.

Flabbergasted, I made no reply.

Connie stomped across the room and smacked the swinging kitchen door. "I'm making us another drink."

I was standing when she returned. "I should leave. I didn't mean to upset you. Maybe I'm bitter. I only meant to be helpful."

"That's OK. It was my fault. I don't want you to go." Connie gave me a gentle shove back into the sofa and resumed her position on the floor, her knees pinning mine to the couch. She smiled at me as she had earlier. The anger surging through her body moments ago was gone. "I'm sorry I sounded off. I just can't stand being told I don't belong. My foster father used to tell me that all the time."

I leaned back into the pillows. Perhaps Connie had had a hard day. My drink was making me mellow, so I wasn't quite sure what had just happened. *I should get going, it must be very late. Michelle might be waiting up for me.*

"Play me some of your favorite songs." Connie's voice broke into my thoughts.

"Is this your guitar?" I asked, caressing the instrument. My fingers seemed less coordinated.

"Not really. It was left with me by a friend, a girl who went into the IHM's. But let's not talk about that. Play something for me, something special that you like."

I found myself strumming Marnie's song. The words flowed freely: "The joys of love are but a moment long/the pain of love endures the whole life long. Your eyes met mine/I saw the love in them shine/you brought me heaven right then/when your eyes kissed mine."

232

Connie's eyes seemed to grow larger in the candlelight, then more distant. But my dizziness felt strangely comforting.

Sometime in the night Connie got me another drink and another. "Do you know the song, 'If I Never Get to Love You'?" Connie's voice drifted up to me as she held me with her eyes.

"I don't think so. Do you have the music? I'll try it."

Connie reached into the coffee table drawer and flipped open a book of songs in front of me. The book was handmade and decorated with Corita prints on the front and back covers. "This is beautiful!" I flipped the pages and saw many of my favorite songs from the convent. "Someone in the IHM's made this. I love it."

"Yes, someone did. Here, play this one." She flipped the pages. I found the music and chords and this time Connie sang,

"If I never get to love you,
It won't be that I ran away.
For as long as you will have me
Close to you I'll stay.
What I wouldn't give to hold you tight!
Never, never let you out of sight!
Be the one you give your first kiss every morning,
Your last kiss every night!"

Her voice was as plaintive as her eyes, which had taken on the deeper color of the ocean that waited for the dawn. My midnight stranger was singing to me. Was I imagining things? The intimacy was overwhelming. The guitar slid flat against my legs, as I fell gently backward against the couch and closed my eyes. I felt so warm. Connie would take care of me. The couch pillows cradled me. The hours flew . . . the stereo was on now. Leonard Cohen soothed, "Suzanne takes you down/to her place by the river . . . "

Connie was lifting me off the couch, "Come lie on the floor, my sweet; you can stretch out. Here, lift your head for the pillow. I'll get a blanket and you can sleep, if you want to."

You're invited to spend the night. I tumbled to the floor. *It's a slumber party, and you're a free adult so you don't have to be home.*

The music curled up with us as Connie returned to tuck us in. She was going to sleep next to me rather than in her bedroom. How sweet! Cohen lulled on, "And she gets you on her wave length/And she lets the river answer/That you've always been her lover."

Were Connie's lips on mine?

Yes. I'm sure of it. I dug my fingers into the carpet to see if I was dreaming. The carpet was like sandpaper against my finger tips. *I'm here. That means Connie's mouth is also. But it's all right.* The softness of her lips brushed both my cheeks and caressed my eyes and chin, then returned to my lips and began another foray across my face. I lay flat on my back as Connie's fingers combed my hair. I closed my eyes and shut out the ceiling. Her hair fell across my eyes. I wanted to run my fingers through it, but I didn't dare move. Her tongue played on my lips like my fingers had on the guitar strings long ago. Her tongue came into my mouth softly, like the tide, inch by inch, searching my lips, my tongue, my teeth, exploring.

A girl is kissing you, my imperious inner friend made another wise observation.

I know what's happening. I turned the voice off. It was not the time for dialogue. Tonight was only magic.

Electricity jolted my body, my back arched with shock as the voltage rippled through my nerves all the way down to my toes. It was Connie's mouth on my breast. The ceiling reeled with urgency and pleasure. I was intoxicated. Could this be the alcohol? I'd never had whiskey whatevers before. But no, I'd been drunk once or twice and felt high and sleepy, not electrified. Connie's hands and mouth were everywhere, my face, my neck, my breasts. My hand reached for her head bringing her more tightly to my chest. Sounds escaped . . . a soft moan. Was that me or her? My body was caught up in its own giving. Connie was part of me now.

Connie's mouth was on my ear. "Are you always so responsive?"

"I've never done *this.*"

"My God, you *are* a virgin!"

"I still will be if we spend the rest of the night talking." I didn't want Connie to get distracted or feel responsible. "Kiss me!"

"Demanding for a virgin, aren't we?" Connie's laughter was stereophonic. She turned me toward her, and slid her arm around my waist. "What's this elastic thing around your waist?" Connie sat up abruptly.

"That's my girdle." I opened my eyes. It's part of the Holy Rule . . . I guess. We all had to wear them in Montecito. I never got the point . . . "

"No, I'm sure you didn't. It's prehistoric. I thought you weren't a nun anymore, so you don't need it, right?"

"I guess not. It's just become a part of me."

"You're wrong about that, my sweet. You have no idea what's a part of you and what isn't!"

"Sure I do! I'm a free adult now, with a car and a job," I asserted.

"How about being a free adult with no girdle?" My perfect stranger murmured in my ear while tugging at my tight wrapping.

"You're right. It's a perfectly stupid thing to wear," I said crawling out of it. "There, take off your shirt too."

"Yes, Ma'am! You're such a natural. I can't believe you've never done this." Connie's hands covered mine on her shirt buttons and together we ripped them open. The blanket fell off her shoulder as she sat up again to shed her blouse. My hands traced her back muscles, her skin softer than cotton. They drifted in aimless delight as lips came down on mine once more. My God, she had such a way with her tongue over my teeth. Odd that a stranger's body could turn me on so easily, so perfectly. With boys, with Denny, my body always held back in the end, paralyzed in some wrenching ambivalence. But there was no cross traffic now, no stop sign. My body was reveling in a life of its own.

Her weight was on me, rocking us; the candles flickered, the apartment floor undulated with our rhythm. Connie's body was mine. When we moved, we flowed together, the boundaries separating us dissolved. She was within me. Somewhere in the

235

dark, one particular moment stretched itself into a forever place. The new music inside me crescendoed under her exquisite stroke. I'd never been touched before.

The dawn wrinkled Connie's window shades as I sat up. Jesus Christ, what the hell happened? I turned for verification to the sleeping form beside me. A woman. She lay next to me, her curved forearm around my waist, her gold hair now stilled on the pillow where mine had been.

What happened last night? I remembered the phone call, Connie at the door, Connie's rug . . . I lifted the blanket covering us. We were both naked. Except, I still had my socks on. Odd. Connie's fingers squeezed my breast. *Christ in a bucket!* Memory flooded.

And yet . . . lying back down next to her felt so natural. My body felt alive, yet strangely at peace. My index finger traced Connie's eyebrows.

You've slept with a woman. The voice was anticlimactic now.

Yes, and I loved it! I felt guilty. *I'm not supposed to enjoy this. Surely there's some part of me that feels . . . sinful?*

I closed my eyes and reconnoitered my heart, my body, my mind and soul. *We feel terrific!* The feeling of wholeness shocked me.

"I had a wonderful time, sweetheart!" Connie leaned across the front seat of her Mustang to kiss me.

My hand pulled the passenger door open. "So did I."

"I've got to go to work. I'll call you." She waved as her car pulled out of Cathedral Chapel's parking lot.

I wobbled to the gate, grabbing the fence and searching my purse for the key. The bag fell off my shoulder. Caught off balance, I followed its direction and fell into the cactus patch next to the gate. *Why was I always falling into cactus at major turning points in my life?*

I demanded the attention of the blossoming golden barrel next to me. *Obviously, this means I'm a homosexual. Yep. That's what I*

236

am. And furthermore, my little friend, I said, patting it gently, *I am delighted! So take that to your roots and pray on it.*

Despite my hang-over, the garden surrounding the back entrance to the holy convent of the Immaculate Heart of Mary sisterhood never looked so full of life, so lovely. Resting there in the cactus patch, I felt like I had the day Mom first took me to the optometrist to be fitted for a pair of glasses. I'd had a childhood of seeing the world in blurred images—street signs fading into the skyline, the basketball hoop never quite where I aimed. I was always the last to see, the last to understand. Until that morning. And until this morning. Connie had ripped the blinders off my eyes and given my heart the freedom to honor what it had always known.

I looked out across my horizon. The parking space lines were arranged in precise parallels, the houses planted precisely down the block. The city and the parking lot had always been so. It was me who was different. Deliciously, irrevocably, simply different. It was me who had crossed the forbidden boundary into my own reality now. Now I had 20-20 vision.

I set my purse on top of the golden barrel, leaned back against the chain link and lifted my chin to soak in the early morning sun. It all made such perfect sense.

No wonder brother Bill and I used to fight over who got Guinevere in the end. No wonder Mom ended my friendship with Cathy Longtree in high school. Some friendship! She'd read Cathy's Valentine card with an eye I didn't possess. I had loved Cathy with all the passion of a sixteen-year-old . . . lesbian, I guess it was called. I wonder what had become of Cathy? Would we have loved each other forever had Mom not broken us apart? Did she love another woman now, or had she married and forgotten me?

No wonder I was so upset when Paul Emanuelle left. It was so easy to tell your friends you were heartbroken about some boy. But you weren't supposed to feel your heart twist over a nun's departure. I was depressed for months when Janie left summer camp. I'd cried myself to sleep. Of course. I'd loved her. Without knowing why, I was so right to tell Denny, "Don't wait for me. It will never be me, nun or no nun."

Of course the other nuns had looked at me strangely and kept their distance. Connie had said, "I can't believe you've never done this." She must have thought I was a homosexual, that I knew I was, that *I* was flirting with *her* on the phone. I must have played the part so perfectly. I *was* the part. I saluted my barrel. *I am the genuine article."*

Was Marnie? Was this why she wasn't admitted into the order? What a bunch of hypocrites the whole damn order was! I was right to leave. What a damn lie. Michelle . . . what about Micki?

I tore my purse off the golden needles and hauled myself, fingers in the chain-link fence, to my feet. I had to go find Michelle.

CHAPTER 25

Tell It to the Pope

"Come in," the weak voice invited my entrance.

"Michelle?" I closed her cell door behind me and turned to stare at my friend sitting upright in bed. She looked delicate in a pink nightgown I'd never seen before.

"Where the hell have you been *all night?*" The anger leapt out of the fragile body.

"What do you mean?" This was a new Michelle. I'd never seen her so upset.

"What else could I possibly mean? I don't mean your shoe laces are untied, I don't mean your hair isn't combed *as usual.* I mean you didn't come home last night. I waited all night for you."

"Oh." I gazed at Michelle. She looked so beautiful in bed, in the soft pink.

"Sit down," Michelle commanded, moving over on her bed.

She slapped the mattress by her thigh.

"I didn't know you cared," I teased with new-found boldness. "I didn't know you waited for me in the night."

Michelle was deadpan. "I always check your room after I come home, Jeanne. You're always there."

"What are you, Mother Inferior? You should talk. I've waited for you until two or three in the morning sometimes. Is that because you're down at Del Martinez's all night?" It finally dawned on me—maybe Michelle was down at Miss Martinez's for the same reason I spent the night with Connie.

"We're talking about where *you* were."

"Why are you home in the middle of the day, Michelle? Are you sick?"

"I'm all right, just run down. Decided to take the day off."

"You're probably exhausted from spending all those nights *working* in Orange County with Del. Do you even sleep?"

Michelle blushed.

"I was at Connie's."

"Connie O'Malley, Luke Zoe's friend? I didn't know you knew her."

"I don't . . . didn't. She called last night. We met on the phone. She came over and picked me up."

"Shit, Jeanne, you are dumb sometimes."

"Maybe I got tired of everyone thinking I'm so naive. I'm not anymore." Sitting there, not twelve inches away, I became mesmerized by Michelle's mouth. I'd never noticed how she ran her tongue over her lips so slowly when she was trying to make a point. I leaned forward and kissed them. *Christ in a bucket, now you are in trouble!*

Michelle's jaw slackened as her mouth opened and pulled mine to her. Her body relaxed against the pillows as her arms wrapped around my neck and she brought my shoulders down against her breast. The pink nightgown clung to my chest. Her tongue never stopped its total concentration on mine.

My God, she's kissing you back!

Her kiss was deep and penetrating, more skilled, more intimate than Connie's. My body melted into Michelle's.

Abruptly, Michelle pushed me away. "Is that what you learned from Connie?"

Hurt and confused, I sat up. "But you kissed me back!"

"Of course I did. I've been wanting to since the day you arrived in Montecito."

"Why didn't you tell me?"

Micki fidgeted with her blanket. "I wasn't sure, I didn't want to corrupt your immortal soul."

"Oh, bullshit. You mean you thought I was too stupid and you didn't want to be responsible for me. Or was it that you were just too busy kissing Sister Dominic Anne? Is that what you were up to in the orchard, Micki? Doing sex, or making love, or whatever it's called? Is that why you were never home? Did you ever really have a brain concussion? For God's sake, Micki, tell me the truth or I'm going to wring it out of you!" I straddled her legs, pulled the pillow out from under her and held it over her head.

"All right, Woman-of-the World, there was no brain concussion! I knew the mezzanine sick-bay was next to the novice cells on the second floor, and Dominic was a nurse. It was the only way. Brilliant, huh?

"You left me all alone at St. Joseph's!" I smacked her lightly with the pillow.

"But, Jeanne, that's no justification for you going to bed with someone you don't even know . . . "

"I like this expression, 'go to bed with.' That's sexy!"

"So now you're a sexual connoisseur."

"Well, it all happened so quickly I didn't have much time to think. Maybe I was too drunk . . . "

"So, she got you drunk. Now that's the lowest trick in the book!"

"It wasn't because we were drunk. She said I was 'responsive,' so there."

"You are, Jeanne." Michelle came toward me to reclaim her

241

pillow. I felt her breath on my neck.

"Well, if you think so," I exhaled slowly, "and I know you really do love me, why didn't you ever . . . "

Suddenly, Michelle leaned back, "Jeanne, go lock my door, and stuff that rug up next to the crack."

I had no trouble with obedience that moment. I sealed the door.

"So you want to know everything now? OK. I'll tell you about the convent and being gay."

Sitting at the foot of the Oracle of Lesbos, the young summer heat suffocating us both, I learned belatedly the homosexual mysteries of convent life.

Curled against the headboard Michelle began. "Remember Sister Paul Emnanuelle? She brought me out at St. Anthony's during my senior year. I was very much in love with her."

"Brought you what?"

"Out. That's what Connie did for you last night."

"Really!"

"Really. Listen to me. Paul Emanuelle told me there are four kinds of gay nuns: those who are and do; those who are and don't; those who are, do and deny it; and those who confined themselves to emotional romance and hand holding."

"Which category was I in?"

"I guess there must be a fifth category: those who don't know what they're doing. Anyway, there are also straight nuns. It's easy to spot them, sooner or later they talk about priests as men, rather than merely holy repositories of St. Peter's trust."

"You mean like Sister Constance Marie who lives downstairs next to me?"

"Hopelessly straight."

Michelle's news was stunning. So much going on while I was stumbling around in chapel wondering why God wasn't talking to me. I eyed my loafers before deciding to kick them off. "I guess Louise and Janis are also 'straight,' as you call it?"

242

"Jeanne, what's the matter?" Michelle sat up and reached for my hand.

"Don't do that."

"Don't do what? One minute we're kissing like the bells of Notre Dame and now you don't want me to touch you?"

"So what kind of love do you and Del Martinez have?"

"Jealous, are we?"

"Quit beating around the burning bush."

"I haven't been to bed with her, Jeanne. She's with someone."

"What does that mean?"

"It means she's got a girlfriend. I even met her."

"Then what have you been doing with her?"

"Talking, yes. Flirting, yes. We kiss. Yes, she holds me at night. But she told me we can't go any further because I'm in the convent. It's too awkward . . . "

"Aw, isn't that heartbreaking."

"We haven't done anything, Jeanne. Listen," Michelle kneeled in front of me on the bed. "I love you," she whispered. "I have for a long time."

I touched Michelle's face, afraid to savor her words.

"I have to know. Why did Lurch and Margaret Rose think I was gay?"

Michelle covered my knees with her palms. "Because you act like it. Because you are! You're sitting here telling me you are."

"But I never *did* anything before last night." My eyes questioned her.

"You look gay. Butch."

"What's butch?"

"Masculine. Short-cropped hair. You stride like a guy when you walk," Michelle explained. "There's a sort of body language," she summarized.

I swept my fingers through my hair flipping the strands back over my ears.

Michelle laughed, catching my elbow. "Just like that! Listen, I'm getting cramps in my knees and I'm not in a praying mood.

Why don't you come settle back with me at my end of the bed. You can hear better if you're closer."

I grabbed my pillow and snuggled in beside her. My arm didn't fit. It seemed to want to go around her shoulders. "I see what you mean, Micki. I must have been a walking telegraph!"

As she curled beside me, I couldn't help noticing that Michelle was not at all masculine.

"But you don't stomp around like I do. And you're a . . . aren't you?"

"I'm just another kind, there are many kinds. I'm just more subtle."

"What do the IHM's say about homosexuality, Micki? I've never heard anyone actually say the word, just references to particular friendships."

"The unwritten, unholy Rule seems to be, 'do it and hide it.' There's no such thing as gay nuns."

"Of course not, what a perfect Catholic myth," I scoffed. "If it doesn't fit into the Pope's view of life everlasting, we'll pretend it doesn't exist."

"Liberal orders like the IHM's and the Maryknolls are much more permissive than the Carmelities or Dominicans. If you're discreet, no one will bother you. Until, of course, you're transferred to one place and your particular love to another. Then you're supposed to go obediently—and quietly."

"But how can that be? You said even some of the top brass have particular relationships that go on for years. Is Sister Luke Zoe gay?"

"No. I don't think so. She's just one of the more honest people around here. She seems to think being gay or straight, being sexual and a nun, is normal. It's how loving you are with other people, your connection to God, that makes a nun a nun."

"Then what's the order's problem, Micki?"

"You were being *obvious*, Jeanne. You broke the rules by blatantly hanging out in my cell late at night. Also, you became friends publicly with Marnie who was a known lesbian!"

244

"It would have been a lot easier if someone had told me the rules."

"I almost did, several times," Michelle chided softly. "Would you have kept them?"

I stared at Michelle. There was so much about her I had never noticed. A passion I'd always suspected was there but could never tap, her fears, the thin, sexy line of her upper lip. "No, Micki. I wouldn't have kept that rule. I think this hypocrisy is blasphemous. Either we're doing something wrong, and nuns, above all, shouldn't do it. Or we're doing something right and beautiful and natural and holy, and we shouldn't lie about it. I can't comprehend what's wrong. I don't feel in my mind or my body that there's anything wrong about loving another girl."

"It's not as simple as that, Jeanne, not in the world, and certainly not in the convent."

"That's where you're wrong, Micki. Did you ever think it's not us who are wrong but the world and the Church?"

"Sure, Jeanne. Go tell it to the Pope! 'Dear Holy Father, would you care to reevaluate your infallible position on the blasphemy of homosexuality? It's only been two thousand years . . . '"

"Micki, that's a great idea!" I jumped up and strode up and down her cell. "I *should* go tell the Pope. Maybe we should boycott the Vatican! I am happy and proud and I feel like standing on top of the Hollywood sign and shouting, 'I'm a queer, and I love it!'"

Michelle groaned.

"It wouldn't be the first time the Catholic Church was totally wrong. They said the earth was flat, the earth was the center of the universe, and birth control is wrong. You watch, Micki, next century they'll change their rules on birth control too. Someday they'll change their not-so-infallible minds about being gay too. Human love is not the forte of the Catholic Church. Sometimes I wonder if they believe in it at all."

"I was afraid you'd say something like that, Jeanne. You'd have made a lousy gay nun. It's a good thing you left."

"A good thing for the convent?"

245

Michelle jumped out of bed and wrapped her arms around my neck. "A good thing for me!" she whispered, her mouth at my ear. "Now that you're not in the convent we can be more free. We can be as close as we've always wanted to be. No more secrets. God knows I need you now, Jeanne. It's been lonely, all these months in hiding, sneaking up and down balconies. All I want is to share it with you."

I cupped her face in both hands and looked into those seductive, haunting, extraterrestrial waters that caught my attention that first day at Montecito. I saw exhaustion in Michelle's face. Her hands were clutching my neck tightly, the space between us ached with the tension of the last year. Keeping up her double life could not have been easy. God knows, those months had been a nightmare for me too.

I smoothed her rumpled hair with my lips and drew her even closer to me. "I'll be your confidante, Micki, your friend, your . . . lover. But hiding is no way to live."

"I can't be a fighter like you, Jeanne," Michelle leaned into me, her face in my shoulder, her small breasts pressing into me. "I'm not ready to give up my vocation. I can help you change the world from the inside, I'll be your secret agent . . . that is, if you love me every day."

"Is that a vow?" I laughed, holding her gently. "If it is, I'll make the same one."

"Let's go back to bed before we wind up loving each other on the holy convent floor."

Michelle lay down, pulling my hands, my arms, my length down on top of her. My heart and my body finally agreed: love was sacred.

The Hollywood sun had long since gone to hide on the far side of the Malibu mountains as I tucked the bedspread around us. I lay there next to her, my eyes wide, staring alternately at the crucifix above her bed and at my new joy. My soul's voice had the last word: *Kicking the habit is only the beginning, Jeanne.*

246

Epilogue

On October 3, 1970, three years, three months, and three days after I walked out of the convent of the Immaculate Heart of Mary, I walked into a meeting of the Daughters of Bilitis, a national lesbian organization.

I'd spent the interim graduating from UCLA in Social Welfare and had just entered their graduate school, where I obtained my M.S.W. (Master of Social Work) in 1972. In the academia of the late sixties I met few lesbians. But I did run from the baton-hurling police when thousands of them invaded UCLA as we protested the invasion of Cambodia. And I did meet Paul, my heterosexual test pad, but found in several months that I was right the first time.

I could find no lesbians who weren't nuns, so ultimately I called the Department of Parks and Recreation looking for a women's softball team, the second-best place to find gay women. I found one.

Her name was Judy. But, in those days being a lesbian feminist, separatist, socialist, journalist, organizer, and radical street demonstrator was not compatible with being a dyke jock. I didn't have time to practice both. I lay down my glove and took to the streets and became president of the L.A. Chapter of the Daughters of Bilitis.

I opened Los Angeles' first Lesbian Center, met a new love with whom I could be political, and founded *The Lesbian Tide*, a national lesbian newsmagazine (1971-1980). In the last twenty years, I've come to understand that I had to leave the convent to be true to my destiny—being a part of an alternative sisterhood and brotherhood fighting for its freedom and salvation.

Michelle Callahan and I have remained friends for twenty-four years, proving that love, sex, and friendship are a viable trinity. Shortly after I left Cathedral Chapel to pursue my life as a social worker in East Los Angeles, our romance melted into friendship. The convent closet came between us. She remained in the order until 1969, finally leaving to "consummate," as she would say, her long love with Del Martinez. Years later, Michelle mused, "It (the convent) was our first failed love relationship. We divorced God." I noticed, however, that Michelle also never fell out of love with social work—or her own machinations. She has spent the last two decades climbing the bureaucratic balconies of a prominent federal welfare agency.

Somewhere during that time we spent another idyllic summer in a brass bed at the Virginia Hotel in Santa Barbara. Now we share process over our mutual loves, political victories, Oreos, hamburgers, and a dull Catholic palate. Ex-nuns don't eat Thai.

Del Martinez and I became closer as we met again as classmates in UCLA's graduate school. The friendship between me and my first father figure remains familial, despite being attracted to the same women more than once. She still tries to tell me when to sit down, and I still stand. She remains, to this day, "the boss lady" at another social work center. She is true to her first and real loves: the ghetto, the young, and the poor. The best in us never changes.

I am grateful to Michelle and Del for coming out in this story of my life and theirs. They, like this book, demonstrate in action how we must all stand proud. If we believe in ourselves enough to live our lives, we must believe in ourselves enough to speak out.

I am also forever grateful to Del Martinez for telling me for more than two decades, "writing is what you do best." Even if it took me twenty-four years to turn her advice into this book.

Marlene Camp, whom I did not see again until a New Age conference in 1987, hasn't changed much either. We argued all the way through lunch . . . and split the bill. I did find out the salient facts: she's straight and is into nails (owns a manicure shop). I did not use her real name in this book as we lost touch with each other again shortly after lunch. Besides, I thought she'd say "no."

Louise Rodriguez left the convent shortly after I did, undoubtedly to marry. I never heard from her again, but my heart tells me she is married, a proud mother, and a sharp businesswoman somewhere.

Janis Engleton also left shortly after I did to marry Brian, her Franciscan monk. They had several holy children.

Donna, our dearly departed dead nun postulant mate, pursued social work in San Pedro in the late sixties with Michelle. I don't know what new habits Donna has acquired since.

Connie was not admitted into the IHM community. We remained in touch, though not closely, for a few years. In 1975, she committed suicide. Some people carry too much pain.

I also don't know what became of Mother Mary Caritas. Lurch and I were not close.

Sister Luke Zoe, a pseudonym, like many of the others, has continued a life of service. She teaches young people and is politically involved with the oppressed in Nicargaua and El Salvador.

Marnie Heathford, a pseudonym, since I cannot locate her, has come in and out of my life several times, always fleetingly.

Novice Lauren David, a pseudonym, did go on to become Sister Lauren David, then left, became a lesbian and a clinical psychologist. I'm not certain of the sequence.

Antonia Marie, a pseudonym, my singing sweetheart, probably never knew how I felt. She also left the convent a year or two after I did, to marry a Franciscan monk.

Mom and Dad remain glued together, a testament to Catholic commitment, love, and habit. They did not have any more children. France did not go to the moon, but she watches her satellites do so from a space agency lab in the Southwest. Bill exchanged his childhood Camelot for a corporate roundtable. Declan Francis Córdova entered the seminary, and left it, in the mid-1980s.

The Immaculate Heart of Mary community continued its political battle with the Cardinal and the Roman Catholic Church until 1970, when they, too, kicked the habit. Their canonical status was revoked by the Catholic Church. The liberal branch of the IHM sisterhood became a lay Christian community and now devotes itself to a broad spectrum of spiritual needs.

The IHM must be credited with gestating talented leadership for the women's, people of color, gay and lesbian, evironmental, peace, and Latin American movements of the last half of the twentieth century.

They still own Montecito, whose La Casa de María Retreat Center now sponsors liberal Christian, New Age, mental health, and self-help retreats. I still enthusiastically recommend the setting for communion with Higher Orders.

Ex-nuns have a private lament. There is an unrequited yearning that comes from breathing, however briefly, the spirit through the flesh. This shared longing, to recapture that temporal sainthood, is recognizable in that place where the brows meet—the third eye, the soul.

After sixteen years of self-avowed agnosticism, I finally heard from God again in 1983—through the voice of my Spirit Guide, Tomasino. Tomasino, an androgynous monk who took her name from the writer saint, Thomas Aquinas, appeared to me at a 12-Step meeting at Cedars-Sinai in Beverly Hills. I've discovered that God, like a true love, recycles and returns, always forgiving and eternally demanding.

But that's another story.